THE PEOPLE OF ATLANTA

The People of Atlanta

A Demographic Study of Georgia's Capital City

C. A. McMAHAN

Associate Professor of Sociology
University of Georgia

THE UNIVERSITY OF GEORGIA PRESS
Athens

Paperback edition, 2009
© 1950 by the University of Georgia Press
Athens, Georgia 30602
www.ugapress.org
Printed digitally in the United States of America

The Library of Congress has cataloged the
hardcover edition of this book as follows:

Library of Congress Cataloging-in-Publication Data

McMahan, Chalmers Alexander.
The people of Atlanta; a demographic study of Georgia's capital city.
xviii, 257 p. illus., maps. 25 cm.
1. Atlanta—Population. [from old catalog] I. Title.
HB3527.A74 M3
50-6929

Paperback ISBN-13: 978-0-8203-3449-3
ISBN-10: 0-8203-3449-9

To My Sons

Jerry and Alex

FOREWORD

Contemporary social life, if more abundant than that experienced by our ancestors, is also more complex. Many problems which in our time confront the governmental administrator, the legislator, the professional, the business man, and, indeed, the private citizen, are both grave and perplexing. The best hope for the avoidance of costly or even catastrophic error in coping with these problems is afforded by a ready and growing body of established facts upon which judicious decisions may be based. To this accumulation of fundamental knowledge, the student of population can contribute much—and, as a matter of record, is already doing so. The widespread recognition of this fact has brought forth in recent years an increasing demand for his analytical and interpretive services.

Accompanying and encouraging the development of this receptive milieu in society for population materials has been the emergence of demography as a scientific discipline. Population study in a broad sense, or perhaps more accurately, reflection on population, has long been an engaging intellectual pursuit. Even the famous Greeks, Plato and Aristotle, who seem to have missed little in the world in which they lived, gave more than passing mention to population in their writings. However, their consideration of population was philosophical or speculative, as was that of other writers who sporadically in the next several centuries made reference to population.

Beginning in the latter part of the seventeenth century, some students (notably John Graunt in London) turned their attention to the study of the meager population data then available with the crude analytical tools at their disposal. For more than two centuries, however, relatively slow progress in empirical research was realized, while the conjectural approach to questions of population continued to hold sway. Gradually, research tools were developed and sharpened, on the one hand, and a more adequate and systematic body of population data which invited investigation was brought into being, on the other hand. But even during the first part of the present century, uninhibited armchair speculation, aimed primarily at startling and terrifying, perhaps enjoyed more widespread popularity than empirical research. Only in the last 25 years has genuine population analysis fully come into its own. During this recent period, the demographer, through the rigorous application of proven statistical and graphic analytical techniques to empirical data, has amassed an imposing array of tested fact and principle. Population study has thus come to rank among the most advanced as well as among the most strategically useful branches of social science.

A heartening example of what an able scholar well versed in population theory and well grounded in the latest research techniques can accomplish is provided by Dr. McMahan's comprehensive study of the people of Atlanta. This work, worthwhile and substantial in its own right, is further enhanced in value by its being one of the first, if not the first, complete and thorough-going demographic analysis of a large urban population. The data and conclusions presented for Atlanta are made more meaningful by their comparison with corresponding materials for the urban population of the United States and for the southern cities of Dallas, Nashville, and New Orleans. Systematic, scientific, and straight-forward in approach, and lavishly illustrated by skillfully designed charts, this scholarly volume clearly shows the masterful influence of Dr. T. Lynn Smith, under whose direction the author gained his basic orientation in demographic research.

McMahan's study is organized in a logical and orderly manner. For the special benefit of the non-technical reader, initial consideration is given to the methods and source materials employed and to the literature pertinent to this investigation. In the analysis proper, attention is first focused upon the number and distribution of Atlanta's population. Following this, their compositional characteristics are brought under scrutiny. Among the attributes of Atlantans singled out for individual treatment are race and nativity, age, sex, marital condition, education, occupation, and religion. Subjected to analysis next are the vital processes of fertility and mortality, Then, migration as it has affected Atlanta's population receives detailed consideration. Finally, the growth which has characterized the city's population is analyzed.

Preparation of this volume has entailed a prodigious amount of work. The task of assembling, sifting, organizing, and analyzing the demographic data concerning Atlanta's population has necessarily been meticulous and time-consuming. It is perhaps in order to explore briefly the worth or utility to contemporary society of the resulting accumulation of tested facts and principles.

Among the benefits which may stem from this undertaking are advancements in the general field of urban population theory. It represents a pioneering, comprehensive, and thorough demographic analysis of a large urban population. The conclusions reached have been carefully examined from the standpoints of known facts, tested relationships, and verified hypotheses. As such, they merit the thoughtful consideration of the student of population.

The impressive compilation of facts and relationships regarding the residents of Atlanta are of interest and value in and of themselves. These data reveal significant truths about the city's most valuable possession—her human inhabitants. Consequently, the findings of this type of study must be counted among the most essential items of information at the command of the well-informed citizen.

Such population facts and principles as those set forth by McMahan are at the roots of many of the bewildering social developments of our time. The rapid growth of urban population has been basic to the acute housing shortage. Increased fertility in the period during and after the recent war, coupled with migration, has accounted for the crowded and inadequate school facilities which our children must now tolerate. Declining mortality rates are not unrelated to the growing significance of old age benefits. Similar concrete examples could be multiplied. The lesson, however, is clear. One who would understand social conditions and changes can not ignore the underlying population factors.

Demographic analyses are assuming a crucial role in the field of public policy and social planning. This is no less true at the local urban level than at the state, national, and international levels. Virtually all fundamental questions confronting any municipal government have their population aspects. Consider the close linkage of one or another phase of population with such perennial urban problems as school construction and consolidation, ascertaining optimum size and location of hospitals and other health facilities, revision of corporate limits, locating parks and recreational facilities, etc. Obviously this reliable body of population information prepared by McMahan will be welcomed by the city fathers of Atlanta, and comparable analyses will undoubtedly be demanded by other progressive municipalities.

The value of this study to private individuals, organizations, and corporations should not be overlooked. Indeed, they all may profit from the careful consideration of relevant demographic data when laying plans for the future. The business man, the professional man, and the religious denomination all are required to make decisions which must to a large extent be based upon such factors as the number, distribution, age make-up, and educational status of the people. All of these and many other relevant topics are analyzed in this study.

Dr. McMahan is to be complimented for this excellent study which represents a substantial contribution to demographic literature. It is particularly pleasing to me that this pioneering demographic analysis of a large urban center was completed at a southern university by a young and promising scholar who received his advanced training in the South. That a university press of this region should publish the study is entirely proper and commendable. I am confident that this splendid analysis will take it place among the several distinguished contributions to the science of demography which have come out of the South in recent years.

Homer L. Hitt, Head
Departments of Sociology and Rural Sociology,
Louisiana State University
Baton Rouge, La.
December 1, 1949

PREFACE

This book presents the results of a study of the population of the city of Atlanta, Georgia. For the most part it is descriptive in nature with some attempt to explain selected findings and relationships. It should be pointed out that this study is not a treatise on urban demography in general, but consists of an elementary population study within a particular frame of reference.

In the field of demography, the period since 1930 has been characterized by the perfection of the tools of population analysis: classifications, indexes, graphic and mapping devices, and similar techniques; it has been further characterized by careful analysis of the completeness and validity of the data involved. During this period the empirical approach has come into its own to produce an understanding of definite demographic relationships as well as the concrete facts. Studies have taken place, for the most part, in connection with the national population, regional analyses, and state studies. As far as the writer knows no investigator to the present time has focused attention directly upon the demographic study of a single large southern city. This study attempts to fill that gap.

Appreciation is expressed to the following persons: to the Head of the Sociology Department at Vanderbilt University, Dr. T. Lynn Smith, for his kind consideration, guidance, criticisms, and suggestions; to the Head of the Sociology Department at The University of Georgia, Dr. B. O. Williams, for his suggestions and continuous encouragement; to Joseph C. Bledsoe, The University of Georgia School of Education, for reading and criticizing the material as it was written chapter by chapter and for many stimulating discussions; to John N. Burrus, Graduate Assistant at Louisiana State University, for reading and criticizing portions of the study and for his encouragement; to Dr. Homer L. Hitt, Head of the Department of Sociology and Rural Sociology, Louisiana State University, for writing the foreword; to Mr. Harry W. Martin and Miss Laura Holmes for aid in preparing the index; to Miss Elizabeth Creighton, secretary, for typing and retyping the manuscript many times; and to my wife, Mable

Shockley McMahan, for preparing parts of most of the figures (except for a few otherwise credited) and for checking computations; and to the many other persons who have aided me from time to time.

Also appreciation is expressed for permission for the use of pictures to the Atlanta Historical Society, The Atlanta Journal, The Atlanta Chamber of Commerce, Georgia Power Company; and to Mr. Walter McElreath for donating several pictures.

Appreciation is expressed to the General Education Board for a grant which made it possible for the writer to spend the school year 1947-1948 in graduate study at Vanderbilt University.

In addition, appreciation is expressed to The Rich Foundation, Inc. of Atlanta, for a substantial grant which made possible this publication.

Also appreciation is expressed to the following publishers for granting permission to reproduce material: Henry Holt and Company, Inc., Johns Hopkins Press; McGraw-Hill Book Company, Inc., The Williams and Wilkins Company; University of Minnesota Press; and University of North Carolina Press.

The initial study was made by the author and the findings were accepted by the faculty of the Graduate School of Vanderbilt University as a dissertation for the degree of Doctor of Philosophy.

C. A. McMahan

Athens, Georgia

TABLE OF CONTENTS

LIST OF TABLES

LIST OF FIGURES

LIST OF PICTURES

(In order of appearance)

THE PEOPLE OF ATLANTA

CHAPTER I

INTRODUCTION

THIS STUDY IS AN ANALYSIS OF THE DATA CONCERNING THE demographic situation and trends of the population of one large southern city, Atlanta, Georgia. The data relating to the population of Atlanta have been analyzed by the application of most of the techniques known to demographers; and in order to make the findings as meaningful as possible, they have been presented in relationship to those of other large urban populations.

OBJECTIVES

The major objective of the study is to analyze the population of one large southern city.

As a part of the over-all objective, it is the intention to present the data in meaningful form in relationship to other large urban populations, particularly to other large southern cities. A further aim is to arrange the presentation of the data so that the reader who is familiar with the field of demography will be spared the necessity of wading through the material on methods and sources of data, although these devices will be described and available if he desires to make use of them. On the other hand, before the reader who is unfamiliar with the field of demography reaches the body of the study (the analysis), he will have had an opportunity to become acquainted with the demographic techniques and types of data involved, thus making the findings more meaningful to him.

SCOPE

The study is an analysis of the enumerated population which is counted as having its usual place of residence in the incorporate (political) limits of the city of Atlanta, Georgia.

For the most part, the study is centered about the year 1940. Some of the data relating to the vital processes are available for more recent years; but since the enumerated data gathered by the Sixteenth Census in 1940 are the latest available at this writing, and particularly since Atlanta became a "tract city" for the first time in 1940, the bulk of the analysis is centered around that year. In many cases, however, trends are shown since 1850.

SOURCES OF THE DATA

The data used in this study are of two basic types: (1) those

3

which have been gathered by enumeration, and (2) those which are products of our registration systems.

For the most part, the enumerated data were gathered by the United States Census Bureau in the Sixteenth Census (1940), although materials from as far back as the Seventh Census (1850) have been utilized. These data of the Census Bureau compose the greatest repository of demographic information in the world.

The facts on the vital processes (reproduction and mortality) have been gathered through our system of birth and death registration. Most of the data in this study relative to the vital processes have been taken from publications prepared under the supervision of the chief statistician for vital statistics and entitled *Vital Statistics of the United States* (for the various years by place of residence). Two other major sources of information on vital statistics are (1) a publication by Forrest E. Linder and Robert D. Grove, *Vital Statistics Rates in the United States: 1900-1940* (appropriate data on publisher, etc., are given where materials from these sources are used); and (2) figures obtained from the statistician in the Atlanta City Health Department.

In addition to these basic sources, numerous studies and publications have been used for information and comparative material.

METHODS AND SOURCE MATERIALS USED

This study has been carried on almost completely by means of the statistical method. Important but simple statistical techniques have been applied to population data obtained from censuses and the registration of vital statistics. Only those techniques are presented which were used to describe the composition characteristics of the population, the birth and death rates, and the life tables with a few of their applications (and one estimate of population).[1]

It is felt that the best method of describing the statistical techniques used is to present the techniques along with a description of the data and their limitations; this is done in Chapter I in order to leave the reader free to study the findings in the main body of the work.

Among the more elementary of the devices used are tables,

1. Generally census and vital statistics data are records (supposedly) of complete enumerations or registrations; thus in this study, no discussion of a sampling situation is necessary.

Data relating to production and consumption are left to the economist, and statistical techniques for analysis of genetic data are left to the biologists.

indexes, ratios, rates, and graphic measures.

The materials are presented by use of a large number of graphic techniques. More than 80 per cent of the figures and charts are used as an aid to analyzing the data, and only occasionally are figures constructed to emphasize the phenomena under consideration. Had these techniques not been used in portraying the data, however, the written material would have been much more voluminous and perhaps less illuminating. Many of the techniques used have been described by Dr. Homer L. Hitt.[2]

Comparison with other urban populations. Most of the findings in this study are compared with the urban population of the United States and certain southern cities, particularly Dallas, Texas; Nashville, Tennessee; and New Orleans, Louisiana.

The basis for selecting Dallas, Nashville, and New Orleans for comparative purposes is the subjective judgment of the writer. It does seem, however, that these cities are most suitable, for several reasons. The author has a first-hand acquaintance with Nashville; New Orleans was the largest "true" southern city in 1940; and since these cities are comparatively "old," Dallas serves as a rather good example of a "recent" city. Dallas also has an economic basis somewhat similar to that of Atlanta in that both are regional distribution and transportation centers.

The number and distribution of the population. One usually judges the importance of a town, city, state, or nation on the basis of size (population and area); and usually the data available on these two items are the most reliable of demographic data.[3] The data concerning demographic phenomena are obtained by means of the census which Fairchild describes as follows:

A periodic enumeration of the population of a political unit. The data secured ordinarily include not only the simple number of persons, but also facts concerning sex, age, race, and a variety of other characteristics which may be very inclusive. The oldest continuous genuine census in the world is that of the United States, which was inaugurated at the beginning of its independent life in 1790, and has been conducted regularly at ten-year intervals ever since.[4]

2. "The Use of Selected Cartographic Techniques in Health Research," *Social Forces*, 26:189-196, December, 1947.
3. T. Lynn Smith, *Production Analysis* (New York: McGraw-Hill Book Company, Inc., 1948), p. 3.
4. Henry P. Fairchild (ed.), *Dictonary of Sociology* (New York: Philosophical Library, 1944), p. 35.

In setting up criteria for determining who shall be counted in a given area of enumeration, three different concepts are used: (1) When the person is found in a certain area on the date of the actual enumeration, he is counted as belonging to that area (a *de facto* population results as in England); (2) when the location of a person's usual home or place of residence is used in determining the area to which a person belongs, he is counted as belonging to the area of his usual residence regardless of where he is found on the day of actual enumeration (a *de jure* population results as in the United States); and (3) a person's legal or voting residence is sometimes used in determining in what area a person should be counted.[5] In compliance with the second criterion above, the population of Atlanta is determined by assigning those persons to the Atlanta population whose residence or home is in Atlanta, Georgia. In many respects the concept *de facto* population would probably be more accurate and more easily counted for a highly urbanized society, but such has never been done for Atlanta or for American cities as a whole.

The density of population which "may be thought of as the average number of inhabitants residing in each square mile of the given area," may be computed by "dividing the number of people of the geographical unit by the land area of that unit expressed in square miles (or square kilometers)."[6]

In order to study cities and neighborhoods more thoroughly, the use of the census tract has been devised. The development of the use of the census tract is included herein and is largely taken from the publication giving data on Atlanta by census tracts.[7]

Around the turn of the century, Dr. Walter Laidlaw saw that population data for areas smaller than wards or boroughs were needed, and that these areas should remain unchanged from census to census. Upon his recommendation, the Census Bureau tabulated data of the 1910 census by tracts for seven cities of over 500,000 inhabitants and for New York City.[8] Today (1940) tract cities have been increased to sixty; for efforts leading to this increase

5. Leon E. Truesdell, "Methods Involved in the Federal Census Population," in Stuart A. Rice (ed.), *Methods in Social Science* (Chicago: The University of Chicago Press, 1931), pp. 199-201.
6. Smith, *op. cit.*, p. 9.
7. *Sixteenth Census of the United States: 1940*, "Population and Housing, Atlanta, Georgia," (Washington: Government Printing Office, 1942), p. 1.
8. *Ibid.*, pp. 1-2.

much credit is due Clarence E. Batschelet, Geographer of the Bureau of the Census, and Howard Whipple Green, Chairman of the Committee on Census Enumeration Areas of the American Statistical Association.

Census tracts may be defined as:

> . . . small areas, having a population usually between 3,000 and 6,000, into which certain large cities (and sometimes their adjacent areas) have been subdivided for statistical and local administrative purposes, through cooperation with a local committee in each case.[9]

The tract areas are generally established to include a comparatively homogeneous population and to obtain uniformity in size as well.[10]

Although Atlanta became a tract city for the first time in 1940, some data from the 1930 census have been retabulated by census tracts; therefore it has been possible in some cases to show trends even by census tracts between 1930 and 1940 within this particular study.[11]

Composition of the population. The static aspects or characteristics of a population which are recorded in a census and with which we are concerned in this study are residence, race, nativity, age, sex, marital status, educational status, occupational status, and religious composition.

(1) *Residence.* As far as residence is concerned, the present study deals with a comparatively small area of the United States, but it is desirable to study the characteristics of the population of this area in detail.

(2) *Race and nativity.* Although considerable data on race and nativity for cities are available prior to 1890, it is with the Eleventh Census that data are available in comparable form for urban areas. Although a criterion of 2,500 inhabitants was not established for urban places until 1910, much of the older data are available because of retabulation procedures included in the 1910 census.

The census data are divided into three major race classifica-

9. *Ibid.*, p. 1.
10. *Ibid.*, p. 1.
11. Works Progress Administration of Georgia Official Project 465-34-3-4, *A Statistical Study of Certain Aspects of the Social and Economic Pattern of the City of Atlanta, Georgia* (n.p.: Works Progress Administration of Georgia, 1939).

tions: white, Negro, and "other races"; the white population is further divided by nativity into native white and foreign-born white.[12] Data are available showing nativity of the nonwhite population; however, since only about 2 or 3 per cent of the nonwhite population of the nation are foreign-born (even less in Atlanta), no such division is made in this study.[13]

In this work Negro and nonwhite can be considered synonymous terms, since other colored people are in negligible numbers in the cities under consideration.

(3) *Age composition.* There are many irregularities in the age distribution which are caused by inaccuracies in the census returns. In all censuses a great many people misstate their ages, and the 1940 census was no exception. Where the age is not accurately known, there is a tendency to find it reported as a multiple of 5 or of some even number. Men appear to concentrate on age 21 and women in certain age groups understate their ages.[14] There is a marked tendency for age to be given as a figure ending in zero, for 5 to be second choice, and for preferring even numbers to odd numbers, except 5.[15]

Such misstatements in reporting age result in errors in all comparisons based on the population by age. The index calculated according to the method described below is useful in determining the accuracy of the reported ages.

The United States Census and those of many other countries present age distribution for single years beginning with under one and ending with 99, or a total of 100 one-year age periods. Omitting the persons whose ages are unknown and those 100 years of age and over, approximately 10 per cent of the remainder normally should be of an age exactly divisible by five, 40 per cent in the other even number ages, and the remaining 40 per cent in the odd number ages other than those ending in five. The effects of each of the known concentrations, i.e., on even years, years ending in 0, is to reduce the proportion of the population in the odd-number ages other

12. *Sixteenth Census of the United States: 1940*, "Population, Vol. II, Characteristics of the Population," Part 2 (Washington: Government Printing Office 1943), p. 4.
13. *Ibid.*, p. 4.
14. *Sixteenth Census of the United States: 1940*, "Population, Vol. IV, Characteristics by Age," Part 2 (Washington: Government Printing Office, 1943), p. 2.
15. P. K. Whelpton, *Needed Population Research* (Lancaster, Pennsylvania: The Science Printing Company, 1938), p. xi.

than those ending in 5. Consequently the ratio of the percentage of the population reporting ages 1, 3, 7, 9, 11, 13, 17, 19, etc., to 40 per cent is a fairly reliable guage of the accuracy of the reported ages. By expressing the observed percentages in these odd-number ages as a percentage of 40 gives an easily understood and useful index number. On such a scale perfect reporting would give a score of 100; and any tendency for the reported ages to concentrate in the even years and in the ages ending with 5 or 0 would reduce the rating.[16]

Although the age of the population of Atlanta is not given by single years, the data are available for the urban population of Georgia. On the index referred to above, the urban population of Georgia made a score of 93.4 out of a possible 100 for the year 1940; the score for the urban portion of the United States was 95.5; and the scores were 96.2 and 95 for the rural-nonfarm and rural-farm areas of the United States. But the racial breakdown within the United States showed a pronounced differential, with the nonwhites scoring 90.1 as compared to 96.1 for the white population.[17] The white population of Georgia scored 95.6 while the nonwhite made a score of only 88.0. In view of the aforementioned data, one could probably assume that the Atlanta population would score about 93.5; that the white population would be somewhat higher than this figure; and that the Negro population would be considerably lower.

Within the urban population of Georgia males made a slightly higher score than females; males made a score of 94.0 and females made one point lower. These figures agree in the main with other studies.[18] It is generally known that females understate their ages, and there seems to be a tendency for the nonwhite female to understate her age to a greater degree than for the white woman.[19]

Inaccuracy in reported ages is usually greater for adults than for children, although the underenumeration of children under 5 and particularly under 1 is quite apparent.[20]

Two simple techniques have been used in presenting the data

16. T. Lynn Smith, "A Demographic Study of the American Negro," *Social Forces*, 28:380, March, 1945.
17. *Ibid.*, p. 381.
18. Smith, *Population Analysis*, pp. 90-91.
19. Smith, "A Demographic Study of the American Negro," p. 381.
20. *Sixteenth Census of the United States: 1940*, "Population, Vol. IV, Characteristics by Age," Part 2 (Washington: Government Printing Office, 1943), p. 2.

on age; namely, the age-sex (population) pyramid and index numbers. In the construction of a population pyramid, "one computes the component percentages each age-sex group is of the total population" and in addition follows certain conventions.[21]

. . . males are represented on the left of the figure and females on the right; a horizontal per cent scale extends in either direction from a zero point in the center; and the 5-year age groups are represented by horizontal bars.[22]

The use of the more refined technique of index numbers makes it possible to point out minor variations (which are usually highly significant from a statistical standpoint, although caution must be used in dealing with small populations) which would ordinarily be passed over lightly.[23] The data are presented in a conventional manner with age variations placed on the horizontal scale and the index numbers on the vertical scale. At a height corresponding to the index number 100, a line is run across the chart to represent the situation in the population selected as the standard.[24] The method of calculating the index number for each age group has been reduced to the following formula:[25]

$$\frac{100}{\text{Per cent of standard population in a particular (y) 5-year age group}} = \frac{X}{\text{Per cent of selected population in a particular (y) 5-year age group}}$$

Any index number less than 100 indicates a relative deficiency of persons in that particular age group in comparison to the standard population; any index number above 100 indicates a relative excess of persons in that particular age group in comparison to the standard population.

Figures 17 and 18 were constructed for comparative purposes only and therefore leave much to be desired in selection of shadings; however, they did seem most useful in the form in which they are presented.

(4) *Sex distribution.* Census officials believe that the sex classifications for the total population are the most dependable of all

21. Margaret Jarman Hagood, *Statistics for Sociologists* (New York: Reynal and Hitchcock, Inc., 1941), p. 754.
22. *Ibid.,* p. 757.
23. Smith, *Population Analysis,* pp. 103-105.
24. *Ibid.,* p. 104.
25. *Ibid.,* pp. 104-105.

the classifications.[26] There is no reason to believe that the sex classification of the Atlanta population should be otherwise except to the extent that smaller numbers of people in census tracts would make the data somewhat less reliable, particularly the very small tracts.

One important error should be pointed out; namely, for Negro children under 5 an excess of females over males is consistently reported in census after census. This is also true for the Negro population of Atlanta, since more females than males are reported for the group under 5. This is not in accord with the data on the sex ratio at birth, and it could not come about by the differential mortality that favors females over males.[27]

In the analysis of the sex distribution of various population units the device most commonly used is the sex ratio; the usual practice being to compute the number of males per 100 females as the sex ratio.[28]

Sex ratios by age are not altogether reliable; however, this is true primarily because of the widespread practice by females of understatement of age.[29] Thus in most census reports, there is a marked decrease in the sex ratio in the age groups 15 to 25 (these ages being the most popular) and a correspondingly large increase in the sex ratio in ages 45 to 65. Most curves showing sex ratio by ages typically resemble a long drawn out "S," with a low point in the 20's, a subsequent gradual rise, and an eventual peak in the 50's or later. This curve is not the very gradual descending non-fluctuating curve which should result if there were no errors in the data, as has been pointed out by Smith.[30] In this study sex ratios by age have been determined and the resulting curves have been plotted; however, these results should be interpreted in the light of the above sources of unreliability. These curves are useful in comparing different populations, since the error noted is fairly consistent for each group within each census.

(5) *Marital status.* Information on marital status for some areas has been available in the census tabulations and publications since 1890, but data for Atlanta were available for the first time in

26. *Fifteenth Census of the United States: 1930*, "Population, Vol. II, General Report and Statistics by Subjects," (Washington: Government Printing Office, 1933), p. 93.
27. Smith, *Population Analysis*, p. 114.
28. Hagood, *op. cit.*, p. 115.
29. Smith, *Population Analysis*, pp. 116-122.
30. *Ibid.*, pp. 116-122.

the census of 1900.[31] The data on marital status refer to the marital condition at the time the census enumeration actually takes place, so that a widowed or divorced person who marries again is counted merely as married; furthermore, many refinements are lacking, particularly number of times married.[32] The general tendency for females to understate their ages introduces the largest error into the data. At certain ages, particularly around 30, the "impossible seems to occur" and the percentage of persons in the single category rises (Negro males are also offenders at this particular age group).[33] In general the data on marital status are fairly reliable even though some of those who actually belong among the divorced are reported as widowed, married, or single, and in spite of the existence of considerable error in the data concerning living with the spouse and living apart.[34]

Age is the most important factor in considering marital status. For adults, the married condition is the normal state followed in order by the single, the widowed, and the divorced.[35] In addition to age, sex and race are definitely related to marital status; so data have been plotted to bring out the differences in sex and race by age.[36] Finally, data on marital status in the censuses from 1910 through 1940 have been analyzed by age classifications in an effort to discover any possible trends in the marital condition of the population of Atlanta.

(6) *Educational status.* Until 1940 about the only measure of educational status was the proportion of persons able to read and write (percentage of literacy). For several reasons this was quite unsatisfactory: (1) Since the measure was often based on entire populations with no refinements, even including children who were too young to have been exposed to schooling; (2) since there was little uniformity in the criteria of the ability to read and write; and

31. *Twelfth Census of the United States: 1900,* "Population, Vol. II," Part II (Washington: Government Printing Office, 1902), p. 308.
32. Smith, *Population Analysis,* p. 133. In view of the small proportion of the adult population which is classified as divorced, no analysis has been made of this classification. There are about twice as many divorced women in Atlanta as divorced men, however. Furthermore, only about 1.5 per cent of the adult population of the United States is classified as divorced; about 2.0 per cent of the Atlanta population 15 years of age and over falls into the divorced classification in the census tabulations.
33. *Ibid.,* p. 134.
34. *Ibid.,* pp. 132-133.
35. *Ibid.,* pp. 134-137.
36. *Ibid.,* pp. 137-144.

(3) since in many parts of the nation and world illiteracy has been reduced to such a low figure that it is useless for comparative purposes.[37]

The Sixteenth Census in 1940 obtained the number of years of schooling completed; so today the following three measures furnish excellent comparative data among the population on educational status: (1) median years of schooling received, (2) percentage with no schooling, and (3) proportion finishing high school.[38]

(7) *Occupational status.* Although data had been collected concerning occupations since 1820, it was not until 1880 that significant data were available for the city of Atlanta.

Occupational statistics concerning the labor force had two serious defects up until 1940:

> . . . (1) the failure to make a primary distinction between those persons who were working on their own account and those who were working for someone else and (2) the lack of a thoroughgoing and consistent procedure for classifying the population along both industrial and occupational lines.[39]

The 1940 census clarified the data considerably.

Although data had been collected in previous censuses to show the relative importance of "wage or salary workers" and "employers and own account workers," it was first published in 1940 (except for certain ones engaged in agricultural pursuits).[40]

The particular occupations are classified into eight large groups in the 1940 census; of these classifications many are somewhat unsatisfactory. The most satisfactory classes (that is, in line with what the name would lead one to expect in urban areas) are "service workers," "craftsmen, foremen, and kindred workers," "clerical, sales, and kindred workers," and "proprietors, managers, and officials." "Professional" and "operatives and kindred workers" are rather heterogeneous and do not serve as completely satisfactory groupings.[41]

The classification of workers according to the industry in

37. *Ibid.*, pp. 153-154.
38. *Ibid.*, p. 154.
39. *Ibid.*, p. 165. (From *Population Analysis*, by T. Lynn Smith. Copyright 1948. Courtesy McGraw-Hill Book Co.)
40. *Sixteenth Census of the United States: 1940*, "Population, Vol. III, The Labor Force," Part 2 (Washington: Government Printing Office, 1943), p. 3.
41. Smith, *Population Analysis*, pp. 166-169.

which they were engaged gives data which are most nearly comparable to previous censuses, but it should be pointed out that the data on occupations as published in the 1940 census volumes are generally not comparable to previous data.[42] For that reason trends have been shown only from 1880 until 1930.

(8) *Religious composition.* Social statistics, including data on religious organizations, have been collected since the census of 1850, although the question of religious preference or affiliation has never been included in the regular census schedule.[43] Such countries as Peru, Germany, India, and Canada do include a question concerning religious affiliation in their regular census schedule; thus it is possible for students of population in those countries to pin down the religious factor when they attempt to determine the relationship between birth rate and occupation, fertility and residence, economic status and migration, and a host of other relationships.[44]

The data on religious status in the United States are not gathered in the Census of Population but are compiled separately in years ending with "6."[45] The data for religious bodies have been gathered four times: *Census of Religious Bodies for 1906, 1916, 1926,* and *1936.* Smith aptly points out that ". . . these materials are very incomplete, lack camparability, and are almost impossible to correlate with other census data."[46] For instance, in this particular study, it is very probable that a large proportion of the membership discussed in this chapter are not residents of the city of Atlanta but are suburban residents; but there is no way to verify this from the data in their present form.

The vital processes. The study of the vital processes includes the analysis of both fertility and mortality data. It seems convenient to begin with the study of reproduction.

(1) *Fertility.* Since such diverse terms have been used to describe the rate of human accretion, it is well that four of those terms be singled out and defined for use in this study: (1) *birth rate,* which refers to one particular manner of measuring the fertility of a population (quite often used in popular speech

---

42. *Ibid.,* pp. 164-174.
43. *Census of Religious Bodies: 1906,* Part 1 (Washington: Government Printing Office, 1910), p. 3.
44. Smith, *Population Analysis,* p. 175.
45. *Ibid.,* p. 176.
46. *Ibid.,* p. 176.

to refer to reproduction);[47] (2) *fertility*, which indicates the actual reproduction of a population;[48] (3) *fecundity*, which denotes the quality or capability of bearing children (potential reproduction);[49] and (4) *natality*, which has not been given a definite connotation and so has not been used in this study.[50]

There are three principal measures of fertility: the birth rate, the fertility ratio, and the net reproduction rate.[51]

(a) *The birth rate.* The crude birth rate is the ratio of the total live births for a given area and time to the total population of that area at the midinterval of the time period; the result is usually multiplied by 1,000.[52] For example, the crude birth rate of Atlanta in 1940 is computed as follows:

$$\frac{\text{Number of births in 1940}}{\text{Population}} \text{ X } 1,000 = \frac{6,344}{302,288} \text{ X } 1,000 = 21.0$$

The population of July 1, should have been used instead of April 1; but in view of inaccuracies in the data, such a refinement would be of little value, for the crude birth rate is very limited in its usefulness as a gauge of human fertility.[53] Since the age and sex composition of a population (as well as age of marriage, etc.,) are so closely related to the crude birth rate, one must make allowances for these differences before making final generalizations. The crude birth rate is useful for making comparisons to indicate the general trend of births for relatively short periods in given areas and for comparing populations with somewhat the same composition, although under-registration of births is likely to give erroneous trends.[54] "Specific rates may be computed for any desired subgroups, such as those for race, urban or rural residence, and age of mother."[55]

47. *Ibid.*, p. 193.
48. Raymond Pearl, *Introduction to Medical Biometry and Statistics* (Philadelphia: W. B. Saunders Company, 1940), p. 199.
49. Sir Arthur Newsholme, *The Elements of Vital Statistics in Their Bearing on Social and Public Health Problems* (London: George Allen and Unwin, Ltd., 1923), p 84, cited by Forrest E. Linder and Robert D. Grove, *Vital Statistics Rates in the United States: 1900-1940* (Washington: Government Printing Office, 1947), p. 54.
50. Smith, *Population Analysis*, p. 176.
51. *Ibid.*, pp. 193-194.
52. Linder and Grove, *op. cit.*, p. 54.
53. Warren S. Thompson, *Population Problems* (New York: McGraw-Hill Book Company, Inc., 1942), p. 163.
54. *Ibid.*, p. 163.
55. Linder and Grove, *op. cit.*, p. 56.

Birth rates are standardized (standardized birth rates) in order to compare the fertility of populations without the results being damaged by the influence of the age and sex composition of the population.[56] The standardized birth rate has not been used, however, in this study.

(b) *The fertility ratio.* Although not a ratio in the strictest sense of the word, this index is calculated by relating the very young children (usually those under 5) to the women of child-bearing ages (women 15-44 or 20-44); then multiplying the result by 1,000.[57] In this study (unless otherwise stated) fertility ratio is the number of children under 5 per 1,000 women aged 15-44.

In comparison to the birth rate, the fertility ratio has several advantages: (1) It is not affected by underregistration of births; (2) it is more refined, since it eliminates women who are too young or too old to produce children and it also eliminates men; and (3) when it is necessary to standardize, it is more easily done.[58] The fertility ratio has the following disadvantages: It depends on census data and so cannot be obtained on a nation-wide basis but once every ten years; and it cannot be applied to some nativity classes, since the mothers fall in one group and the children in another. Sometimes it proves imperfect in comparing Negroes in the South, since mothers often leave children on the farm and move to the city, placing mothers and children in different residential classifications.[59] Birth statistics, however, are so unreliable that the fertility ratio is the most practical and reliable of our measures of fertility.[60]

(c) *Replacement ratios.* The replacement ratios indicate the trend of total fertility by holding the age-specific rates constant although the age make-up itself may be changing. The first of these rates is the gross reproduction rate.

The gross reproduction rate is the figure obtained by computing the number of children that would be born to 1,000 women (1) passing, without losses by death, through the reproductive period, and (2) subject to the prevailing rates of reproduction at the several age periods. For the population to maintain its number on this basis, it would be

56. Smith, *Population Analysis*, pp. 194-196.
57. Hagood, *op. cit.*, p. 123.
58. Smith, *Population Analysis*, p. 198.
59. *Ibid.*, p. 198.
60. *Ibid.*, p. 198.

16

necessary for 1,000 mothers to have 1,000 daughters. . . . This represents the absolute minimum compatible with a self-sustaining population. The gross reproduction rate leaves no place for improvement in mortality, for it assumes the ideal of no deaths for these women from birth to the end of their reproductive period.[61]

"In their most useful form the data on the fertility of a population are related to those on mortality and expressed as a percentage of that necessary to maintain a stationary population. This is called the net reproduction rate."[62]

The net reproduction is obtained by allowing for the losses by death of the original cohort of 1,000 women. This group is made subject to prevailing death rates from age 0 to the end of the reproductive cycle and, on the basis of the actual age-specific fertility rates, the number of female births to all women remaining alive is calculated. The average number of daughters thus computed for each woman of the original cohort gives the net reproduction rate If the rate is equal to 1, the population is just replacing itself (remains stationary); if it is more than unity, it is increasing. A net reproduction rate below unity indicates a decreasing population. However, this prediction holds good only after the present fertility and mortality have been held constant long enough to build up a population in which the age composition is due entirely to the operation of these two factors.[63]

In Chapter XII life tables have been constructed and the stationary populations set up for both the white and the Negro "races" of Atlanta; thus with just a few more computations, the net reproduction rate could be obtained if live births by age of mother, race, and sex were available for the population of Atlanta. Unfortunately the exact net reproduction rate cannot be computed, since live births by age of mother, race, and sex for the population of Atlanta are not available. Nevertheless, in order to obtain a figure as close to the true net reproduction rate as possible, female births to Atlanta mothers by race and age have been calculated by using the sex ratio of births in the white and the Negro population of Georgia; thus it is possible to obtain approximately

61. Rupert B. Vance, *All These People* (Chapel Hill: The University of North Carolina Press, 1945), p. 90.
62. Smith, *Population Analysis*, p. 198.
63. Vance, *loc. cit.*

17

the number of female births to the cohort under consideration. For the period 1939-1941 the sex ratio at birth of the white population of Georgia was 1.06196 and of the Negro population, was 1.03021. The number of female births to mothers in each 5-year age group was found by dividing 2.06196 and 2.03021 into the total births to Atlanta mothers of the white and the Negro races respectively. No correction was made for underregistration.

All of the calculations made for computing the gross and net reproduction rates are in accordance with procedures outlined by Hagood.[64]

In addition to the net reproduction rate, data calculated in this study as well as an index of net reproduction are used; and some rather old data are used for comparative purposes. The index of net reproduction is calculated "by relating the ratio of children under five per 1,000 women aged 20-44 in the actual population to the same ratio in the stationary population."[65]

(d) *The data on fertility.* The data by age and sex for the city of Atlanta have been available since the census of 1890, and thus it is possible to compute the fertility ratios for the last 50 years.

The collection of birth statistics in the United States was initiated in 1915 although the birth registration area was not complete until 1933.[66] Data on births are available for Georgia since 1928 although they were not tabulated by both place of residence and place of occurrence until 1937. For the city of Atlanta, birth statistics by residence are available since 1937. Underregistration of births has plagued demographers in dealing with fertility data, so "more complete registration is now the most important goal in the improvement of birth statistics."[67]

It was estimated that birth registration for the white population of Georgia was about 83.6 per cent complete during the period December 1, 1939, to March 31, 1940. Birth registration for the Negro population of Georgia was only 77.6 per cent complete.[68] For the United States as a whole, the percentage completeness of birth registration for whites and Negroes was

64. *Op. cit.,* pp. 890-896.
65. *Ibid.,* p. 92.
66. Linder and Grove, *op. cit.,* p. 1.
67. Smith, *Population Analysis,* p. 207.
68. *Sixteenth Census of the United States: 1940,* "United States Life Tables and Actuarial Tables: 1939-1941," (Washington: Government Printing Office, 1946), p. 102.

93.98 and 81.87 respectively.[69] Since birth registration is usually more complete in urban areas than in rural, one would expect the completeness of birth registration for Atlanta to be considerably above the average of Georgia. The percentage completeness of birth registration in Atlanta for the period December 1, 1939 to March 31, 1940 was as follows: all classes, 95.7; whites, 97.2; and Negroes, 92.3.[70] No corrections have been made in this study for underregistration, however.

(2) *Mortality*. The three principal measures of mortality are (1) the death rate, (2) the expectation of life, and (3) the infant mortality rate.[71] The last mentioned is an especially good index of the general welfare of the population.

(a) *Crude death rate*. There are many kinds of death rates. Hagood makes a basic classification of "observed death rates," "corrected death rates," and "standardized death rates."[72] The crude death rate for Atlanta in 1940 may be calculated by use of the following formula:[73]

$$\frac{\text{Number of deaths occurring during}}{\text{Population of Atlanta, 1940}} \text{ X } 1,000 = \frac{3,679}{302,288} \text{ X } 1,000 = 12.2$$

Of course the crude death rate could be based on deaths tabulated by occurrence or by residence. The population used above should have been for the mid-year 1940 rather than for April 1. Crude death rates are not accurate or refined enough to give valid results for all comparisons.[74] They are useful, however, for comparing similar populations for similar periods of time; for example, the comparison of cities as used in this study. Nevertheless, one must always bear in mind the extent to which crude death rates are related to the influence of the sex and age make-up of the population.

(b) *Other death rates*. To make the data concerning death rates more accurate, they must be standardized by age and sex; the

69. *Ibid.*, p. 103.
70. Robert D. Grove, "Studies in Completeness of Birth Registration," *Vital Statistics—Special Reports*. 17:242, April, 1943.
71. *Sixteenth Census of the United States: 1940*, "United States Life Tables and Actuarial Tables: 1939-1941," pp. 234 and 248.
72. *Op. cit.*, pp. 821-822.
73. Smith, *Population Analysis*, p. 234.
74. *Ibid.*, p. 235.

process used is the same as that for the birth rates. In addition to standardized death rates, useful rates are those for specific age and sex groupings, which are called age-specific death rates.

(c) *The expectation of life*. Smith gives an excellent description of the life table and expectation of life.

> Perhaps the most useful manner of combining the age-specific death rates is to construct what is called a *life table*. Such a table shows the average duration of life for persons born at the same time and for persons of any given age who are alive at the same time. It indicates the average number of years that those of any given age from birth on up may expect to live. This average is called the *expectation of life*. . . .[75]

Life tables are very useful and are needed in this study particularly to measure mortality, to measure the gross and net reproduction rates in Atlanta, and to measure replacement rates. Life tables are available for state populations and have been constructed for selected states by sex, race, and residence. To the writer's knowledge, however, life tables are not available for the state of Georgia by sex, race, and residence nor for the city of Atlanta by race and sex.

In view of the need for life tables for the population of Atlanta, they were constructed. The life tables in this study were prepared according to the Reed-Merrell Method.[76] Considerable difficulty was encountered, as the age distribution of the city of Atlanta was not given beyond 75 years, by 5-year age groups. Since the age distribution above 75 years was not available for Atlanta, the next best source would have been age-specific death rates for the urban portion of the Georgia population for the advanced age groups. This information was not available without considerable effort in correcting the data both for the age groupings as well as for the reported deaths (the latter being especially necessary for the nonwhite group). In view of the fact that life tables had been constructed for the urban population of Mississippi by

75. *Ibid.*, pp. 235-236. (From *Population Analysis*, by T. Lynn Smith. Copyright 1948. Courtesy of McGraw-Hill Book Co.)
76. Lowell J. Reed and Margaret Merrel, "A Short Method for Constructing an Abridged Life Table," *Vital Statistics—Special Reports*, 9:681-712, June, 1940; and Hagood, *op. cit.*, pp. 856-915. The statement that the construction of a life table by "the Reed-Merrell method . . . involves only 1 or 2 hours of work" is found in Linder and Grove, *op. cit.*, p. 76. After constructing many life tables in the study of population, the present writer seriously doubts that a life table can be constructed by this method in 2 hours.

20

sex and race in 1948, and since the life expectancy at birth of the white populations of these two southern states corresponded fairly closely (Georgia: males, 61.72; females, 67.46; Mississippi: males, 62.26; females, 67.17), it was decided to use the specific death rates of the Mississippi urban population for the advanced ages.[77] The life tables from which the data were taken were prepared by Vernon Davies and John C. Belcher.[78] Even though the populations of Georgia and Mississippi are not entirely comparable, and although it is known definitely that the urban population of Mississippi is not so highly urbanized as the population of Atlanta, the writer thinks that the amount of error introduced will not be considerable.

In computing the age-specific death rates, the July 1, 1940 population was used; this was calculated by linear extrapolation.[79] Although this method is simple, it was probably quite accurate since very little time had elapsed since the census date (only three months removed).

No effort was made to make correction for the age distribution of the Atlanta population nor for the underregistration of deaths. It is felt that the errors involved here are slight for the white population of Atlanta; and even though they may be considerable in the case of nonwhites, the size of the error is not known.[80]

(d) *Infant mortality*. The infant mortality rate is usually computed by relating:[81]

$$\frac{\text{Deaths of infants under one year of age (exclusive of stillbirths) during a specified time period (usually one year)}}{\text{Total number of live births occuring during the same period}} \times 1,000$$

77. Metropolitan Life Insurance Company, *State and Regional Life Tables: 1939-41* (Washington: Government Printing Office, 1948), pp. 106-109 and 158-161.
78. *Mississippi Life Tables by Sex, Race and Residence: 1940* (Jackson, Mississippi: Mississippi Commission on Hospital Care, 1948), pp. 4-5 and 8-9.
79. Hagood, *op. cit.*, pp. 790-797.
80. For a discussion of errors involved see *Sixteenth Census of the United States: 1940*, "United States Life Tables and Actuarial Tables: 1939-1941," (Washington: Govenment Printing Office, 1946), pp. 1, 10, 101-107.
81. Linder and Grove, *op. cit.*, p. 43.

The infant mortality rate for the city of Atlanta in 1940 was, for example, calculated as follows: $\dfrac{305}{6{,}344} \times 1{,}000 = 48.1$

The saving of the lives of children and infants has been responsible for the great decline in the death rate in recent years and as a result the expectation of life has increased considerably.[82] Thompson states that the four factors most responsible for lowering infant mortality are:

> . . . (a) the better care that children are receiving at home, that is primarily, the improvement in the methods and sanitation of infant feeding; (b) the decline in the number of children born to a large portion of the mothers, thus enabling them to give their children better care both before and after birth; (c) the more expert medical care of children; and (d) the generally more comfortable circumstances in which a large part of the people in the more advanced nations now live.[83]

Smith has pointed out that the paramount reason the infant mortality continues to be an excellent measure of the general welfare of a population, is that ". . . people that lack the knowledge or the desire to care for their helpless offspring will hardly have the knowledge or the will to care for themselves."[84]

(e) *Causes of death.* In regard to causes of death, in many cases the "causes of death are as yet lacking in precise scientific definition and standardization,"[85] however, with this limitation, fairly complete data for recent years are available for Atlanta.

(f) *The data.* Although some data for mortality have been collected by enumeration in the past (1850-1900), the Twelfth Census taken in 1900 was the last to collect data with the regular population enumeration.[86] Data are now collected under a registration system, which was an outgrowth of the Census Act of 1902. Georgia did not permanently enter the death-registration area until 1928; thus data are available only from that time.[87]

82. Thompson, *op. cit.*, p. 220.
83. *Ibid.*, pp. 221-222. (From *Population Problems*, by Warren S. Thompson. Copyright 1942. Courtesy of McGraw-Hill Book Co.)
84. *Population Analysis*, p. 248.
85. *Ibid.*, p. 247.
86. United States Census Office, *Census Reports*, "Vol. III, Vital Statistics," Parts I and II (Washington: Government Printing Office, 1902).
87. Linder and Grove, *op. cit.*, pp. 583 and 605.

Furthermore, the data were not classified by residence until the publication for 1937 of a volume combining both natality and mortality even though some partial tabulations had been made irregularly since 1915.[88] Thus, fairly accurate and usable data on mortality are available for the city of Atlanta since 1937 only, and complete data are still not available.

Migration. The term *migration* is used in this study to refer to the movement of people in physical space; it is understood that such movement involves a change in residence.[89] There are two main types of migration that will be considered here: international migration and internal (inter- and intrastate) migration.

The most accurate data on migration to the city of Atlanta are contained in the census publication, *State of Birth of the Native Population*.[90] These data are presented in Figures 63 to 70 for Atlanta and three other southern cities. The most accurate data on foreign immigration to Atlanta are contained in tabulations showing country of birth of the foreign-born white population (these data have been examined also under race and nativity).

In 1940 about 76 per cent of the native white population of Atlanta was born in Georgia; while nearly 94 per cent of the native-born nonwhite population of Atlanta was born in Georgia. The Atlanta native-born white population represents about 9.5 per cent of the native white population of Georgia; while the Negro population of Atlanta is 9.6 per cent of the Negro population of the state of Georgia. If migration were not selective of age and sex, the Atlanta population should be about 9.5 per cent of the Georgia population at all ages.

In order to determine whether migration to Atlanta, with respect to the Georgia population, is selective of age and sex, a technique suggested by T. Lynn Smith has been used. Figures 71 and 72 have been made according to conventional patterns; age is shown on the horizontal scale and the percentage is shown on the vertical scale. The population of Atlanta has been related to the population of Georgia by age and further divided by sex. The heavy line on the chart represents the situation for the population of Atlanta in relation to the population of Georgia.

88. *Vital Statistics of the United States: 1946*, Part II (Washington: Government Printing Office, 1946), p. vi.
89. Smith, *Population Analysis*, p. 293.
90. *Sixteenth Census of the United States: 1940*, "Population, State of Birth of the Native Population," (Washington: Government Printing Office, 1944).

For example, the first point on the chart for native white males in Figure 71 is found by dividing the number of native white males 0-4 in Atlanta by the number of males 0-4 in the Georgia native white population. As discussed under the chapter of "migration," this device definitely shows that the migration processes are selective of age and sex.

In 1940 considerable data were collected on internal migration by color, age, and sex of migrants as well as by economic characteristics of migrants. The writer has not made use of these data because he felt that they were basically faulty for use here.[91]

The growth of population. No effort is made in this study to deal with any so-called mathematical laws of population growth. The growth of the city of Atlanta is traced from the time it first became a city of 2,500 persons in 1850 until 1948.

The growth of population has been presented upon semilogarithmic paper. This type chart is useful where the proportion or rate of change is the feature to be emphasized.[92] Smith points out that:

> Plotting the population or the dependent variable on a logarithmic scale has two advantages: (1) it helps keep the diagram within reasonable dimensions; and (2) since a variable that increases at a uniform rate gives a straight line when plotted on semilogarithmic paper, it enables one to tell at a glance whether the rate of increase is holding its own or falling off and just as readily to compare the rates of population increase. . . .[93]

Although it has not been necessary to make an estimate of population, in the study of growth of population, it can be rather easily and simply done by means of the death rate. Since the

91. *Sixteenth Census of the United States: 1940*, "Population, Internal Migration 1935 to 1940, Color and Sex of Migrants," (Washington: Government Printing Office, 1943); *Sixteenth Census of the United States: 1940*, "Population, Internal Migration 1935 to 1940, Age of Migrants," (Washington: Government Printing Office, 1946); *Sixteenth Census of the United States: 1940*, "Population, Internal Migration 1935 to 1940, Economic Characteristics of Migrants," (Washington: Government Printing Office, 1946); and *Sixteenth Census of the United States: 1940*, "Population, Internal Migration 1935 to 1940, Social Characteristics of Migrants," (Washington: Government Printing Office, 1946). For an excellent discussion of these materials see *Smith, Population Analysis*, pp. 296-299.
92. Hagood, *op. cit.*, p. 84.
93. *Population Analysis*, pp. 372-373. (From *Population Analysis*, by T. Lynn Smith. Copyright 1948. Courtesy of McGraw-Hill Book Co.)

number of deaths for the city of Atlanta is known for 1947 and, in view of the fact that death rates change very slightly from year to year, the population could be estimated by the formula for the death rate.[94]

$$\text{Death rate} = \frac{\text{number of deaths}}{\text{population}} \times 1,000$$

Since no estimates are made, it seems unnecessary to explain methods of interpolation and/or extrapolation.

SIGNIFICANCE OF THIS STUDY

This study is important because it represents an inroad into the use of a vast wealth of population data which for the most part are as yet unanalyzed.

In the second place, most of the analytical techniques of demography and the tract city are products of the twentieth century; therefore they were not available until rather recently. Thus, it is an opportunity to get results from the application of such techniques as the sex ratio, the life table, the net reproduction rate, the fertility ratio, and the many other analytical techniques to data on a tract city.

Third, many of the analytical techniques have been applied previously either in their entirety or in part to total populations or rural populations and to a limited extent to urban populations. This has come about largely within the last twenty years and a considerable portion of this work has been done by rural sociologists. Such studies include that which Hamilton carried on in North Carolina on migration; Williams' study of mobility in South Carolina; the study of Beegle and Smith on differential fertility in Louisiana; Smith's analysis of the composition of the population of Louisiana; and among other studies, the National Resources Committee's analysis of data relating to the urban United States.[95]

94. *Ibid.*, p. 186.
95. C. Horace Hamilton, *Rural-Urban Migration in North Carolina 1920 to 1930*, North Carolina Agricultural Experiment Station Bulletin 295, Raleigh, 1934; B. O. Williams, "Mobility and Farm Tenancy," *Journal of Land and Public Utility Economics*, 14:207-208, May, 1938; J. Allan Beegle and T. Lynn Smith, *Differential Fertility in Louisiana*, Louisiana Agricultural Experiment Station Bulletin 403, Baton Rouge, 1946; T. Lynn Smith, *The Population of Louisiana: Its Composition and Changes*, Louisiana Agricultural Experiment Station Bulletin 293, Baton Rouge, 1937; National Resources Committee, *Population Statistics, 3. Urban Data* (Washington: Government Printing Office, 1937).

And in the fourth place, even though John Graunt[96] made a good start in 1662 toward analyzing the population of the city of London, as far as the writer can ascertain, never have all the modern demographic techniques been applied to the population of one city and particularly to a southern city (especially a tract city).

ORDER OF PRESENTATION

The first and second chapters are devoted to the introduction and to a review of the literature respectively. The last chapter in the study is a summarizing chapter. The remainder of the work is devoted to five major topics: (1) the number and distribution of the population of Atlanta; (2) the composition of the population; (3) the vital processes; (4) migration; and (5) growth of population.

Chapter III is an analysis of the first of these topics, the number and distribution of the population. The next seven chapters are devoted to the second topic; that is, the composition of the population and the particularly distinguishing features of race and nativity, the age profile, the sex distribution, the marital status, the educational status, the occupational status, and the religious status of the Atlanta population. The vital processes, which is the third major topic, are covered in Chapters XI and XII. These two chapters are concerned with factors having to do with reproduction and mortality respectively. Migration, which is the fourth topic, is covered in a single chapter (Chapter XIII); while Chapter XIV is devoted to the final topic, the growth of population.

GENERAL ORIENTATION TO THE CITY

Without adhering to strictly conventional terminology, the following orientation will aid the reader in understanding the physical layout of Atlanta.

The Metropolitan District of Atlanta is composed of the central city of Atlanta and its satellite incorporated cities and suburban unincorporated areas. These satellite cities include Decatur (population 16,561) on the east and northeast; East Point (population 12,403), College Park (population 8,213), Hapeville

96. Walter F. Willcox, editor, *Natural and Political Observations Made Upon the Bills of Mortality by John Graunt* (Baltimore: The Johns Hopkins Press, 1939), pp. 1-90.

26

(population 5,059) on the south and southwest; Brookhaven, Chamblee, Clarkston, and Doraville on the northeast; and Avondale Estates on the east of Decatur. The suburban unincorporated areas tangent to Atlanta include the populous northern residential section of Buckhead (estimated 1948 population, 75,000), Center Hill (population 12,155) west of the central city; and Lakewood, south of the city. In 1940, the metropolitan area included a large portion of Fulton and DeKalb Counties and small portions of Cobb and Clayton Counties.

The happenings and developments of time become visible within the central city of Atlanta. The downtown retail trade area has grown up around the railroads which run in the general direction of east and west, in this central part. The general shape of the downtown area is an elongated rectangle with the main lines of traffic running north and south. This area stretches some one-and-a-half miles north and south by about six blocks east and west, and there is considerably greater movement of vehicular and pedestrian traffic in the generally north-south direction. The southern part of the city developed much earlier than did the section north of the railroad tracks. However, this southern area is "ringed in" by several large industries, the Federal Penitentiary, and the satellite cities of East Point and Hapeville. Thus, within the twenty years preceding 1940 there was a very rapid development northward. The southern portion of the city contains much more industry than does the northern portion.

Within the downtown trade area, the shops south of the railroad tracks still do a greater proportion of the retail and wholesale trading for the city. Many of the "smarter" and more expensive shops, however, are congregated in the northern trade area. Most of the downtown theatres are located on Peachtree Street in the northern shopping district. On Marietta Street, leading northwest from the heart of the city, are situated many of Atlanta's small industries. The large stock yards and most of the abattoirs of the city are found in this northwestern region.

The heart of the city is "Five Points," where five streets form a junction; from this point, the city has developed in every direction. The city's government centers are concentrated a few blocks south of the "heart" of the city in the "older" part of town and are within two blocks of one another; these include the State

Capitol, located on a prominent high point, the City Hall, and the Fulton County Court House.

In Atlanta, as in other southern cities, whites and Negroes are usually segregated (by custom). Around the downtown retail trade area, there appears to be a belt of Negro population in all areas except that directly north of this area. In addition, the western and southwestern parts of the city contain a large proportion of Negroes. In the western part of the city are located several large Negro universities; this appears to be the section where the "elite" within this racial group are concentrated. The sections of West End (southwest) and Inman Park (northeast) were at one time choice white residential sections; both are now densely populated and include many persons who rent rooms, homes, and apartments. Among residential areas characterized by homes for higher income-level white families are the Ansley Park section (northeast), the Druid Hills section (northeast), and the Piedmont Park section (north). Middle-income families, where the characteristic pattern is the small home, owned by the occupant, dominate in the following sections: Kirkwood (southeast), Sylvan Hills (southwest), and East Atlanta (east).

With this orientation to the city of Atlanta, and the previous introduction to the methods used in this study, it is proper that a review of the literature related to urban population analysis be undertaken before beginning the analysis proper.

CHAPTER II

REVIEW OF THE LITERATURE

It is the purpose of this chapter (1) to review some of the literature relative to population study but particularly relating to city populations, and (2) to select some of those writings which represent a distinct contribution to the field of urban population study. There is, in one place or another, an abundance of maps, tables, essays, studies, and other information relating to city populations; but nowhere can one find a critical examination and summary of the more important findings and statements relating to urban population analysis.

A general survey of the literature in the field of population has suggested to the investigator that he must of necessity limit and even select the contributions which are reported in this review. This is necessary because of the great number of "studies" in the field of population down through the years.

The Greeks apparently began the writings commonly referred to as population theory; Plato wrote in his *Republic* concerning the relationship of population increase to warfare; Aristotle advocated control of offspring in order to regulate population to resources. Except for a few writings here and there, however, no population theory was evolved from Greek antiquity to modern times.[1] This study of Atlanta is not concerned with philosophical population theory; nor does it stress the study of the urban population from the pathological point of view. Within this work the stress is upon the analysis of urban populations in general and upon the analysis of the population of one city in particular.

It appears that the development of the body of knowledge in the field of urban population analysis can, with considerable justification, be divided into three basic periods. The first period extended from the time of John Graunt's study of the bills of mortality in London in 1662, through the first quarter of the nineteenth century and the publication of the essays of Malthus. Although including an interval of considerable inactivity, the second period covered the remainder of the nineteenth century

1. A. B. Wolfe, "Population," *Encyclopedia of the Social Sciences*, first edition, XII, 248-9.

and extended through the first quarter of the twentieth century. The present period began with Thompson's study in 1931 of the ratio of children to women in 1920. (There might be considerable justification for beginning the modern period with the work of Willcox and/or the work of Billings relating to the declining birth rate in the United States. The writer preferred the foregoing division, however.)

The first of these periods was characterized by some rather speculative writings, but the real intent was to understand population movements. The second period amounted to a time of development of techniques. The third period now affords an opportunity for the application and the further development of those techniques.

From Graunt Through the Essays of Malthus

As far as the writer could ascertain the first known attempt to estimate the population of a city was made in 1662 by John Graunt in his publication, *Observations on the London Bills of Mortality*. With Graunt's work as a point of departure, there follows a review of the literature in more or less chronological order. It should be pointed out that the subdivisions in this chapter are not indicative in all cases of the importance of the study or author under consideration; for in the interest of economy of space and time, it has been necessary merely to mention many important writers and their literature by means of footnotes.

John Graunt's Observations on the London Bills of Mortality.[2] Walter F. Willcox clearly summarizes Graunt's contribution as follows:

> Graunt is memorable mainly because he discovered the numerical regularity of deaths and births, of the ratios of the sexes at death and birth, and of the proportion of deaths from certain causes to all deaths in successive years and in different areas; or in general terms, the uniformity and predictability of many important biological phenomena taken in mass. In doing so he opened the way both for the later discovery of uniformities in many social or volitional phenomena like marriage, suicide and crime, and for a study of these uniformi-

2. Walter F. Willcox, editor, *Natural and Political Observations made upon the Bills of Mortality by John Graunt* (Baltimore: The Johns Hopkins Press, 1939), pp. 1-90.

30

ties, their nature and their limits; thus he, more than any other man, was the founder of statistics.[3]

Graunt started out by referring to his sources of data (the weekly Bills of Mortality) and their shortcomings. He was aware that the bills were little used, but he gathered all that the parish clerks were able to afford him and reduced them to tables. Even Graunt found that deaths were reported more accurately than births (christenings); and he accounted for this by the following reasons: (1) religious attitude against baptizing of infants as unnecessary or unlawful; (2) ministers lacking authority to have names placed on registers; and (3) the necessity of fees. Graunt observed that burials exceeded christenings from the period 1603 to 1644. According to these records the population of London should have declined; but instead, he knew that it was growing because of increase of buildings, housings, foundations, and other such indications. Thus he realized that the country surrounding London must be furnishing this increase in population (rural-urban migration). He further found that in the country the christenings exceeded the burials, and of particular interest is the way he accounts for this differential birth rate.

. . . Now that the Breeders in London are proportionally fewer then those in the Country arises from these reasons, *viz.*

1. All that have business to the Court of the King, or to the Courts of Justice, and all Country-men coming up to bring Provisions to the City, or to buy Foreign Commodities, Manufactures, and Rarities, do for the most part leave their Wives in the Country.

2. Persons coming to live in *London* out of curiosity, and pleasure, as also such as would retire, and live privately, do the same, if they have any.

3. Such, as come up to be cured of Diseases, do scarce use their Wives *pro tempore.*

4. That many Apprentices of *London*, who are bound seven, or nine years from Marriage, do often stay longer voluntarily.

5. That many Sea-men of *London* leave their Wives behind them, who are more subject to die in the absence of

3. *Ibid.*, p. xiii.

their Husbands, then to breed either without men, or with the use of many promiscuously.

6. As for unhealthiness it may well be supposed, that although seasoned Bodies may, and do live near as long in *London*, as elsewhere, yet new-comers, and Children do not, for the *Smoaks*, *Stinks*, and close *Air* are less healthfull then that of the Country; otherwise why do sickly Persons remove into the Country *Air*? And why are there more old men in Countries then in *London*, *per rata*? And although the difference in *Hackney*, and *Newington*, above-mentioned, be not very notorious, yet the reason may be their vicinity to *London*, and that the Inhabitants are most such, whose bodies have first been impaired with the *London Air*, before they withdraw thither.

7. As to the causes of Barrenness in *London*, I say, that although there should be none extraordinary in the Native *Air* of the place, yet the intemperance in feeding, and especially the Adulteries and Fornications, supposed more frequent in *London*, then elsewhere, do certainly hinder breeding. For a Woman, admitting 10 Men, is so far from having ten times as many Children, that she hath none at all.

8. Add to this, that the minds of men in *London* are more thoughtfull and full of business then in the Country, where their work is *corporal* Labour, and Exercizes. All which promote Breedings, whereas *Anxieties* of the minde hinder it.[4]

Contrary to findings today, Graunt pointed out that there were more males in the city than females; however, he did point out that males tend to outnumber females in long distance migrations (which is in agreement with present-day findings).[5] He noted as the city grows, the boundaries of the city push outward; and that there is an increase in the number of parishes and the number of deaths. He was interested in fertility and estimated that every wedding produced four children. He remarked about live and still births and even went so far as to set up "life tables" which pointed out the high death rates in the very early ages.[6]

Although Graunt and the writers that followed him differed on several points, all of them agreed that:

. . . the cities were less healthful than the country; that

4. *Ibid.*, pp. 55-56.
5. *Ibid.*, p. 58.
6. *Ibid.*, p. 71.

the city population was poorer from the standpoint of vitality than the country population; and that the mortality rate of the city population was higher and the birth rate lower than that of the rural people—some exceptions to this rule, stressed by Justi, Halley, and Deparcieux were, in their own opinions, not real exceptions, but mere results of migrational factors and difference in the age composition of the city and the country population. They all stressed that, without migration from the rural districts, the cities would be unable to grow and would be doomed to decrease in population and eventually disappear, because of the excess of deaths over births. In connection with this, some of them discussed the age, sex, and other characteristics of the cityward migrants and the "export" of the babies to the city.[7]

William Petty (1623-1685). Concerning the vital processes Petty came to conclusions similar to those of Graunt; however, he gave additional **data** concerning London and Dublin. He pointed out that the proportion of breeders in the country was greater than in the city; that the number of births in London was about five-eights that of the burials; and that if London were not supplied with migrants from the country, it would decrease and finally disappear.[8]

Gregory King (1648-1712). King differed from the above writers in his findings concerning London in that he found a larger proportion of married persons. In spite of this the fertility per marriage was lower in the city than in the country, and so he corroborated the conclusions of Graunt and Petty concerning the lower reproduction rate of the city population.[9] He found, however, a larger proportion of females in the city and a larger proportion of males in the country.

Edmund Halley (1656-1742). Edmund Halley held that London and Dublin were not representative cities, since so many strangers died therein; therefore he selected Breslau as a representive city. He attempted to show that births were not more numerous than deaths and that there was no differential rate in the vital processes in the city and in the surrounding territory.

7. Pitirim A. Sorokin, Carle C. Zimmerman, and Charles J. Galpin, *A Systematic Source Book in Rural Sociology*, Vol. I (Minneapolis: The University of Minnesota Press, 1930), pp. 96-97.
8. *Ibid.*, p. 99.
9. *Ibid.*, pp. 101-102.

By subsequent studies, however, this contention of Halley was given a meaning corroborating in essence the conclusion of his predecessors, in this sense; that the infusion of the immigrants to the city from rural parts was not to be regarded as a factor which increased the mortality rate of the city but decreased it. The data supplied by Richard Price, J. Sussmilch, Deparcieux, and partly by Justi established this point.[10]

Richard Price. Richard Price published in 1769 his *Observations on Reversionary Payments* and included therein many figures and life-expectation tables. He came to the conclusion that if there were no migration from the country to the city, the mortality rates in the city would still be higher and the birth rates lower than in the country; and furthermore, the country rates would be still more favorable.[11]

Arthur Young. Arthur Young, in his *The Farmer's Letters to the People of England* (1768) showed a differential mortality rate of infants of 14-16 per 100 in villages to 60-70 per 100 in the cities; and that the urban residents were not nearly so prolific as the country people.[12]

Deparcieux (1703-1768). Deparcieux found that in the French cities of Paris, Lyon, Rouen, Bordeaux the deaths did not exceed the births; however, in analyzing and standardizing the data he did not mean that the vital statistics were any better than the country or even as good as the country, but he accounted for this phenomenon by a series of migrations and other reasons.[13]

Johann Peter Sussmilch. His conclusions were similar to those already explored, but he did generalize particularly when he stated that the proportion of males did predominate in the rural areas and that within the cities the proportion of females was conspicuously higher.[14]

Thomas R. Malthus (1766-1834).[15] Malthus published his first essay on population in 1798 and he published several later essays.

10. *Ibid.*, pp. 102-103.
11. *Ibid.*, pp. 103-106.
12. *Ibid.*, pp. 106-107.
13. *Ibid.*, pp. 107-109.
14. *Ibid.*, p. 111.
15. James Bonar. *Malthus and His Work* (New York: The Macmillan Company, 1924); Sorokin, Zimmerman, and Galpin, *op. cit.*, pp. 129-132; Warren S. Thompson, *Population Problems* (New York: McGraw-Hill Book Company, Inc., 1942), pp. 18-31.

Although his ideas were not entirely original, his thinking was dominated by his concern for the welfare of men, and his theories of population came as a result of trying to understand how human welfare was related to population growth.

The main idea of his work was that population tends to increase faster than the means of subsistence. He believed (1) that man was not likely to undergo any radical changes with regard to his "passions"; (2) that man's material needs and his sex passions were in essential conflict; (3) that subsistence limited population growth; and (4) that subsistence increased in arithmetical ratio, while population tended to increase in geometrical ratio.

One would gather from his work that Malthus never thought of contraception as a means of limiting population.

Thompson points out that:

> . . . Malthus presented so clearly a useful point of view for the study of population that his work well deserves to be considered the point of departure for our study of population. . . . It should be borne in mind that in some parts of the Essay Malthus couched on most of the present-day problems of population and that in nearly every case this treatment is enlighting if not final.[16]

It may well be true that the essays of Malthus deserve to be considered as a point of departure for the study of "population problems," but it seems to the investigator that Malthus' writings had just the opposite effect on the analytical approach to population study. The very fact, as Dr. Thompson points out, that the treatment was "final" seemed to answer the questions and act as an opiate. Thus, one would probably be safe in stating that the modern period in analytical population studies began with Thompson's (the author of the foregoing statement) *Ratio of Children to Women*: *1920*.

FROM MALTHUS TO THOMPSON

In the century after the death of Malthus in 1834 considerable inroad was made into the bounds of knowledge; and even though there was a general lack of direct analytical study of population, many studies appeared which had tremendous influence in the

16. *Ibid.*, p. 30. (From *Population Problems*, by Warren S. Thompson. Copyright 1942. Courtesy of McGraw-Hill Book Co.)

field of demography. Among the earlier writers of this period who contributed either directly or indirectly to population study were Marx, Galton, Darwin, Mendel, Booth, Tylor, Pearson, and Whipple.[17]

In the late nineteenth century, Ravenstein, Livi, and Weber made significant contributions to the field.

E. G. Ravenstein. Ravenstein summarized some of the most thoroughly established principles of migration based on studies in England (64 British cities), Europe, and the United States. He found (1) that the majority of migrants move very short distances, although migrants moving long distances tend to go immediately to large industrial and commercial centers; (2) that the process of dispersion is the process of absorption in reverse; i.e., there is a compensating counter current set up for each main current of migration; and (3) that the process of absorption works like this: the attractive force of the city "pulls in" those nearest the city first; the gaps thus created are filled by migrants from a greater distance from the central city, until the magnetic force of the city is felt all over the area.[18]

R. Livi. Although many have generalized concerning the differences of urban and rural populations, the Italian scholar, Livi, has demonstrated the hypothesis probably better than others; that is, the city population will be more heterogeneous than the surrounding rural population because of recruiting of the city population from different and remote places.[19]

17. Karl Marx, *Capital: A Critique of Political Economy* (Frederick Engels, editor, New York: The Modern Library, 1936); Sir Francis Galton, *Natural Inheritance* (London: The Macmillan Company, 1889); Charles R. Darwin, *The Descent of Man and Selection in Relation to Sex* (New York: D. Appleton and Company, 189?); W. Bateson, *Mendel's Principles of Heredity* (Cambridge: University Press, 1913); Charles Booth, *Life and Labour of the People of London* (London: The Macmillan Company, 1892-1897); Edward B. Tylor, *Anthropology: An Introduction to the Study of Man and Civilization* (New York: D. Appleton and Company, 1898); Karl Pearson, *The Grammar of Science* (London: Adam and Charles Black, 1900): and George C. Whipple, *Vital Statistics* (second edition; New York: John Wiley & Sons, Inc., 1923).
18. E. G. Ravenstein, "On the Laws of Migration," *Journal of the Royal Statistical Society*, 48:167-235, 1885. For exceptions to some of Ravenstein's findings, see Sorokin, Zimmerman, and Galpin, *op. cit.*, p. 218.
19. Pitirim Sorokin and Carle C. Zimmerman, *Principles of Rural-Urban Sociology* (New York: Henry Holt and Company, 1929), pp. 108-110 and 142.

Adna Ferrin Weber.[20] Weber, in studying the growth of cities in the nineteenth century, presented definite data concerning causes of city growth, rate of growth of cities, and even the process of decentralization; i.e., the tendency for residents of the central zones of the city to move farther out to escape the congested areas. Thus according to Weber there is a tendency for the central zones of the city to lose population. Weber has also pointed out the social significance of city growth. Atlanta, Georgia, was not included in her list of 27 cities of "25,000 or more inhabitants which gained more than 60 per cent" in the decade 1890-1900.

Louis I. Dublin and Alfred J. Lotka. Dublin studied causes of death by occupation; and since most occupations other than agriculture are in the city, his investigation has special significance for this study. One of his most significant findings indicated that professional men have death rates about one-half as great as common laborers.[21] Dublin, working with Lotka, worked out a formula for the true rate of natural increase by using specific birth rates and specific death rates.[22]

Sorokin and Zimmerman demonstrated that the cities contain high proportions of the foreign elements.[23]

Robert R. Kuczynski. Kuczynski has popularized a method for measuring the balance of births and deaths which yields a "net reproduction rate." He shows how many daughters a birth cohort of 100 females will have during their life-time at the age specific birth rates and death rates of a given time.[24]

FROM THOMPSON TO THE PRESENT

This is the period in which the empirical approach came into

20. A. F. Weber, *The Growth of Cities in the Nineteenth Century*, Studies in History, Economics, and Public Law, Vol. XI (New York: Columbia University, 1899); and Adna Ferrin Weber, "The Significance of Recent City Growth; The Era of Small Industrial Centres," *The Annals of the American Academy of Political and Social Sciences*, 23:223-236, March, 1904.
21. Louis I. Dublin, "Causes of Death by Occupation: Occupational Mortality Experiences of the Metropolitan Life Insurance Co., Industrial Department, 1911-1913," (Washington: Government Printing Office, 1917), pp. 1-88.
22. Louis I. Dublin and Alfred J. Lotka, "On the True Rate of Natural Increase as Exemplified by the Population of the United States, 1920," *American Statistical Association Journal*, 20:305-339, September, 1925.
23. *Principles of Rural-Urban Sociology*, p. 23.
24. Robert R. Kuczynski, *The Balance of Births and Deaths*, Vols. I and II (New York: The Macmillan Company, 1928-1931).

its own to produce an understanding of the concrete facts and definite demographic relationships. The period is characterized by the perfection of the tools of population analysis: classifications, indexes, graphic and mapping devices, and similar techniques; it is further characterized by careful analysis of the completeness and validity of the data involved.

For the most part the foregoing developments took place in connection with studies of the national population with Thompson in the forefront; but it was extended to regional analyses (especially the South, with Vance leading the way); and a very substantial part of the advancement came out of state studies in which rural sociologists, who for the most part used urban data for comparative purposes only, were the ones in the lead.

So far, however, no one seems to have focused attention upon the urban population in general, nor upon the demographic study of any single southern city, in particular. But the accumulation of data, the perfection of the analytical devices, and the importance of the demographic factors in all social and economic analyses make this failure in applying the modern methods of demography to the urban field one of the outstanding examples of cultural lag in our times. Thus the present study provides a long needed analysis in an area in which little comprehensive systematic work has been done.

The most significant findings of a number of studies of immediate relevance to the present investigation covering the period since 1930 are presented briefly in the following paragraphs.

Warren S. Thompson. In the writer's opinion, the true analytical population studies began in 1931 when Thompson analyzed the ratio of children to women as reported in the 1920 census.[25] Here he used the fertility ratio (although he was not the first investigator to use it) which in many respects was superior to the birth rate, and he set the pattern for scientifically analyzing the vast data which are included in the official publications of the Census Bureau.

Thompson and Whelpton have pointed out that the small town and open-country population in the United States is

---

25. Warren S. Thompson, *Ratio of Children to Women*, Monograph XI (Washington: Government Printing Office, 1931).

composed largely of native stock.[26]

Walter F. Willcox. Since the beginning of the nineteenth century, the fertility of the population has been declining. Willcox definitely established this fact in his work and in the data he cited.[27]

Calvin F. Schmid. In his studies of Minneapolis and St. Paul and later Seattle, Schmid has collected and analyzed much information about these three cities; and he has related many social and economic characteristics to population data.[28]

Conrad F. Taeuber. In a study of migration in selected German cities, Taeuber concluded that most migrants travel only short distances, but that "distance of migration to and from cities . . . tended to increase with skill and social rank of migrant."[29]

C. Horace Hamilton. In a study on North Carolina, Hamilton found that the age groups 20 to 30 contained about one-half the net migration loss to farms (much of which went to cities); and that the age groups 15 to 35 could account for three-fourths of the net migration loss.[30]

Harold F. Dorn. Dorn found more deaths registered than births in 145 counties in the United States; three-fourths of the population of these counties was located in the highly urbanized areas of the Pacific Coast and the Middle Atlantic States.[31]

Robert M. Woodbury. Infant mortality rates in cities seem to be lower than rates for rural areas. Woodbury found that the urban rate for 1934 was 10 per cent lower than for rural areas;

26. W. S. Thompson and P. K. Whelpton, *Population Trends in the United States* (New York: McGraw-Hill Book Company, Inc., 1933), p. 45.
27. Walter F. Willcox, *Introduction to the Vital Statistics of the United States, 1900 to 1930* (Washington: Government Printing Office, 1933). See also J. S. Billings, "The Diminishing Birth Rate in the United States," *The Forum*, 15:467-477, June, 1893.
28. Calvin F. Schmid, *Social Saga of Two Cities* (Minneapolis: Minneapolis Council of Social Agencies, 1937).
29. Conrad F. Taeuber, "Migrations to and From Selected German Cities," (unpublished Doctor's dissertation, University of Minnesota, Minneapolis, 1931), cited by Noel P. Gist and L. A. Halbert, *Urban Society* (New York: Thomas Y. Crowell Company, 1947), p. 264.
30. C. Horace Hamilton, *Rural-Urban Migration in North Carolina 1920 to 1930*, North Carolina Agricultural Experiment Station Bulletin 295, Raleigh, 1934.
31. Harold F. Dorn, "The Natural Decrease of Population in Certain American Communities," *Journal of the American Statistical Association*, 34:106-109, March, 1939.

the position was reversed in 1915.[32]

National Resources Committee. In 1909 The Country Life Commission "explored the problems of rural living for the first time in a systematic fashion."[33] The report, *Our Cities—Their Role in the National Economy*, examines urban conditions in a similar manner. A wide range of relevant subjects is called to the attention of the reader, especially in the relationship of cities to our national scheme.

> . . . The number of cities or urban places in the United States has increased from a mere half dozen in 1790 to 3,165 in 1930. The Nation's urban population has risen from only 3 per cent of the total population in 1790, 7 per cent in 1830, 26 per cent in 1880 to 56 per cent in 1930. The family has grown smaller and the older-age group larger. American cities instead of maintaining a birth rate sufficient to reproduce themselves must recruit from the country. . . .
>
> . . . In 1930 almost one-half of the Nation's population— that is, 54,753,000 persons or 45 per cent of the total— resided in the 96 metropolitan districts with at least 100,000 inhabitants in each. These 96 metropolitan districts contain within their large central cities 37,814,000 urbanites; while 17,000,000 of our people have become suburbanites.
>
> . . . Of more than 3,000 counties of the country, the 155 which contain the larger industrial cities embraced, in the year 1929, 74 per cent of all industrial wage earners, 81 per cent of all salaried employees, 79 per cent of all wages paid, 83 per cent of all salaries paid, 65 per cent of all the industrial establishments, and 80 per cent of the value added to manufactured products. . . .[34]

Furthermore, urban governments employ one and one-fourth million persons who constitute one-third of all public employees (1930).[35]

Lowell J. Reed and Margaret Merrell.[36] In 1939 Reed and

32. Robert M. Woodbury, "Infant Mortality in the United States," *Annals of the American Academy of Political and Social Sciences*, 188:97, November, 1936.
33. National Resources Committee, *Our Cities—Their Role in the National Economy* (Washington: Government Printing Office, 1937), p. 1.
34. National Resources Committee, *Our Cities*, p. vii.
35. *Ibid.*, p. viii.
36. Lowell J. Reed and Margaret Merrell, "A Short Method for Constructing an Abridged Life Table," *Vital Statistics—Special Reports*, 9:681-712, June, 1940.

Merrell published a relatively short method of constructing an abridged life table. This method has been of untold value to students of demography.

J. Allan Beegle and T. Lynn Smith. In a study of differential fertility in Louisiana, Beegle and Smith found that in cities the white population seemed to be reproducing more rapidly than the Negro population; however, they believe that the apparent racial differentials are merely reflections of the degree of urbanity to which each is exposed rather than "race" itself.[37]

Louise Kemp. The fertility ratio cannot in every case be used to measure accurately reproduction of Negroes in the South. Kemp found that young Negro females tend to leave their children on the farm with their grandparents while they (the young females) work in the cities.[38]

Frank W. Notestein. Notestein found that in all types of urban areas the lower classes reproduced at higher rates than did the upper classes.[39] Thompson, in his Butler County, Ohio, study, further substantiated Notestein in that where economic status was measured by family rentals, the higher the economic status, the lower the average number of children.[40]

Howard W. Green. Green likewise found the birth rate higher for women in low-rent areas (103.1 per 1,000 women 15 years old or older in low-rent areas and only 49.2 for high-rent areas).[41] In a study of fertility in Baltimore, Pearl found fertility decreased as one ascended the economic scale for both white and Negro women.[42]

Although it is generally true that the fertility decreases as the economic scale is ascended, some exceptions have been noted.

37. J. Allen Beegle and T. Lynn Smith, *Differential Fertility in Louisiana,* Louisiana Agricultural Experiment Station Bulletin No. 403, Baton Rouge, 1946, p. 27.
38. Louise Kemp, "A Note on the Use of Fertility Ratio in the Study of Rural-Urban Differences in Fertility," *Rural Sociology,* 10:312-313, September, 1945.
39. Frank W. Notestein, "The Differential Rate of Increase Among the Social Classes of the American Population," *Social Forces,* 12:17-33, October, 1933.
40. Warren S. Thompson, *Average Number of Children per Woman in Butler County, Ohio, 1930—A Study in Differential Fertility* (Washington: Government Printing Office, 1941), p. 9.
41. Howard W. Green, "Cultural Areas in the City of Cleveland," *American Journal of Sociology,* 38:356-367, November, 1932.
42. Raymond Pearl, "Fertility and Economic Status," *Human Biology,* 4:525-553, December, 1932.

Edin[43] in a study of Stockholm, and Lamson[44] in a study of Chinese cities found that those in the higher economic and social positions have higher rates of fertility.

T. Lynn Smith. Smith has done a tremendous amount of work in the field of population, emphasizing at all times the analytical empirical approach rather than the philosophical and/or pathological attack. In one of his publications, *Population Analysis*,[45] he summarizes much of what is known about the subject of population and gives the sources of his data as well as the methodology used to determine the relationships. Probably his greatest contribution is the use of cartographic techniques as analytical tools in the field of population.

Among the significant contributions relative to urban populations which have been made by Smith are the following: (1) He has definitely shown that the apparent concentration of females at certain ages can be accounted for by the tendency of women to understate their ages: (2) he has pointed out that the extremely low sex ratios of Negroes largely account for the low sex ratios in southern cities; (3) he believes that the age make-up (a great scarcity of children, high proportions in the productive ages, and relatively few aged people) of the urban population can be accounted for by the shorter expectation of life in the city, the migration of young adults to the city, and the tendency for aged persons to return to the rural areas; and (4) by a very searching analysis of data on marital status, he has concluded that the urban population lives in the married state to a much less extent than the rural populations, divorced people and single persons are concentrated in the cities, widows tend to concentrate in the cities, and the proportion married among the Negroes is less than that among whites.

THE LITERATURE FOR WHICH DETAILED SUMMARIES ARE NOT INCLUDED

It was pointed out at the beginning of this chapter that some of the material relative to urban population analysis would be reviewed. A great wealth of material has been covered; out of

43. K. A. Edin, "The Birth Rate Changes," *Eugenics Review*, 20:259, 1929.
44. Herbert D. Lamson, "Differential Reproduction in China," *Quarterly Review of Biology*, 10:308-321, September, 1935.
45. *Population Analysis* (New York: McGraw-Hill Company Inc., 1948). The writer has patterned this study after the approach used by Smith.

that mass of studies, selected summaries have been included in this chapter. The basis for including or leaving out detailed reviews has been the subjective judgment of the writer. He has no valid reason unless it be in the interest of economy of space for not including a more detailed report in the case of many studies. The studies herein presented appear to the writer to be most relevant to the purposes of the immediate investigation. Among studies not discussed herein which appear to have some bearing on the problem under consideration but of less immediate relevance or which have been included in more inclusive reviews are the following: Hitt and Bertrand on hospital planning in Louisiana, and Hitt on the use of selected cartographic techniques;[46] Vance on the measurement of migration;[47] and of course there are innumerable others.

In addition to the literature in the field of demography, considerable other material has been reviewed in an attempt to determine what, if any, attention had been paid to the Atlanta population in those writings; and to determine further what material was available that would aid in the interpretation of the findings of this study.[48] One study made by the Works Progress Administration has furnished excellent material for comparative purposes and for showing trends.[49] The authors of that study made no attempt to interpret their findings. Much of the material therein was related directly to this work; in fact, some of the figures have been reproduced and are included herein.

46. Homer L. Hitt and Alvin L. Bertrand, *Social Aspects of Hospital Planning in Louisiana*, Louisiana Agricultural Experiment Station and the Office of the Governor, Louisiana Study Series No. 1, Baton Rouge, 1947; Homer L. Hitt. "The Use of Selected Cartographic Techniques in Health Research," *Social Forces*, 26:189-196, December, 1947.
47. Rupert B. Vance, *Research Memorandum on Population Redistribution Within the United States* (New York: Social Science Research Council, Bulletin 42, 1938).
48. Wallace P. Reed, *History of Atlanta, Georgia* (Syracuse, New York: D. Mason & Co., Publishers, 1889); *City of Atlanta* (Louisville, Kentucky: The Inter-State Publishing Company, 1892-93); Atlanta City Council and the Atlanta Chamber of Commerce, *Handbook of the City of Atlanta* (Atlanta, Georgia: The Southern Industrial Publishing Co., 1898); The Pioneer Citizens' Society of Atlanta, *History of Atlanta* (Atlanta, Georgia: Byrd Printing Company, 1902); and John R. Hornady, *Atlanta Yesterday, Today, and Tomorrow* (n.p.: American Cities Book Company, 1922).
49. Works Progress Administration of Georgia Official Project 465-34-3-4, *A Statistical Study of Certain Aspects of the Social and Economic Pattern of the City of Atlanta, Georgia* (n.p.: Works Progress Administration of Georgia, 1939).

It will be apparent to the reader that nowhere in the literature can there be found a complete analysis of the population of a large southern city. The analysis that follows is an attempt to fill that gap by the application of the most recent techniques of demography.

CHAPTER III

THE NUMBER AND DISTRIBUTION OF
THE POPULATION OF ATLANTA

In view of the fact that more interest is manifested in the number of inhabitants and their distribution in space than in any other demographic phenomena, these two aspects of Atlanta's population are treated together. It is the purpose of this chapter then to show how the Atlanta population compares in size to other large urban communities of the United States and particularly of the South; to determine how the density of the Atlanta population ranks in comparison with other large cities; and to compare the distribution among various areas within the city itself.

The fact that centers of population exist or that there is a high density of population does not thereby make a center urban. Rather, the fact that people live close together usually makes them more dependent upon each other and there emerges a social and economic organization out of this interdependence that is characteristically urban. Size and density are among the several factors which are related to the level of living of a population. In our American society, the fact that one city is larger than another makes it more important, *per se;* this is true probably because we seem to value "bigness."

The Sixteenth Census of the United States, as of April 1, 1940, enumerated 302,288 persons in the city of Atlanta.[1] The Atlanta, Georgia, Metropolitan District had 442,294 inhabitants in April, 1940; based upon a sample population survey, it was estimated that the population was 498,109 in April, 1947. The chances are 19 out of 20 that a complete census would yield a figure between 472,000 and 525,000 for the total population.[2]

In the United States in 1940 about 56.5 per cent of the population resided in urban areas; there were 3,454 urban places, of which five places had a million or more inhabitants, nine places had between 500,000 and 1,000,000 persons, 23 places had between 250,000 and 500,000 (Atlanta was included in this group), and

---

1. *Sixteenth Census of the United States: 1940,* "Population, Vol. I, Number of Inhabitants," (Washington: Government Printing Office, 1942), p. 32.
2. Bureau of the Census, *Current Population Reports—Population Characteristics,* Series P-21, No. 6, August 19, 1947, p. 5.

55 places had between 100,000 and 250,00 inhabitants.[3]

From the point of view of comparative size of cities, in 1940, New York ranked number one (the largest city); New Orleans ranked fifteenth; Atlanta ranked twenty-eighth; Dallas ranked thirty-first; Birmingham, thirty-fifth; and Nashville ranked fiftieth.[4]

By examining Table I, it may be noted that the Atlanta Metropolitan District had a more dense population per square mile than the average of similar districts in the United States; the central city of Atlanta also was more densely populated than the average of similar cities in the nation or the other southern cities to which it is compared; and finally, the area outside the city (suburban Atlanta) had a higher density than similar areas of the nation and particularly the areas just outside other southern cities.

TABLE I
POPULATION DENSITY OF SELECTED METROPOLITAN DISTRICTS
OF THE UNITED STATES, 1940

Metropolitan Districts	Population per Square Mile
Total (140 Districts)	1,411.0
In Central Cities	7,813.1
Outside Central Cities	515.2
Atlanta	1,717.6
In Central City	8,711.5
Outside Central City	628.4
Dallas	684.9
In Central City	7,259.5
Outside Central City	160.7
Nashville	765.3
In Central City	7,609.2
Outside Central City	253.0
New Orleans	1,617.8
In Central City	2,480.1
Outside Central City	338.5

Source: *Sixteenth Census of the United States: 1940*, "Population, Vol. 1, Number of Inhabitants," (Washington: Government Printing Office, 1942), pp. 58-59.

3. *Sixteenth Census of the United States: 1940*, "Population, Vol. I, Number of Inhabitants," p. 26.
4. *Ibid.*, p. 32.

Figures 1 and 2 indicate that in general the density of population increases as the center of the city is approached. Exceptions are census tracts F-27 and F-35, which include the greater portion of the central retail trade and business districts. It may also be observed that there has been very little appreciable change in the density of the individual census tracts during the decade 1930 to 1940. This is true even though the average density increased from 7,939 in 1930 to 8,711 in 1940.[5]

5. Works Progress Administration of Georgia Official Project 465-34-3-4, *A Statistical Study of Certain Aspects of the Social and Economic Pattern of the City of Atlanta, Georgia* (n.p.: Works Progress Administration of Georgia, 1939), p. 16; and *Sixteenth Census of the United States: 1940,* "Population, Vol. 1, Number of Inhabitants," (Washington: Government Printing Office, 1942), pp. 58-59.

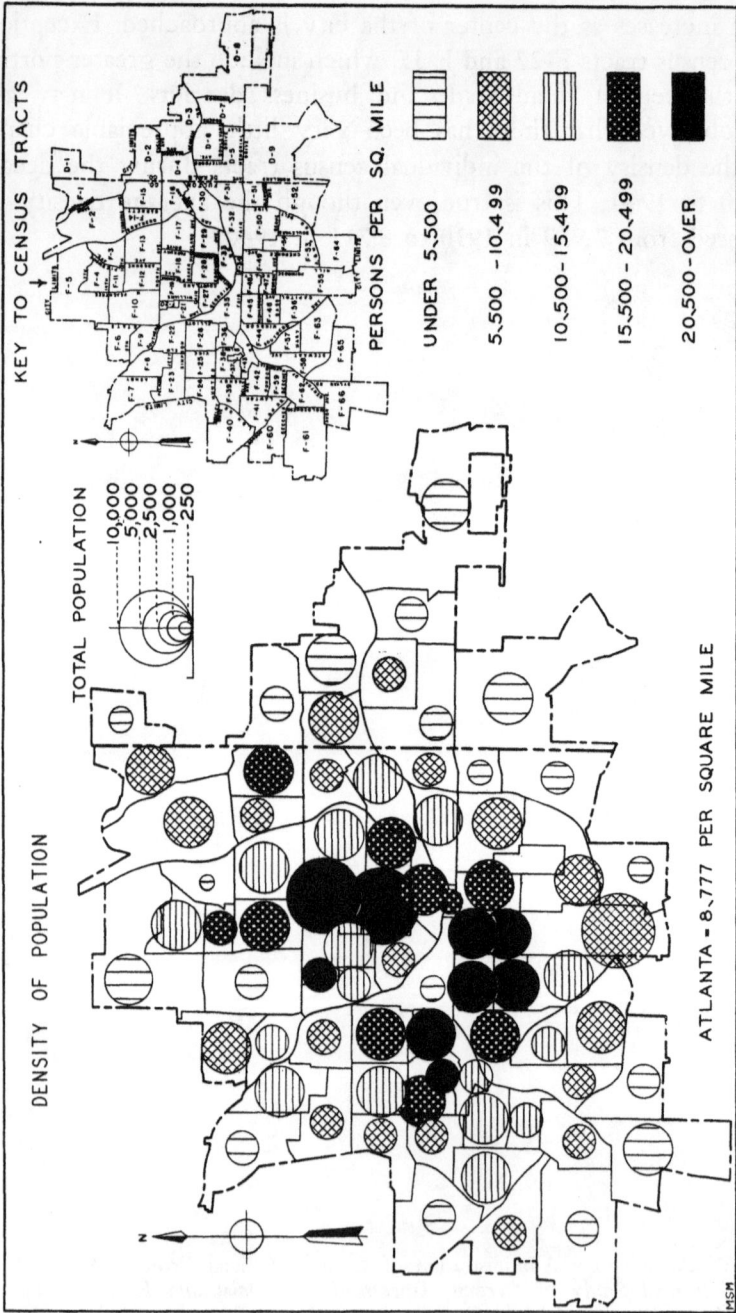

FIGURE 1. Density of population of the city of Atlanta, by census tracts, 1940.

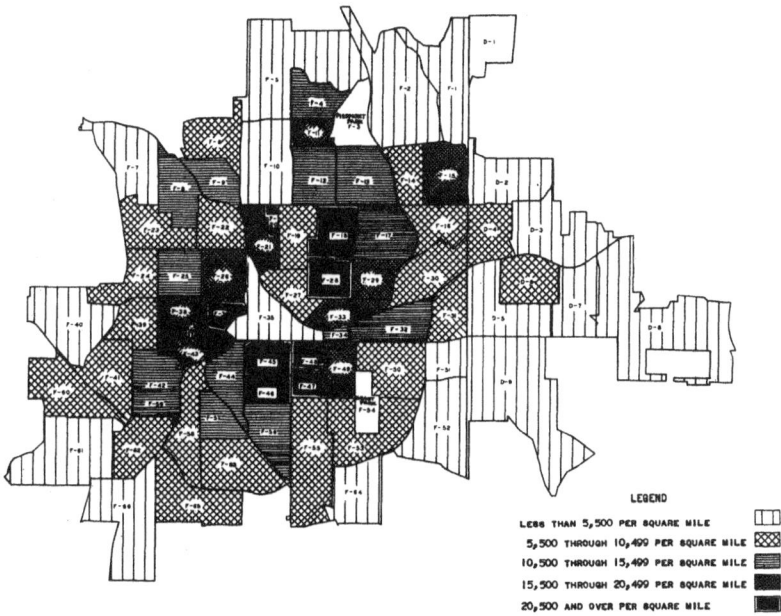

FIGURE 2. Density of population of the city of Atlanta, by census tracts, 1930. (Reproduced from WPA of Georgia official project 465-34-3-4.)

CHAPTER IV

RACE AND NATIVITY

FOLLOWING THE FOREGOING ANALYSIS (CHAPTER III) OF THE number and distribution of the Atlanta population, it is proper that the composition of the population be considered. In a localized urban study the subject of race and nativity should be discussed first because differences in racial composition and nativity have far-reaching effects politically, socially, and economically; the influence of these differences is often quite subtle and all-pervasive, and many demographic phenomena vary appreciably among the so-called racial groups. This statement does not mean to imply, however, that all demographic phenomena are related to racial characteristics *per se*.[1] Until the influence of race and nativity are defined, very few reliable comparisons can be made regarding other demographic phenomena.

It is the purpose of this chapter to point out the various racial and nativity elements and their importance in the Atlanta population; to show how Atlanta compares in these respects with the urban United States population and the population of other southern cities; to demonstrate the variations within the different sections of the city; and to show the responsible factors related to race and nativity as well as the trends in racial and nativity composition since 1890.

As indicated previously, census data are divided into three major race classifications: white, Negro, and "other races." The white population is further divided by nativity into native white and foreign-born white.[2]

The Atlanta population in 1940 was 64 per cent native white, 1.4 per cent foreign-born white, and 34.6 per cent was Negro.

Atlanta had a much smaller proportion of its population classified as native white than did the urban United States. The same is true when Atlanta is compared with Dallas, Nashville, and New Orleans. In the urban United States 12.3 per cent of the white population was foreign-born while Atlanta had only 1.4

1. Warren S. Thompson, *Population Problems* (New York: McGraw-Hill Book Company, Inc., 1942), pp. 113-114.
2. *Sixteenth Census of the United States: 1940*, "Population, Vol. II, Characteristics of the Population," Part 2 (Washington: Government Printing Office, 1943), p. 4.

per cent. This figure was lower than all the other southern cities studied except Nashville. Atlanta's population with 34.6 per cent contained a larger proportion of Negroes than any of the other southern cities examined, but New Orleans was a close second with 30.1 per cent classified as Negroes. In comparison to the urban population of the United States, Atlanta had more than four times the average proportion of Negroes.

In order to show how the various race and nativity groups vary within the city and the surrounding area, Figures 3, 4, and 5 were prepared. Figure 3 shows rather clearly where the non-white population lived; it is plain that Negroes lived close to the center of the city. By comparing Figure 3 with Figure 1 it will be noted also that the Negroes lived in the most congested part of the city. The percentage of nonwhites in the suburban areas of Atlanta (see Figure 4) is considerably less than in the center of the central city.

The Atlanta foreign-born white population of 1940 was composed of 4,293 persons (2,399 males and 1,894 females); it will be interesting to note that of this group about one-fourth was Russian (U.S.S.R.).[3] It might be well to point out here that the largest groups of Russians were concentrated in tracts F-13, F-17, F-45, and F-56; all of these tracts contained 75 or more persons from Russia.[4] The second most important foreign-born white group was the Greeks who numbered 440; and people from Germany, Poland, and England and Wales made up the first five in that order.[5]

TRENDS IN RACE AND NATIVITY

When Figure 5 is compared to Figure 3, it is noted that the distribution of the colored population in 1940 had about the same general characteristics as the distribution in 1930; that is, the areas nearer the central trade area (the heart of the city) contained a higher proportion of Negroes than did the outlying areas.

In order to get an overview of race and nativity and to be able to see the race and nativity trends in urban populations

3. *Sixteenth Census of the United States: 1940,* "Population and Housing, Atlanta, Georgia," (Washington: Government Printing Office, 1942), p. 19.
4. *Ibid.,* p. 19.
5. *Ibid.,* p. 19. The investigator believes that the data do not adequately distinguish between persons born in Russia and those born in Poland.

52

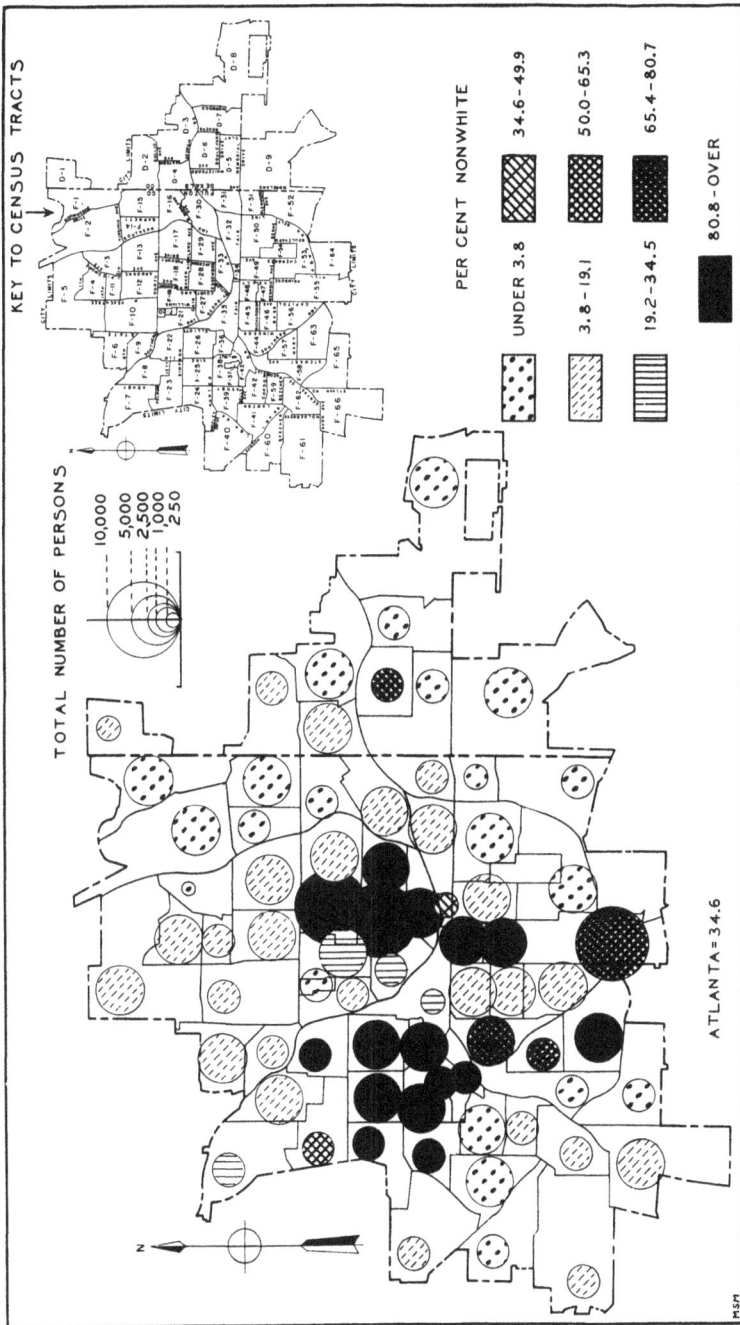

FIGURE 3. Relative importance of nonwhites in the population of Atlanta, by census tracts, 1940.

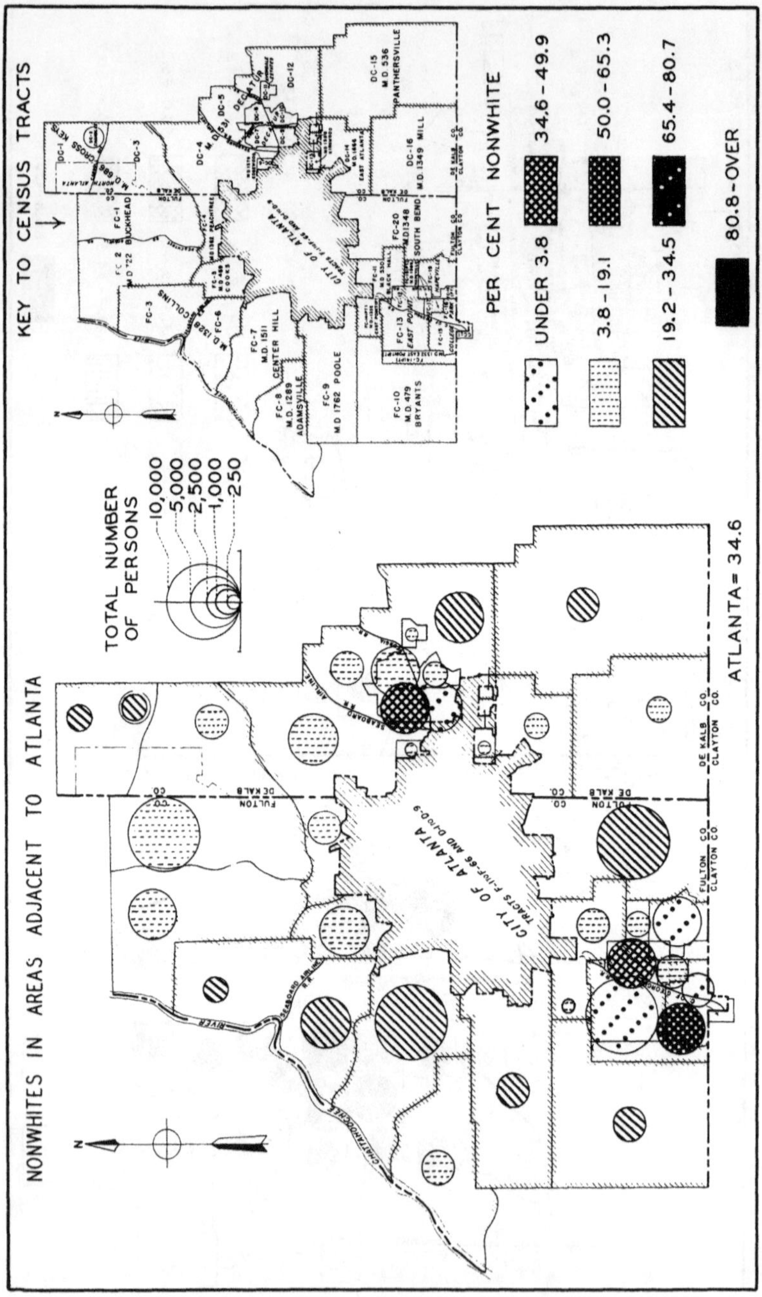

FIGURE 4. Relative importance of nonwhites in the population of suburban Atlanta, by census tracts, 1940.

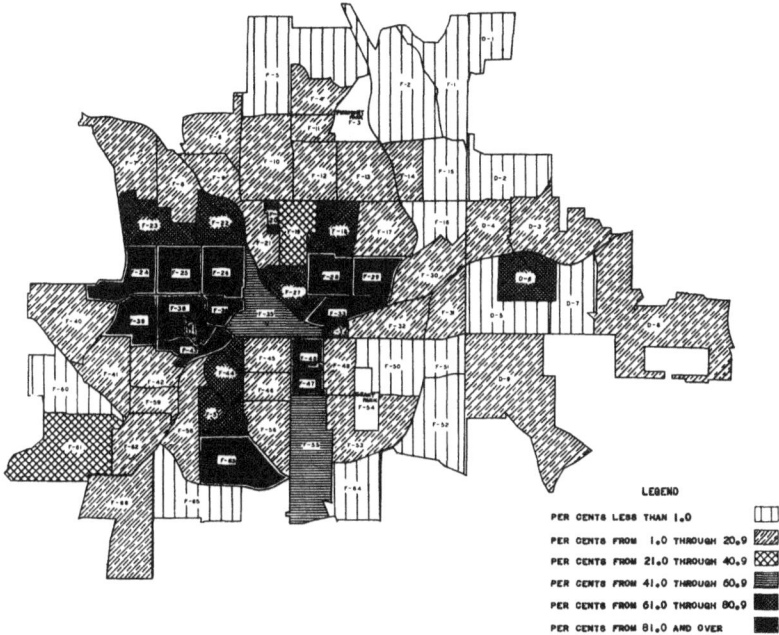

DISTRIBUTION OF COLORED POPULATION
BY CENSUS TRACTS
CITY OF ATLANTA
1930

LEGEND

PER CENTS LESS THAN 1.0

PER CENTS FROM 1.0 THROUGH 20.9

PER CENTS FROM 21.0 THROUGH 40.9

PER CENTS FROM 41.0 THROUGH 60.9

PER CENTS FROM 61.0 THROUGH 80.9

PER CENTS FROM 81.0 AND OVER

SOURCE: U.S. BUREAU OF THE CENSUS.

FIGURE 5. Distribution of the nonwhite population of the city of Atlanta, by census tracts, 1930. (Reproduced from WPA of Georgia official project 465-34-3-4.)

of the United States and particularly of the South, Table II and Table A, Appendix, have been prepared. Concerning race and nativity, one notes in general the following: (1) The foreign-born urban population of the United States reached a maximum in 1930; the Atlanta and Dallas foreign-born populations reached a maximum in 1920; and the foreign-born populations of Nashville and New Orleans have been consistently decreasing since 1890; (2) the percentage that the foreign-born population is of the total urban populations under consideration has rather consistently declined; (3) white, native white, and Negro populations have consistently increased; (4) the proportion of native whites has consistently increased in the urban population of the United States and Dallas, while the proportion reached a peak in 1920 in Atlanta, and in 1930 in Nashville and New Orleans (same as 1920); and (5) with the exception of Atlanta, there has been a general increase in the proportion of native whites of native parentage.

Negroes. As an aid to analysis, the data on the Negro population are presented in compact form in Table B, Appendix, for the period of 1850 to 1940. The data since 1890 indicate that with one exception, each decade has seen the urban populations of the United States made up of larger and larger proportions of Negroes although the Negro population has become a smaller portion of the total population of the United States, with the exception of 1940. In Atlanta in 1850, about 1 out of 5 persons was a Negro; by 1870 nearly 46 out of each 100 were Negroes; the proportion of Negroes then declined until 1920 and for the last two decades there has been a slight increase so that in 1940 a little more than one-third of the population was Negro. Dallas has the smallest proportion of Negroes of any of the cities included in this study, the proportion at the present time being just a trifle more than 1 out of 6 persons. In 1850 one-fourth of the Nashville population was Negro and although not increasing consistently, by 1890, 38.6 per cent of the population was Negro; since 1890 the proportion of Negroes decreased to 27.8 per cent in 1930 and there was a slight increase in 1940. From 1870 to 1930 the proportion of Negroes in New Orleans varied between 26.4 per cent and 28.3 per cent, while in 1940 the proportion increased to about 30 per cent.

TABLE II

PER CENT DISTRIBUTION OF SELECTED URBAN POPULATIONS BY COLOR, NATIVITY, AND PARENTAGE, 1890-1940

City, Color, and Nativity	Per Cent Distribution					
	1890	1900	1910	1920	1930	1940
Urban United States:	100.0	100.0	100.0	100.0	100.0	100.0
White	93.2	93.2	93.5	93.2	91.1	91.3
Native	68.4	71.1	70.8	74.1	75.6	79.1
Native parentage	39.7	40.2	41.9	45.2	48.6	—
Foreign or mixed parentage	28.7	30.9	29.0	28.9	27.0	—
Foreign parentage	—	—	20.6	20.8	18.8	—
Mixed parentage	—	—	8.3	8.1	8.2	—
Foreign born	24.8	22.2	22.6	19.1	15.6	12.3
Negro	6.5	6.5	6.3	6.6	7.5	8.4
Other Races	0.3	0.2	0.2	0.2	1.3	0.3
Atlanta:	100.0	100.0	100.0	100.0	100.0	100.0
White	57.1	60.2	66.4	68.7	66.7	65.4
Native	54.3	57.5	63.6	66.3	64.9	64.0
Native parentage	49.9	52.5	59.4	62.3	61.6	—
Foreign or mixed parentage	4.4	5.0	4.2	4.0	3.3	—
Foreign parentage	—	—	2.4	2.4	1.9	—
Mixed parentage	—	—	1.8	1.6	1.4	—
Foreign born	2.8	2.7	2.8	2.4	1.7	1.4
Negro	42.9	39.8	33.5	31.3	33.3	34.6

57

TABLE II (Continued)

PER CENT DISTRIBUTION OF SELECTED URBAN POPULATIONS BY COLOR, NATIVITY, AND PARENTAGE, 1890–1940

City, Color, and Nativity	Per Cent Distribution					
	1890	1900	1910	1920	1930	1940
Dallas:	100.0	100.0	100.0	100.0	100.0	100.0
White	78.8	78.7	80.4	83.1	82.8	82.9
Native	68.6	70.9	74.7	79.0	80.3	80.4
Native parentage	57.7	57.3	64.9	70.8	73.9	---
Foreign or mixed parentage	10.9	13.6	9.9	8.2	6.4	---
Foreign parentage	---	---	5.6	4.7	3.4	---
Mixed parentage	---	---	4.1	3.5	3.0	---
Foreign born	10.3	7.8	5.7	4.1	2.5	2.5
Negro	21.0	21.2	19.6	15.1	14.9	17.1
Nashville:	100.0	100.0	100.0	100.0	100.0	100.0
White	61.4	62.8	66.9	69.9	72.2	71.7
Native	56.5	59.1	64.2	67.9	71.0	70.8
Native parentage	48.3	50.2	57.7	62.5	67.4	---
Foreign or mixed parentage	8.1	8.9	6.5	5.3	3.6	---
Foreign parentage	---	---	3.8	3.1	2.0	---
Mixed parentage	---	---	2.7	2.2	1.6	---
Foreign born	4.9	3.7	2.7	2.0	1.2	0.9
Negro	38.6	37.2	33.1	30.1	27.8	28.3

TABLE II (Continued)

PER CENT DISTRIBUTION OF SELECTED URBAN POPULATIONS BY COLOR, NATIVITY, AND PARENTAGE, 1890-1940

City, Color, and Nativity	Per Cent Distribution					
	1890	1900	1910	1920	1930	1940
New Orleans:	100.0	100.0	100.0	100.0	100.0	100.0
White	73.3	72.8	73.6	73.7	71.4	69.7
Native	59.3	62.5	65.4	67.1	67.1	66.7
Native parentage	29.1	35.9	43.5	49.2	52.8	----
Foreign or mixed parentage	30.2	26.5	21.9	17.8	14.3	----
Foreign parentage		----	13.5	10.8	8.0	----
Mixed parentage		----	8.4	7.1	6.3	----
Foreign born	14.0	10.3	8.2	6.6	4.3	3.0
Negro	26.6	27.1	26.3	26.1	28.3	30.1

Sources: *Eleventh Census of the United States: 1890* (Washington: Government Printing Office, 1892), pp. 672-673; *Twelfth Census of the United States: 1900*, "Population, Vol. II," Part II (Washington: Government Printing Office, 1902), pp. 123-149; *Thirteenth Census of the United States: 1910*, "Population, Vol. I," (Washington: Government Printing Office. 1913), pp. 184-224; *Fourteenth Census of the United States: 1920*, "Population, Vol. II, General Report and Analytical Tables," (Washington: Government Printing Office, 1922), p. 79; *Fifteenth Census of the United States: 1930*, "Population, Vol. II, General Report, Statistics by Subjects," (Washington: Government Printing Office, 1933), pp. 27, 34, 73-79; *Sixteenth Census of the United States: 1940*, "Population, Vol. II, Characteristics of the Population," Part 1 (Washington: Government Printing Office, 1943), pp. 20 and 114.

CHAPTER V

AGE COMPOSITION

AMONG THE MORE USEFUL AND INTERESTING DATA IN THE FIELD of demography are those relating to age. The function of this chapter is to point out the significance of the age distribution of Atlanta; to show the important features of the age make-up of the population; to show how the age distribution of Atlanta compares to other large urban populations and particularly to other southern cities; to present the differences in age make-up of the different portions of the city; to determine the differences in age distribution according to race and nativity and by sex; and finally to show how the age distribution has been changing.

Employers, planning boards, welfare organizations, government bureaus, military authorities, school officials, social scientists, and many others in the business and professional world as well as people in general are tremendously interested in the age of individuals and groups of people. In extremely subtle ways, age conditions many of the aspects of social phenomena. In addition, it is necessary for demographers and social scientists to eliminate effects resulting from age before comparing groups or populations in regard to fertility and mortality rates.

From an economic point of view, the chief significance of age data is that in populations with low proportions of persons in the productive ages of life and high proportions of persons in the dependent ages (that is the very young and the very old), there is a tremendous strain to furnish a high level of living. A classic example is the high proportion of dependency in rural areas as compared to urban areas. There are large variations in age distributions, however, among urban populations.

Age distribution and concentration at certain ages are also important outside the economic field. From an institutional standpoint, a shortage of persons in the productive years means lack of leadership in the community; or as is the case of high concentration in the productive ages, it means great opportunities and, in our society, strenuous competition. Educationally, in urban communities which have low proportions of persons in the very young age groups, it means that it is possible to educate better those persons which they do have. Yet urban communities must

61

realize that to receive well-trained persons in the productive ages, they must share their productivity with the rural areas from which their future population must come. Finally, the very type of life, conservative or radical, depends largely on whether there are concentrations of old people or of young adults.

The data on age are presented by the use of three techniques: (1) the age and sex pyramids, (2) index numbers of ages, and (3) dependency ratios. The first two have been previously explained, but it is convenient at this point to explain the dependency ratio. Generally speaking, persons aged 15 to 64 must support those persons less than 15 years of age and those 65 and over. Thus the ratio of dependents to contributors is a useful index.[1]

$$\frac{\text{Dependents (under 15 and 65-over)}}{\text{Contributors (15-64)}} \text{X } 1,000 = \frac{\text{Dependency}}{\text{Ratio}}$$

The outstanding features of Atlanta's age distribution can be noted from the pyramid showing all classes of the population in Figure 6. The age and sex pyramid for the total population of Atlanta suggests an urban population which does not reproduce itself (as indicated by the lack of children); the pyramid bulges in the productive age groups, particularly ages 15-45, and especially so on the female side (indicative of a population receiving large numbers of migrants and especially female migrants who normally travel relatively short distances); the older age groups are considerably heavier on the female side, a condition due largely to short-distance migration to the city and lower mortality rates for females.[2]

These features are characteristic of urban populations throughout the world. For example, they are generally true of many European cities, Paris[3] in particular, as well as many Latin-American cities, such as the *Distrito Federal*[4] of Venezuela (with the exception of a high proportion of very young children).

Included in Figure 7 is the age-sex pyramid for all classes of

1. T. Lynn Smith, *The Sociology of Rural Life* (New York: Harper and Brothers, 1947), p. 77.
2. Noel P. Gist and L. A. Halbert, *Urban Society* (New York: Thomas Y. Crowell Company, 1941), pp. 268-278 and 255-261.
3. M. Huber, H. Bunle, and F. Boverat, *La Population De La France—Son Evolution Et Ses Perspectives* (Paris: Librarie Hachette, 1939), pp. 33-47.
4. Juan Alvarado Franquis, *Comentarios Al VII Censo de Poplacion de Venezuela* (Caracas, Venezula: Ministerio de Fomento, Direction General de Estadistica, 1947), pp. 17-26.

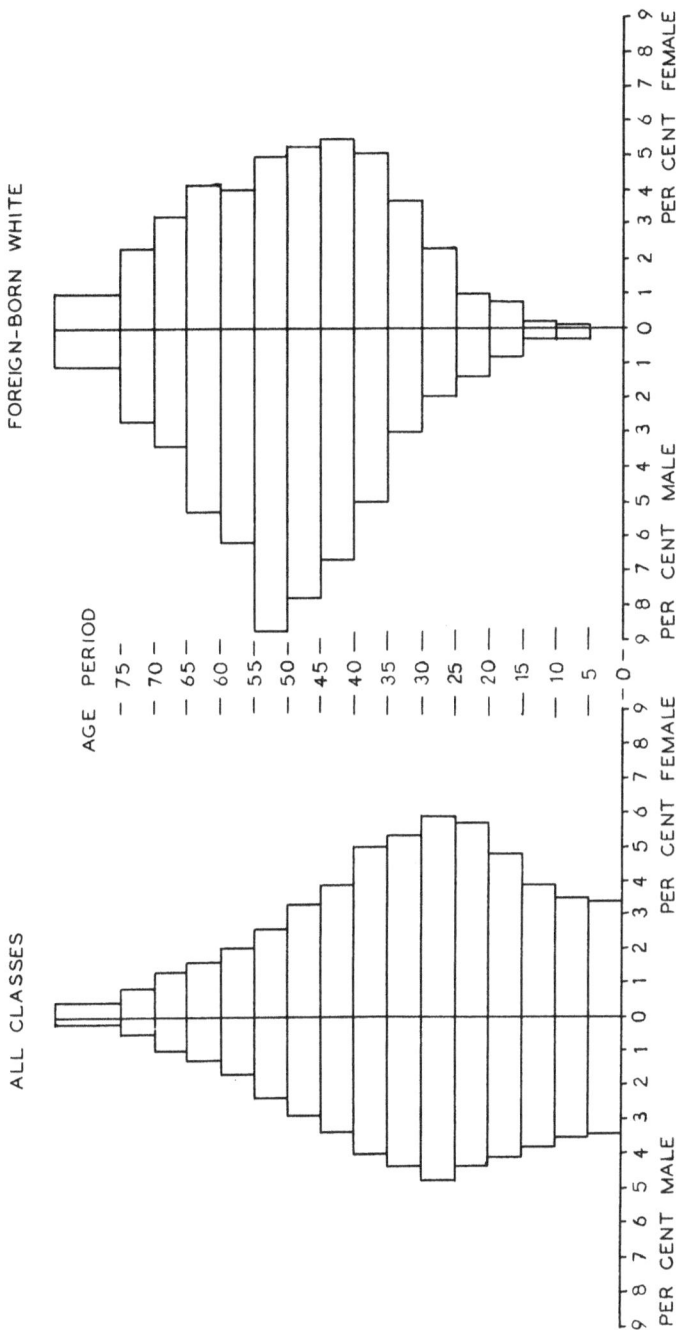

FIGURE 6. Age-sex pyramids for the total (all classes) and the foreign-born white populations of the city of Atlanta, 1940.

the Atlanta Metropolitan District (includes the city proper, also). It will be immediately noted that there is a considerable increase in the percentage of children, and that the bulge in the productive ages is somewhat less prominent.

ATLANTA COMPARED TO OTHER URBAN POPULATIONS

In order to reveal significant variations in the age structure a somewhat more refined device (index numbers) has been used in Figures 8 and 9.[5] The age distributions of Atlanta, Nashville, New Orleans, and New York are compared with each other and with the total urban population of the United States as well. Atlanta has a greater proportion of children under 10 than the urban United States, New York City, or New Orleans, but less than Nashville; only New York City has a smaller proportion of young people in the age group 10-14 than Atlanta. Atlanta shows the highest concentration in the young adult age groups, particularly 25-30; and finally Atlanta has a smaller proportion of persons over 50 than any of the other populations compared in the figure.

When the various segments of the Atlanta population are compared to the urban population of Georgia (which includes Atlanta), Figure 9, the heavier concentrations come in the somewhat later age groups, which probably indicates that people migrate to Atlanta somewhat later in life than to the other cities which go to make up Georgia's urban population.

RACE AND NATIVITY DIFFERENCES

Returning to Figure 6 the pyramid for the foreign-born white is the "top-shape" pyramid of an immigrant population characterized by (1) a noticeable lack of children; (2) a heavy concentration in the productive age groups (particularly heavy for males who usually move long distances in greater proportions than females); and (3) a higher proportion of old people than the population as a whole.[6] One notes that the heaviest concentration comes in the male group aged 50-54. This probably indicates that the greatest ingress of foreign migrants came to Atlanta about 30 to 35 years ago (1905-1910).

The age and sex pyramid for the native white population resembles rather closely the pyramid for the total population;

5. T. Lynn Smith, "A Demographic Study of the American Negro," *Social Forces*, 23:379-387, March, 1945.
6. Gist and Halbert, *op. cit.*, pp. 268-278 and 255-261.

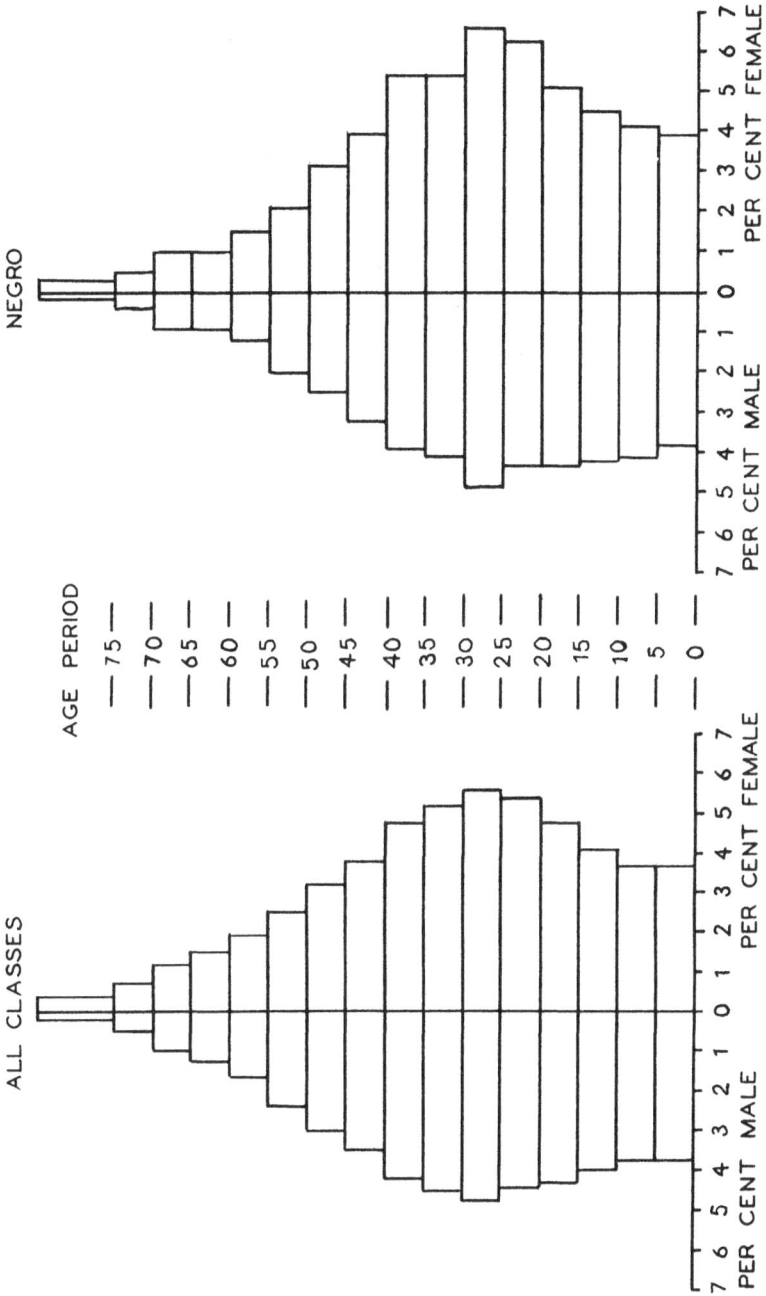

FIGURE 7. Age-sex pyramids for the total (all classes) and the Negro populations of the Atlanta metropolitan district, 1940.

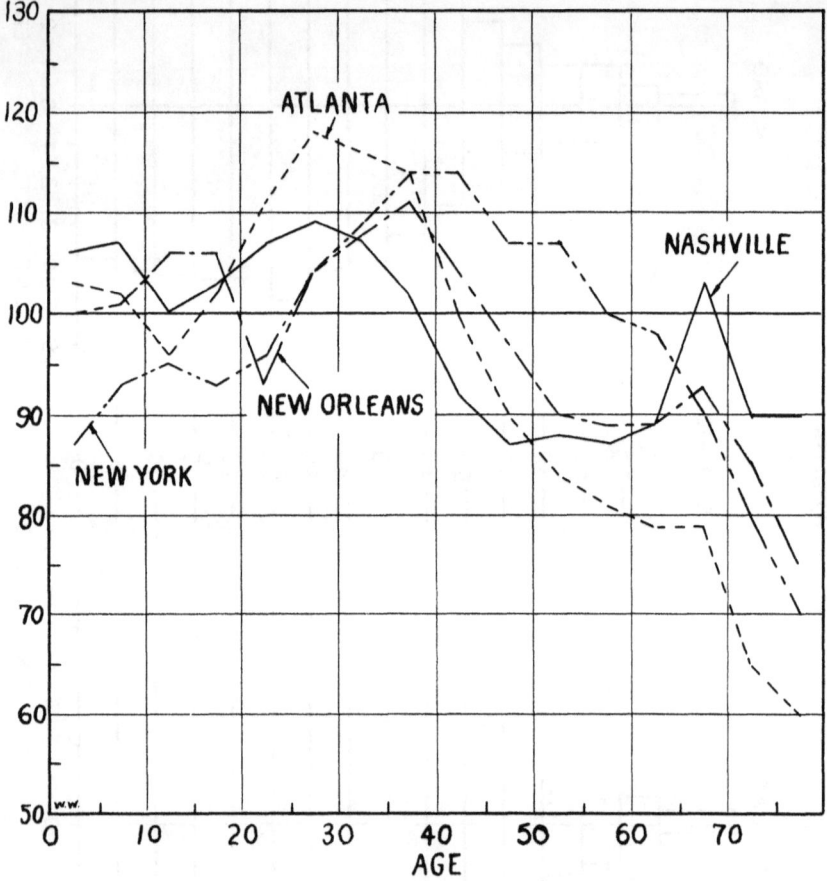

INDEX NUMBERS

ATLANTA

NASHVILLE

NEW ORLEANS

NEW YORK

AGE

FIGURE 8. Index numbers showing the relative importance of each age group in the populations of selected cities of
the United States, 1940 (urban population of the United
States = 100).

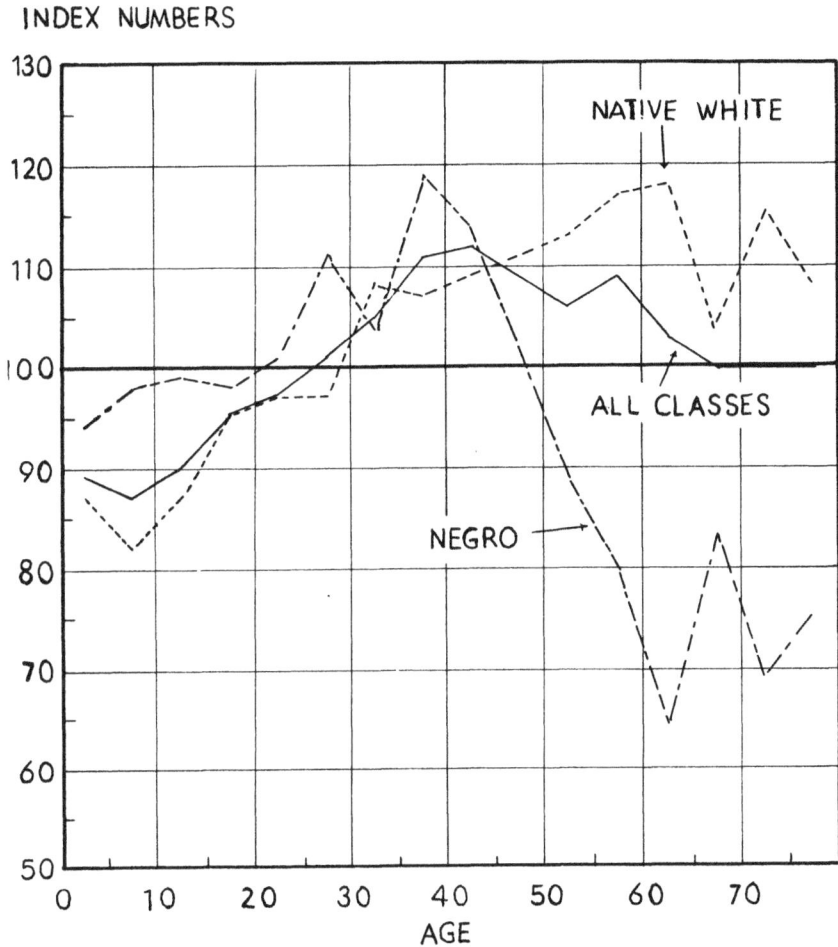

INDEX NUMBERS

FIGURE 9. Index numbers showing the relative importance of each age group in the total (all classes), native white, and Negro populations of the city of Atlanta, 1940 (urban population of Georgia = 100).

however, Figure 10 shows a great dissimilarity in the Negro population. Especially noteworthy is the concentration of Negro females and the lack of a proportionate number of Negro males in the Atlanta population. This phenomenon can best be accounted for by the long-distance migration of Negro males to northern cities and to the west coast (usually long distance migrations are heavily selective of males), and the comparatively short-distance migration of Negro females into Atlanta from the surrounding smaller urban as well as the rural areas.[7]

The Negro population is characterized by its concentration in the early years of life and by the extreme shortage of persons in the older age groups; on the other hand, the native white population has a much higher proportion of old people than the city average or, for that matter, the average of the urban population of Georgia. This latter fact is brought out vividly in Figure 11.

Figure 12 presents the contrast of the native white and foreign-born white population in the Metropolitan District of Atlanta. The same general characteristics of the immigrant population enumerated above in connection with the central city are apparent in the pyramid for the foreign-born population in the Metropolitan District.

AGE VARIATIONS BY SEX

In Figure 13 the relative importance of each age group in the population of Atlanta is shown by sex; the basis for comparison is the urban population of the United States: It is noted that neither males nor females are relatively so important in Atlanta at the older ages as in the average urban population of the United States. In the age groups 20 to 40, both males and females are proportionately greater in numbers than the national average for urban. This finding further confirms the previous conclusion reached in analysis of Figure 8, that Atlanta has a relatively "young" population with greater proportions concentrated in the productive age groups.

In Figure 14 one finds some rather startling facts. In the age groups under 10 the males are in considerably higher proportions than the females; this is in line with demographic phenomena in general, but the Negro male is considerably more important than

7. Smith, "A Demographic Study of the American Negro," pp. 379-387.

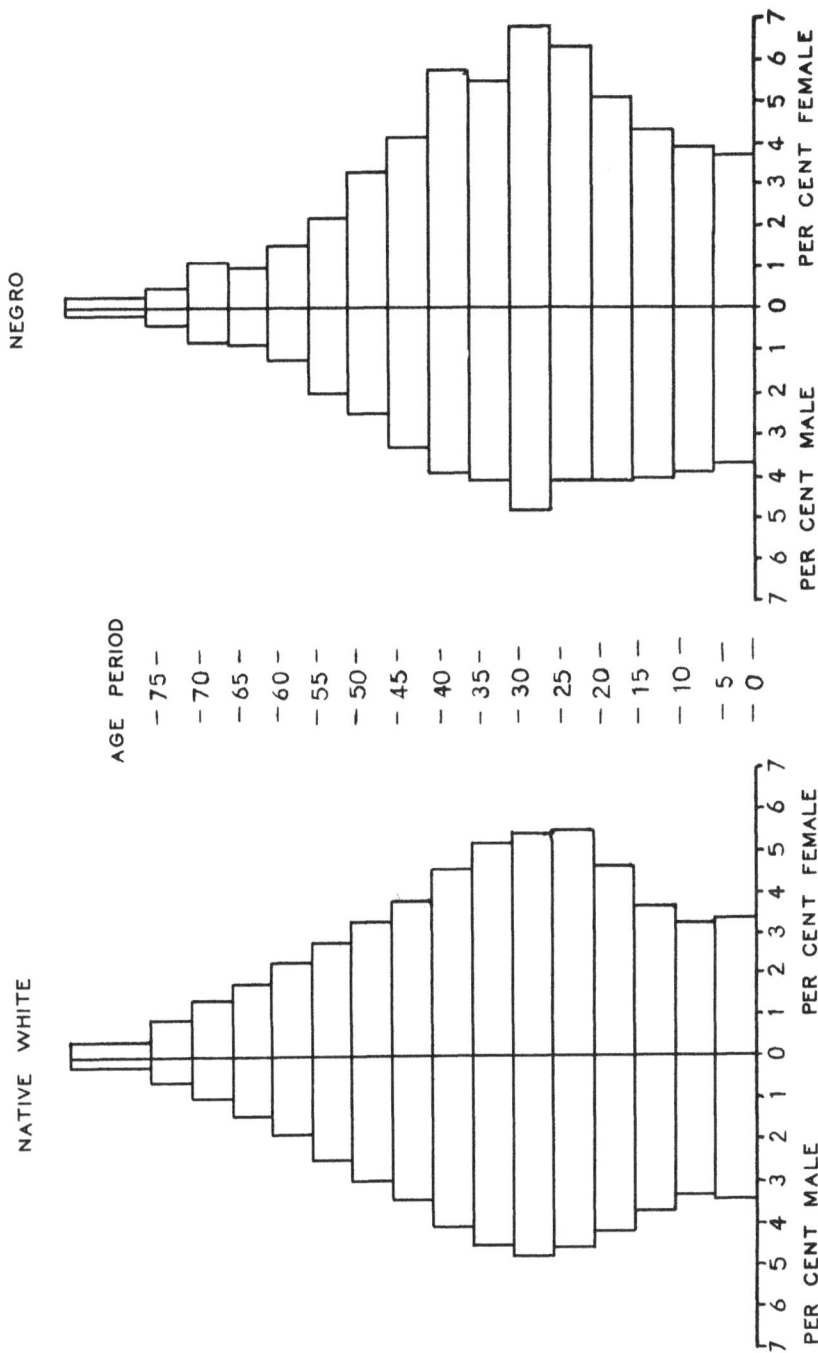

FIGURE 10. Age-sex pyramids for the native white and the
Negro populations of the city of Atlanta, 1940.

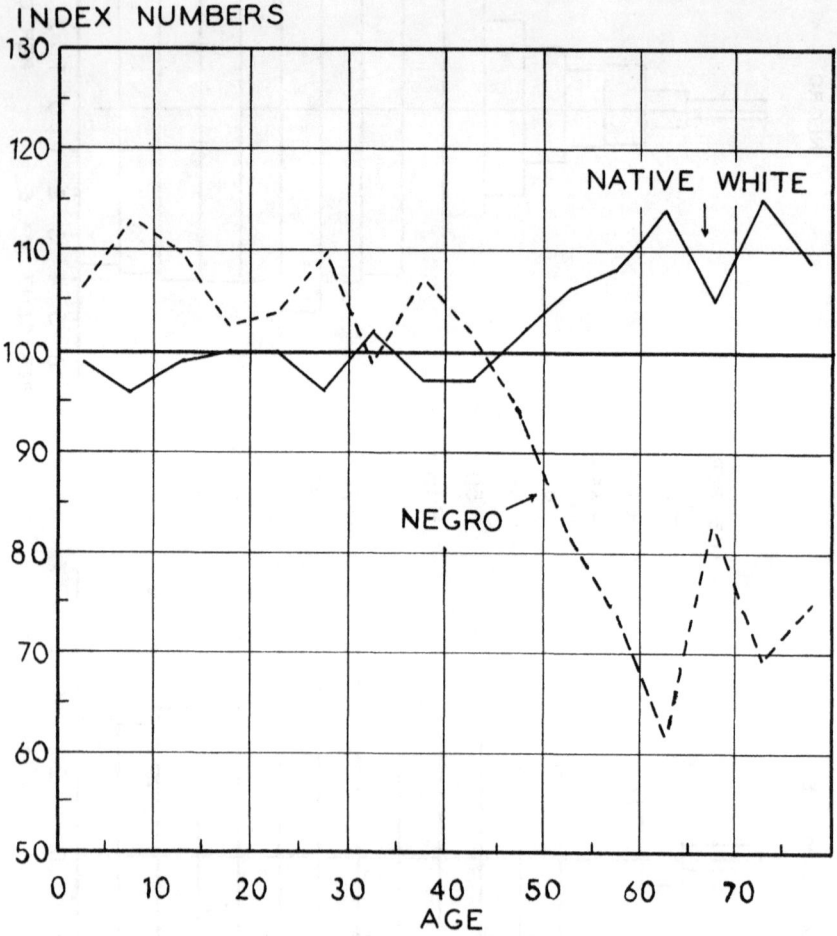

FIGURE 11. Index numbers showing the relative importance of each age group in the native white and Negro populations of the city of Atlanta, 1940 (all classes, city of Atlanta = 100).

Courtesy of the Atlanta Historical Society.

Collier's Store and The Post Office in 1845—Located at What is Now Known as "Five Points."

Skyline of Atlanta in 1864.

Courtesy of the Atlanta Historical Society.

View of Decatur and Peachtree Streets From Marietta Street (September 2, 1864)—Known Now As "Five Points."

Atlanta Depot in 1864—One of the Finest in the United States When Built in 1853; Rammed Down by General Sherman, November 14. 1864.

First Kimball House—Probably the Largest and Most Magnificent Hotel in the South When Erected in 1870—Unique for a Town Almost Completely Burned Less Than Five Years Before.

Central Building of International Cotton Exposition 1881—First Southern and Second American World's Fair and Probably a Stimulus to the Growth of Atlanta.

Courtesy of the Atlanta Historical Society.

Wall Street Showing "Commercial Center" East From Broad Street Bridge to Car Shed and Including The Depot, Kimball House, and National Hotel (1887).

West Side of Peachtree North From Ellis Showing Capital City Club and the Handsome Abbott Residence (1890)—Present Site of Davison-Paxon Company.

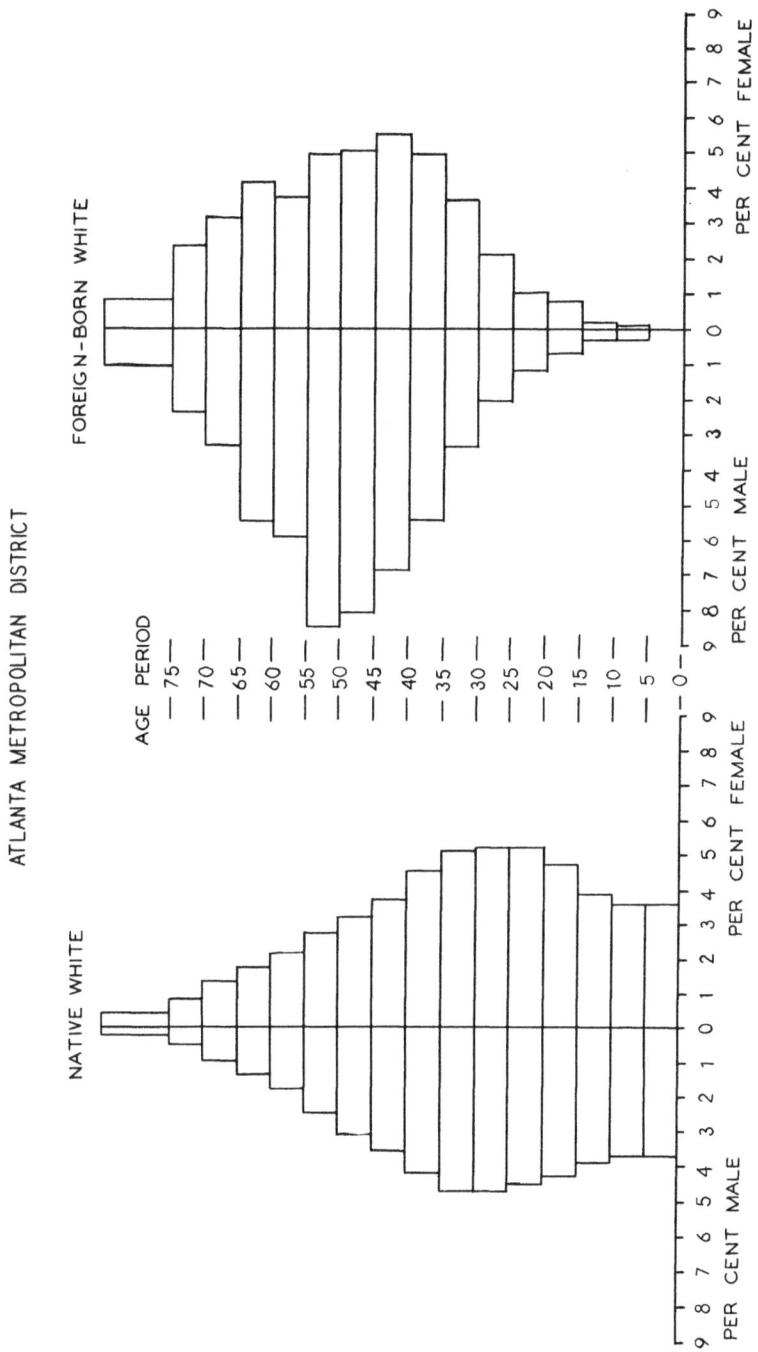

FIGURE 12. Age-sex pyramids for the native white and the foreign-born white populations of the Atlanta metropolitan district, 1940.

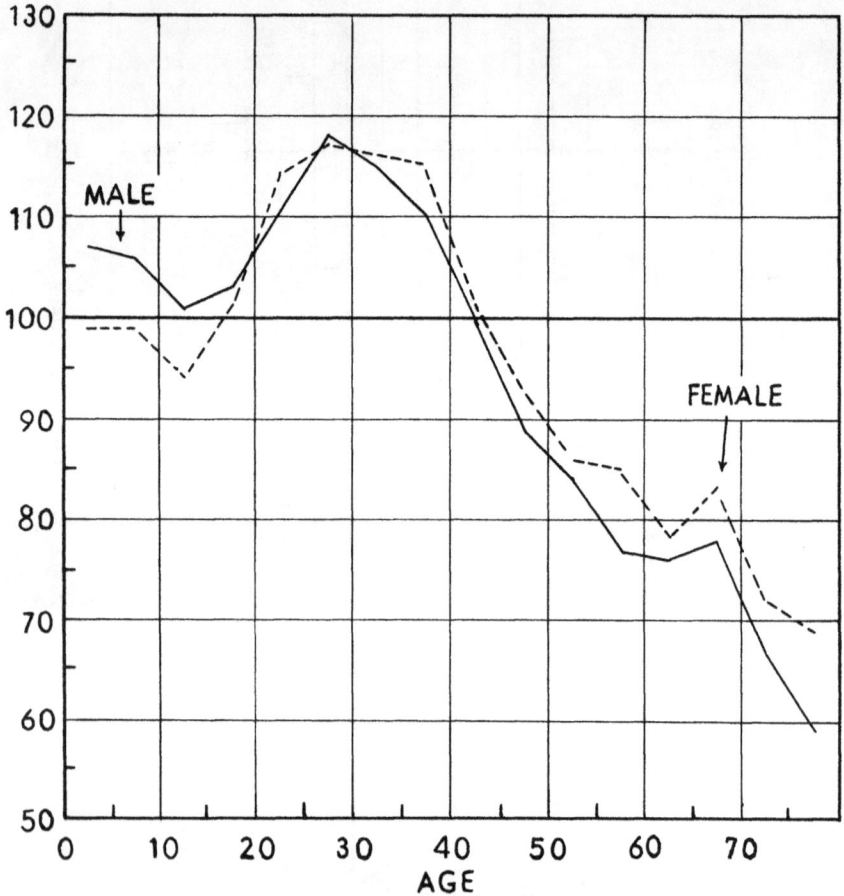

INDEX NUMBERS

FIGURE 13. Index numbers showing the relative importance of each age group in the population of the city of Atlanta, by sex, 1940 (for males, urban male population of the United States = 100; for females, urban female population of the United States = 100).

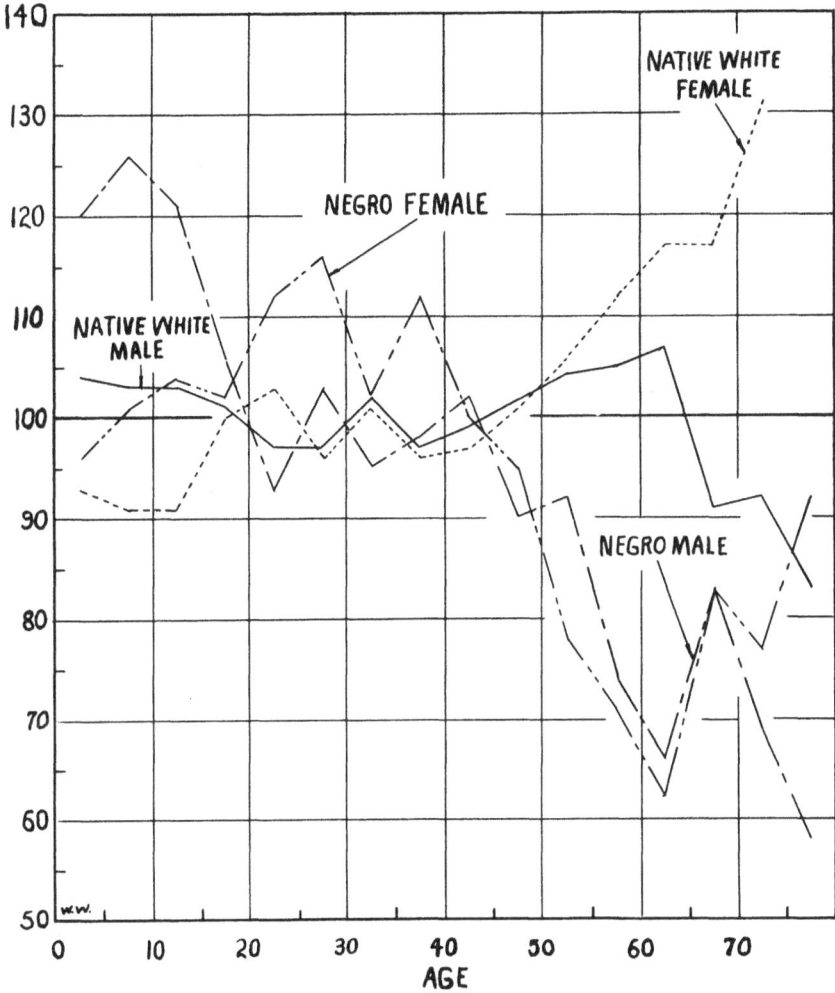

FIGURE 14. Index numbers showing the relative importance of each age group in the native white and Negro populations of the city of Atlanta, by sex, 1940 (total population, city of Atlanta = 100).

the white male which is *not* in accordance with known ratios at birth and known mortality differentials. In the productive age groups the Negro female is by far the more important while the native white female is more important beyond age 30. As one would expect in view of differential mortality rates between whites and Negroes, the whites are represented in greater proportions in the older age groups; however, within the Negro population in the age group 50 to 70 the Negro male is more important than the Negro female. Since it is generally known that mortality rates are higher for males than for females and that life expectancy is shorter for males, this finding is somewhat unusual. The writer offers the conjecture that this result may have been brought about by the misstatement of ages by Negro men.

DEPENDENCY RATIOS

To emphasize the importance of the differences shown by the index numbers, Table III was prepared showing the number of dependents per 1,000 contributors, by race, for selected urban populations in 1940. An analysis of this table shows that in the native white populations examined Atlanta's productive population did not have as many dependents as the average urban place nor as many as New Orleans or Nashville, while Dallas and Atlanta had about the same burden. In the Negro population, only

TABLE III

DEPENDENTS PER 1,000 CONTRIBUTORS, BY RACE, FOR SELECTED URBAN POPULATIONS, 1940

Population	Dependents per 1,000 Contributors	
	Native White	Negro
Urban United States	427	397
Atlanta	351	376
Dallas	346	338
Nashville	415	383
New Orleans	374	422

Source: *Sixteenth Census of the United States: 1940*, "Population, Vol. II, Characteristics of the Population," Part 1 (Washington: Government Printing Office, 1943), pp. 23, 119-120, 125, and 135-136.

Dallas had a smaller proportion of persons in the dependent group than did Atlanta.[8]

The variations, by census tracts, of dependents per 1,000 contributors are shown in Figures 15 and 16 for the white and Negro populations of Atlanta. The highest dependency ratios for the white population are found in the south central and northwestern portions of the city; while most of the lower ratios are found in the northern portion of the city. For Negroes, the pattern is not quite as distinct although there seems to be a slighter degree of concentration of persons in the productive ages near the center of the city.

SPATIAL DISTRIBUTION OF THE VARIOUS AGE GROUPS

In order to show the spatial distribution of the various age groups Figures 17 and 18 were prepared. In 1940 the population under 5 years of age was noticeably small in the northeastern portion of the city. The highest proportions were found in tracts F-32, F-34, and F-20 in the central portion of the city; one of these tracts, F-20 contains a Federal housing project (Techwood) in which the population is rather dense. The other heavy concentrations of persons under 5 were found on the periphery of the city in tracts F-6, F-8, F-57, F-63 and F-64.

By again referring to Figures 15 and 16 it is possible to note where the productive age groups are concentrated.[9] The tracts having the lighter shadings generally indicate high proportions of persons in the age groups from 15 to 64. White persons in the productive age groups are found concentrated in the northern portion of the city as well as in tracts F-27, F-33 and F-35. Negroes in the productive ages of life are found in high proportions and large numbers in tracts F-28 and F-37 particularly.

The distribution of old people is shown in Figure 18. The best that can be done here is to point out that definitely lower than average proportions of old people are found in all tracts

8. Although there was a considerable differential among the urban populations studied, the greatest differential is found between urban and rural populations. For example, in Georgia in 1940 in the rural farm population the dependency ratio was 713, while for the urban population it was 409. See C. A. McMahan, "A Study of the Population of Georgia by Sex, Age, Color, Residence, and Selected Social-Economic Factors, 1940," (unpublished Master's thesis, The University of Georgia, Athens, 1946), p. 35.

9. See Appendix B for the distribution of some of the productive age groups in 1930.

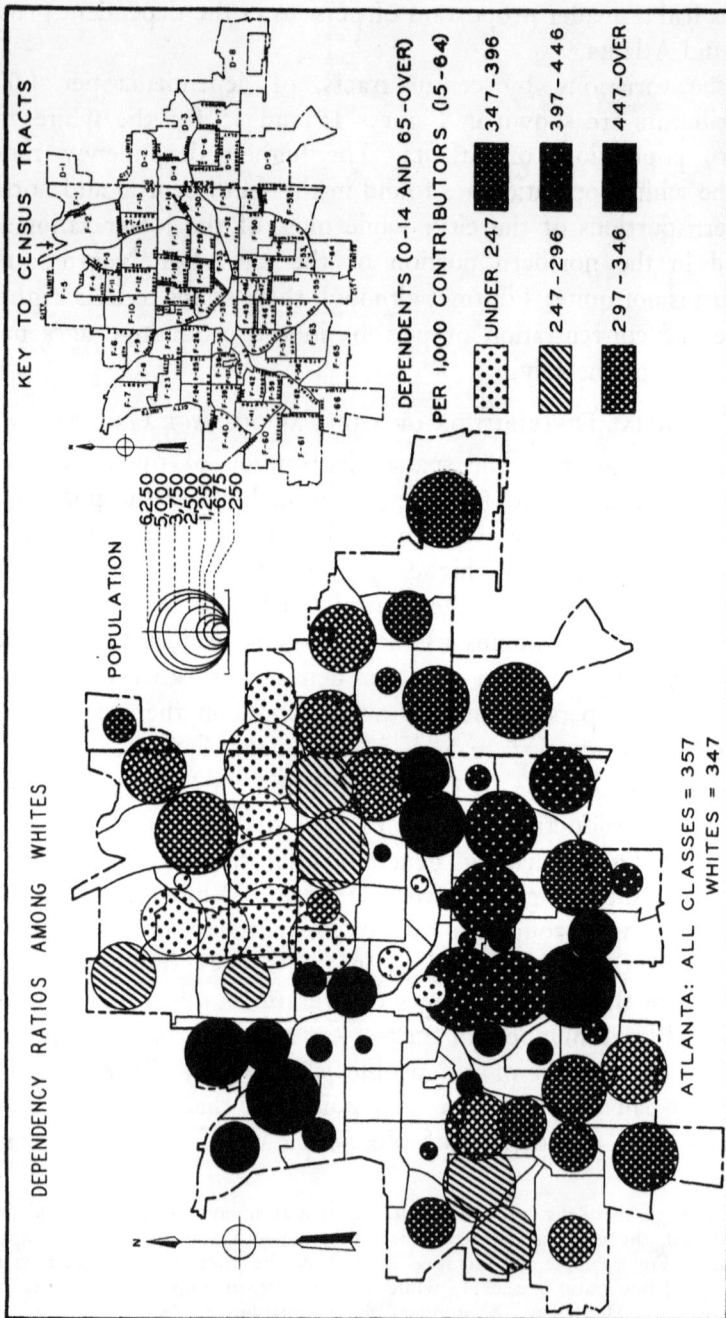

FIGURE 15. Dependents per 1,000 contributors in the white
population of Atlanta, by census tracts, 1940.

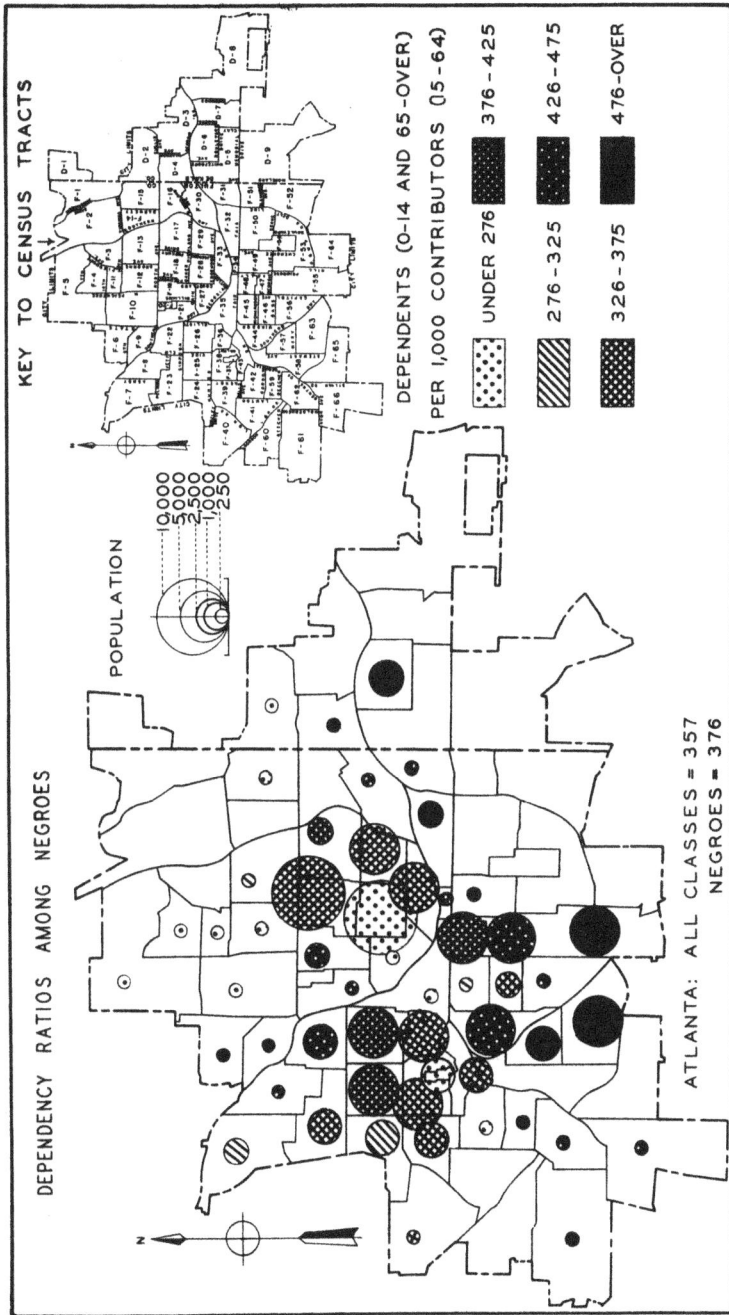

FIGURE 16. Dependents per 1,000 contributors in the Negro population of Atlanta, by census tracts, 1940.

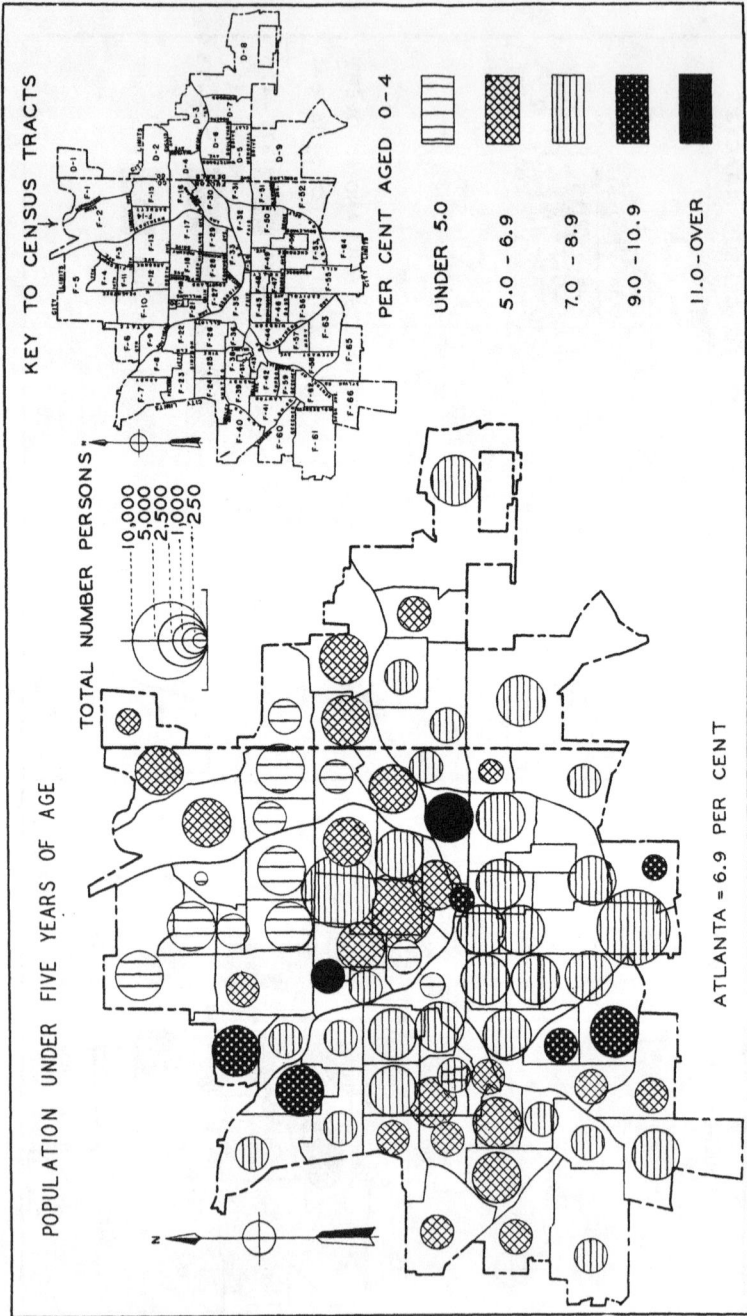

FIGURE 17. Distribution of the Atlanta population under five years of age, by census tracts, 1940.

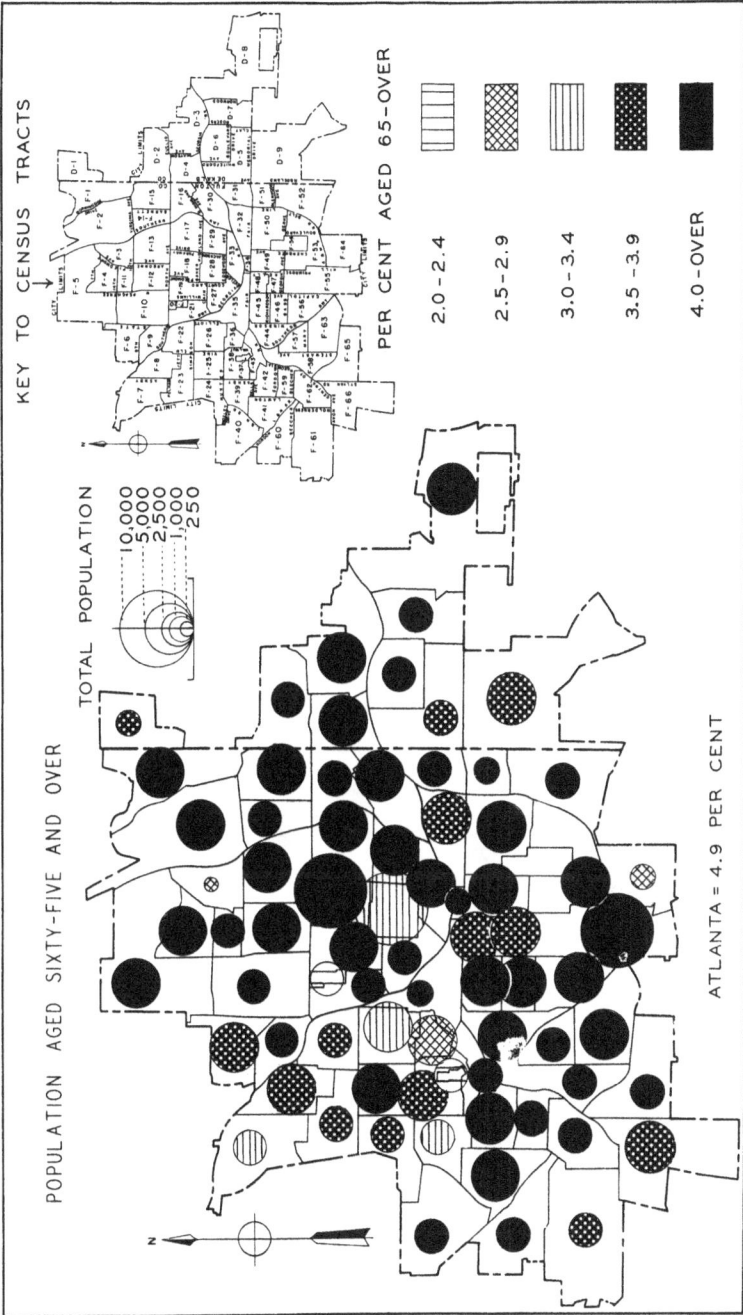

FIGURE 18. Distribution of the Atlanta population aged 65 years and over, by census tracts, 1940.

79

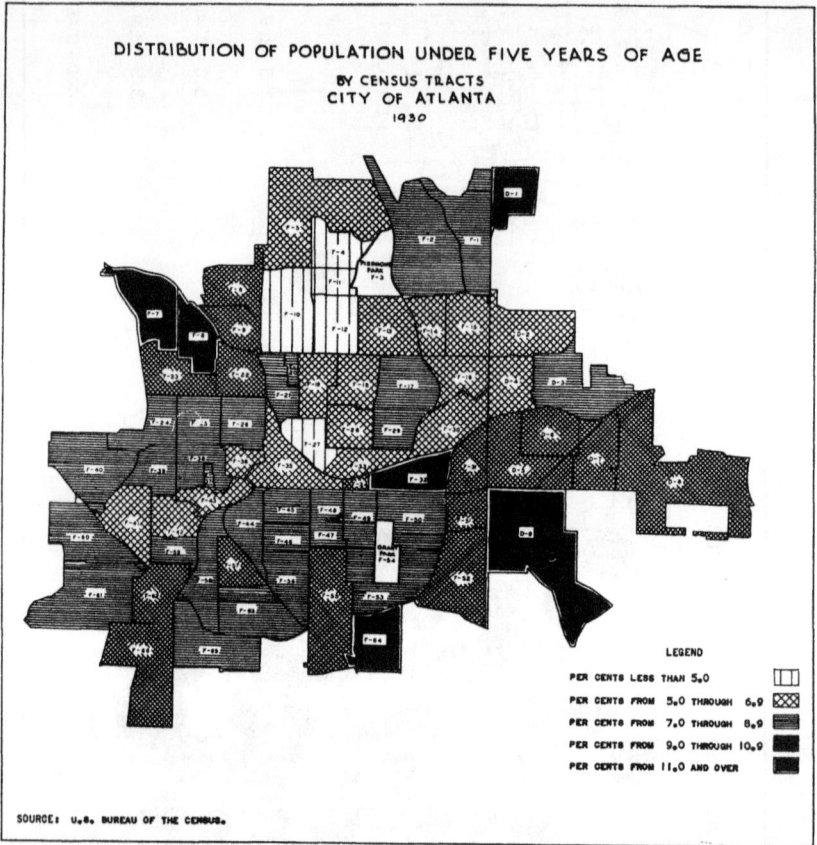

DISTRIBUTION OF POPULATION UNDER FIVE YEARS OF AGE
BY CENSUS TRACTS
CITY OF ATLANTA
1930

LEGEND

PER CENTS LESS THAN 5.0
PER CENTS FROM 5.0 THROUGH 6.9
PER CENTS FROM 7.0 THROUGH 8.9
PER CENTS FROM 9.0 THROUGH 10.9
PER CENTS FROM 11.0 AND OVER

SOURCE: U.S. BUREAU OF THE CENSUS.

FIGURE 19. Distribution of the Atlanta population under five years of age, by census tracts, 1930. (Reproduced from WPA of Georgia official project 465-34-3-4.)

80

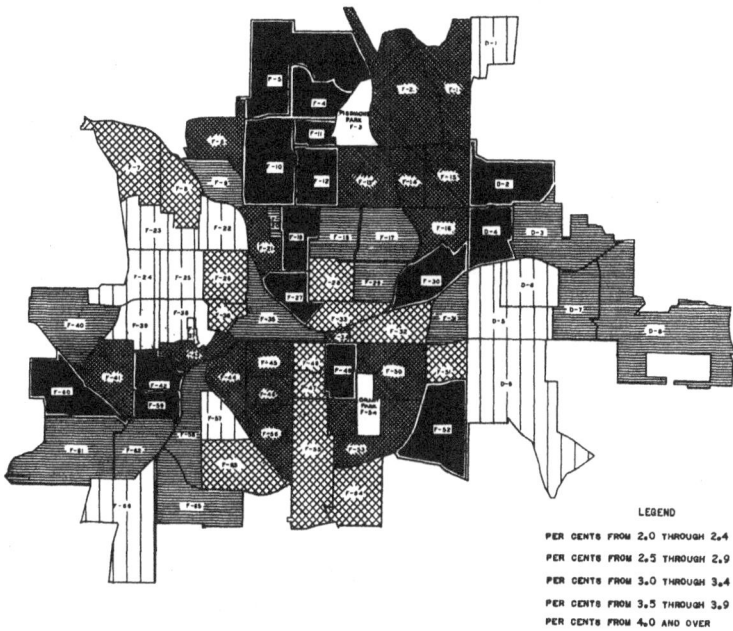

DISTRIBUTION OF POPULATION SIXTY-FIVE YEARS OF AGE AND OVER
BY CENSUS TRACTS
CITY OF ATLANTA
1930

LEGEND

PER CENTS FROM 2.0 THROUGH 2.4
PER CENTS FROM 2.5 THROUGH 2.9
PER CENTS FROM 3.0 THROUGH 3.4
PER CENTS FROM 3.5 THROUGH 3.9
PER CENTS FROM 4.0 AND OVER

SOURCE: U.S. BUREAU OF THE CENSUS.

FIGURE 20. Distribution of the Atlanta population aged 65-over, by census tracts, 1930. (Reproduced from WPA of Georgia official project 465-34-3-4.)

except the black shadings; particularly small proportions of persons over 65 are found in tracts F-28, F-26, F-36, F-39, and F-64.

TRENDS IN AGE COMPOSITION

In order to point out the changes in age composition between 1930 and 1940, Figures 19 and 20 are presented. It will be noted in Figure 19 that with only one exception, the highest percentage of the very young was located in census tracts near the periphery of the city. In comparing the 1940 data with 1930 by use of Figures 17 and 19, one will discover that there have been significant changes in tracts D-1, F-7, and D-9; these may be merely outstanding differences that indicate the general aging of the Atlanta population, since in 1940 only 6.9 per cent of the population fell in the age group under 5 years of age in comparison to 7.7 per cent in 1930.[10]

Now turning to the other extreme, the very old in the population, when Figure 18 is compared with Figure 20, it will be seen that Figure 18 is considerably darker; thus it is indicated that the Atlanta population of 1940 had a much larger proportion of its population in the very advanced ages than was the case in 1930. In 1940, 4.8 per cent of the population was 65 years of age or older, whereas in 1930 only 3.4 per cent fell in that classification. This is substantiating evidence that the average age of the population of Atlanta is rising (becoming older).[11]

10. *Sixteenth Census of the United States: 1940*, "Population, Vol. II, Characteristics of the Population," Part 2 (Washington: Government Printing Office, 1942), p. 374.
11. *Ibid.*, p. 374.

CHAPTER VI

SEX COMPOSITION

THE SEX COMPOSITION OF A POPULATION IS ONE OF THE MOST BASIC aspects of its structure. The ratio of males to females affects many demographic phenomena; for example, the birth rate, marriage rate, amount and extent of migration, and finally the death rate. The social life of a community is greatly affected by the balance between the sexes; in mining, frontier, and steel towns the reckless life results largely in a scarcity of women and also stems from the same fact. The lack of men in textile centers and certain residential cities and even the nation's capital during the war years has tremendous influence on the type of life and even the mores.

It is the object of this chapter to discuss the balance between the sexes in Atlanta, other southern cities, and urban portions of the United States. These data are analyzed by race and nativity, and in addition the differences existing between census tracts in the city of Atlanta are pointed out. Finally, trends in the sex ratio since 1850 are analyzed.

In 1940 the sex ratio for the Atlanta population was 85.5; this is one of the lowest sex ratios of any large city in the nation. Furthermore, sex ratio among persons of all ages in Atlanta, including children, among whom the sex ratio is very high, is at least ten points below the urban average of the United States and lower than any other city studied or known to the writer (even Washington, D. C., for 1940).

In order to compare Atlanta with other large urban populations, Table IV was prepared. This table shows Atlanta's total population to have the same sex ratio as Nashville and a much lower ratio than the other populations studied.

RACE AND NATIVITY DIFFERENCES

From Table IV, it is noted that the foreign-born white populations have the highest sex ratios, the native white populations next, while the Negro populations have the lowest sex ratios of all. In fact, the extremely low sex ratios of the southern cities are largely due to the low sex ratios among their Negro populations. In 1940 the sex ratio among Negroes was 83.7 in Charlotte; 82.5

83

in Nashville; 84.9 in Richmond; 85.8 in New Orleans; and 78.7 in Atlanta.[1]

In spite of the limitations of sex ratios by age, the data are useful for comparing similar populations, and so Figures 21 and 22 have been constructed. One should note particularly the following points: (1) The lowest sex ratios seem to be at ages 20-25, and the Negro population reaches an extreme low at this age group; and (2) the foreign-born population is predominantly masculine although there is no known reason for the very high sex ratios at the very young ages in this group (very small numbers, possibly, make this a chance variation).

TABLE IV

Sex Ratios in Selected Urban Populations, 1940

Population	All Classes	Native White	Foreign- Born White	Negro
Urban United States	96	94	107	88
Urban Population of Ga.	87	90	127	80
Atlanta	86	89	127	79
Nashville	86	87	113	83
New Orleans	90	90	131	86
New York	97	96	104	82

Source: *Sixteenth Census of the United States: 1940*, "Population Vol. II, Characteristics of the Population," Parts 1, 2, 3, 5, and 6 (Washington: Government Printing Office, 1942).

Variations of Sex Ratios by Census Tracts

In order to try to determine how the sex ratio varies in the different areas of the city and in the areas immediately adjacent to the city, Figures 23 and 24 have been prepared. The highest sex ratios are found in Tracts F-7 (a highly industrialized section); F-27 and F-35, both downtown districts (central trade area); and F-64, on the edge of the city. The lowest ratios are found in Tracts F-43 and F-4; both of these tracts are densely populated residential areas with a high proportion of rooming-houses for young women.

When one examines Figure 24 he is immediately impressed by the smaller circles and the darker shadings indicating smaller

1. T. Lynn Smith, *Population Analysis* (New York: McGraw-Hill Book Company, Inc., 1948), p. 128.

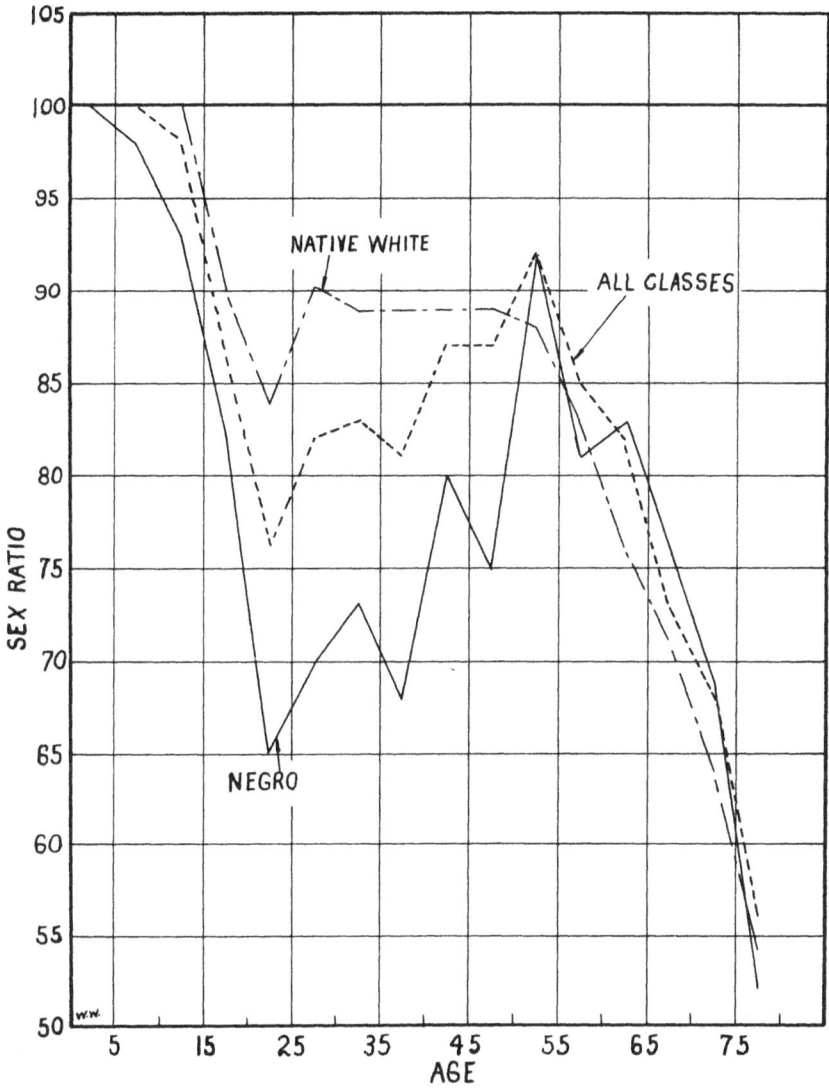

FIGURE 21. Sex ratios by age for the total (all classes), native white, and Negro populations of the city of Atlanta, 1940.

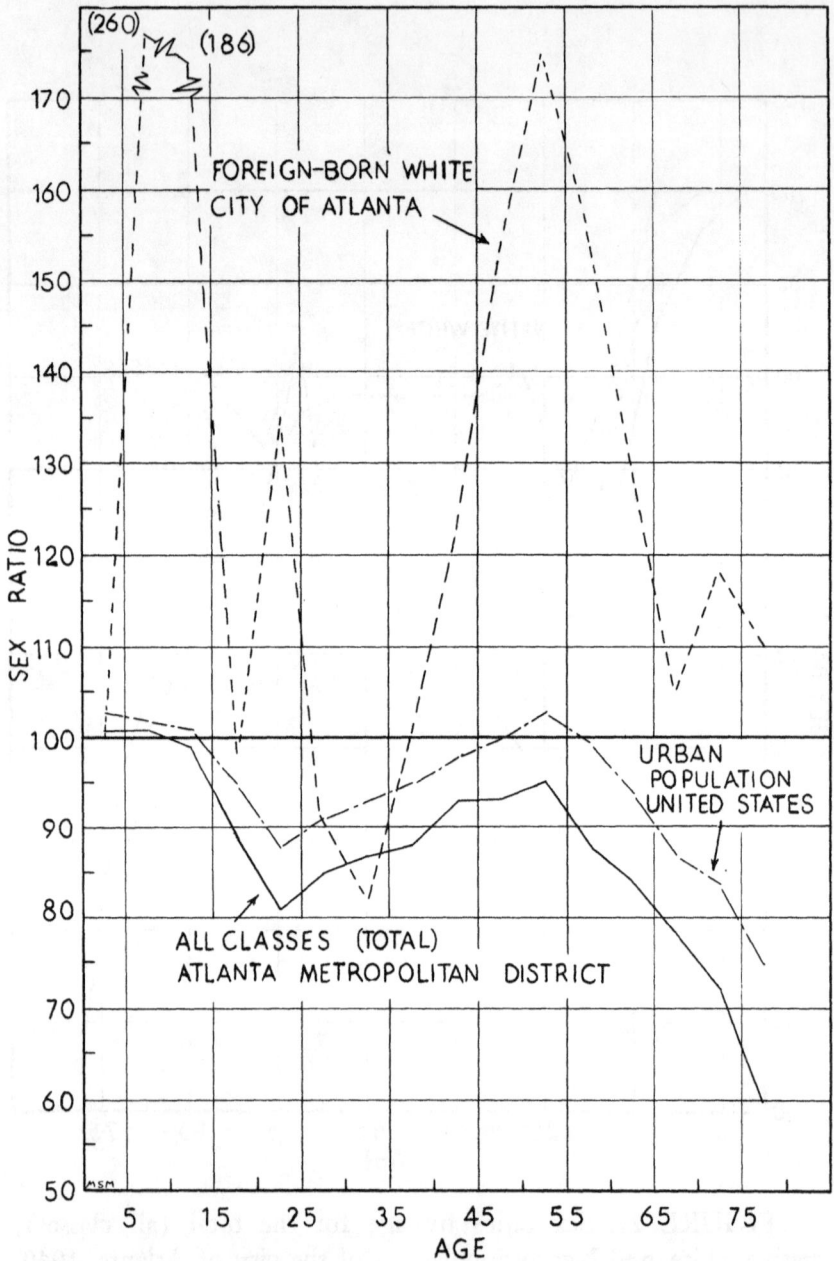

FIGURE 22. Sex ratios by age for the Foreign-born white population of the city of Atlanta, the total (all classes) population of the Atlanta metropolitan district, and the urban population of the United States, 1940.

numbers of people and higher sex ratios. From a comparison of Figures 23 and 24, one may generalize by stating that as urbanity increases, for the Atlanta area at least, the sex ratio tends to fall.

It might be well at this point to compare directly Figure 3 with Figure 23. It will be noted in making this comparison that census tracts which have high proportions of Negroes also tend to have sex ratios below the average for Atlanta.

TRENDS IN THE BALANCE BETWEEN THE SEXES

When Atlanta became a "city" exceeding 2,500 (attaining this number for the first time at the census of 1850), the sex ratio was approximately 100, indicating that the sexes were evenly distributed. At that time, however, the white population was heavily masculine as indicated by a sex ratio of 107, and the Negro population was extremely feminine with a sex ratio of only 77 (Table C, Appendix).

The sex ratio of the Atlanta white population has varied from the highs of 107 and 108 for the censuses of 1850 and 1860 respectively, to a low of 89 in 1940. The census of 1870 showed a sharp drop to 94, which probably reflects the casualties of the then recent war; the sexes evened up around 1900 with a somewhat irregular decline to the 1940 figure.

The Negro population of Atlanta has never had a sex ratio higher than 86; it has always been dominated by the female, reaching its extreme low in 1900 with only 71 males per 100 females. The sex ratio climbed rather steadily until the high was reached in 1920 (rather unusual when one generally thinks of the tremendous migrations of Negroes to the northern cities immediately following World War I), then has declined for the past two decades.

For the total population of Atlanta, the last year of a reported sex ratio of 100 or higher was 1860. Each census since that date has reported more women than men in the city. Although the sex ratios for the total population show some fluctuation from 1870 to 1920, the trend has been generally downward, i.e., toward a lower sex ratio. Thus sex ratios dropped from 93 in 1910 and 1920 to 88 in 1930, and to about 86 in 1940.

It may be noted from Table C, Appendix, that the sex ratio for the white population exceeds that for the Negro in each census year for which data are available. The amount of difference

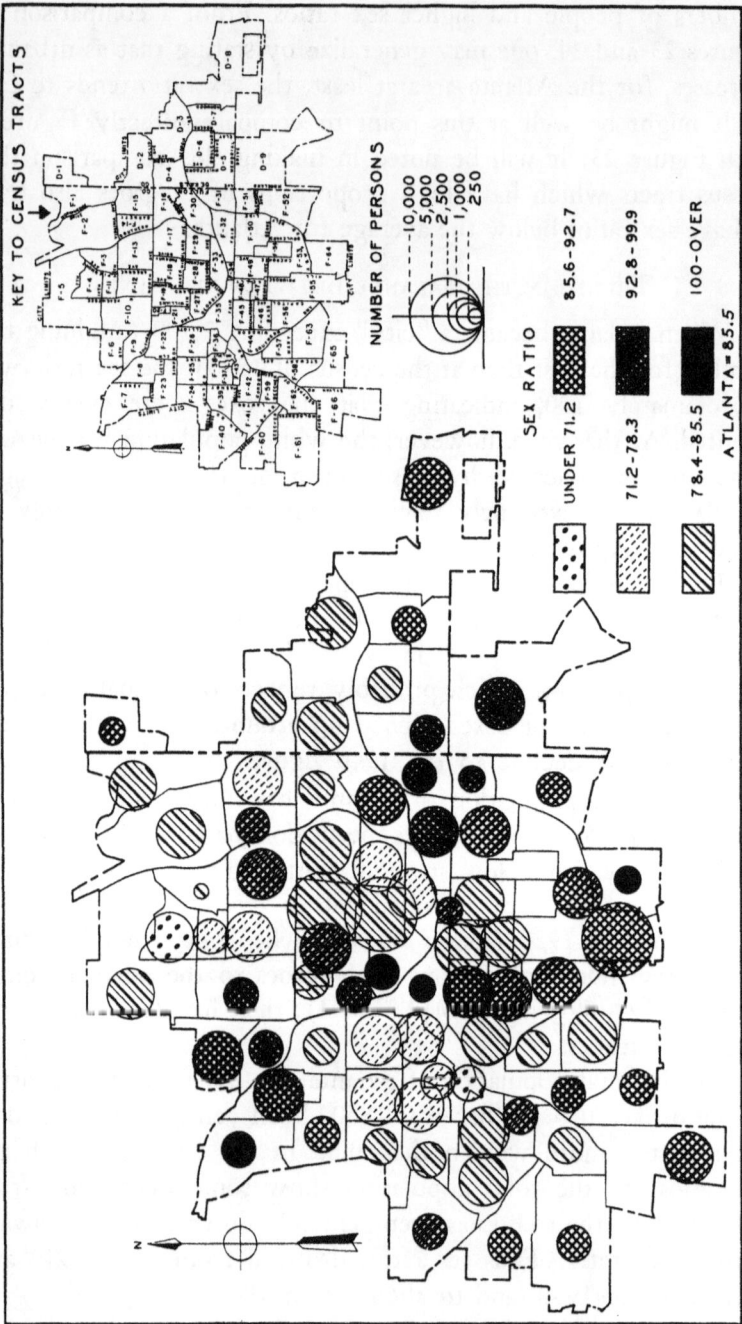

FIGURE 23. Sex ratios among the population of the city of Atlanta, by census tracts, 1940.

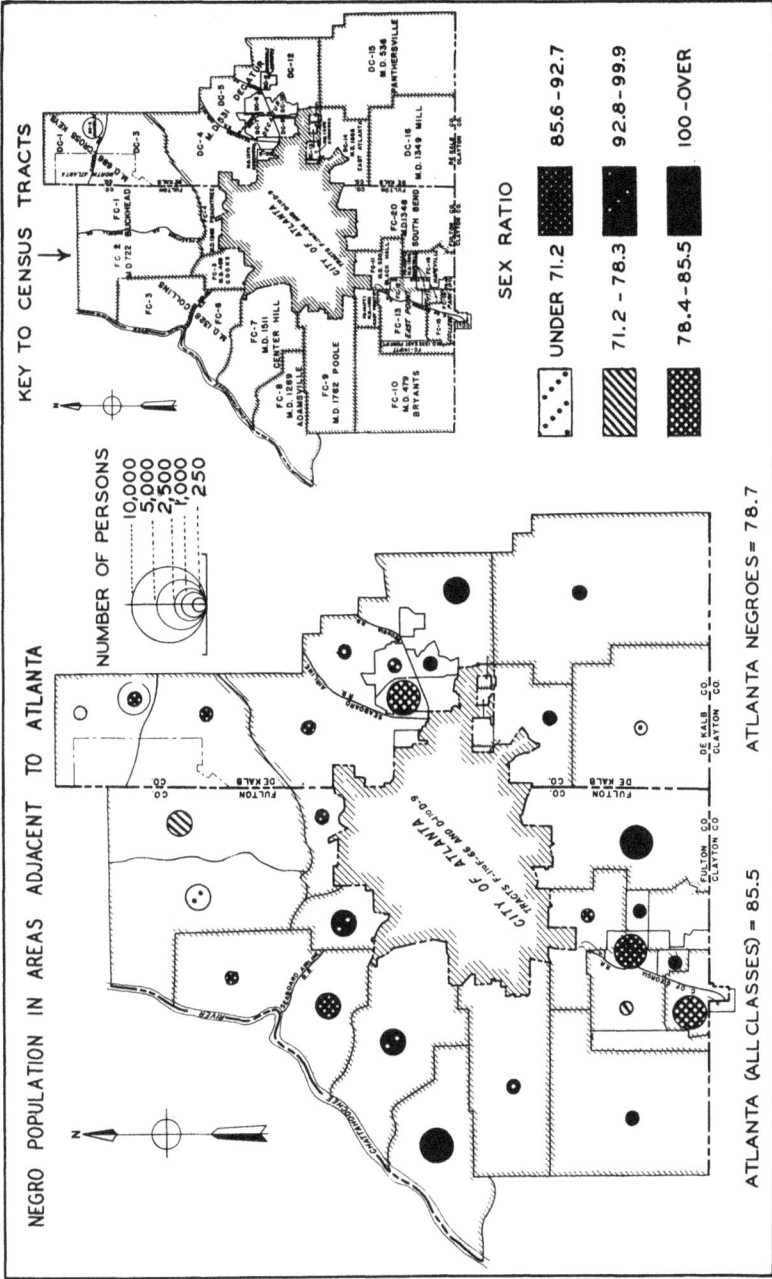

FIGURE 24. Sex ratios among the Negro population in areas adjacent to Atlanta, by census tracts, 1940.

between the sex ratios for the two groups varies from 10 points in 1920 and 1940 to 25 points in 1900, and 30 points in 1850. Thus it appears that the white population group of Atlanta has a consistently higher proportion of males than does the Negro group. This is in general agreement with the findings of other demographers.[2]

When the findings of this chapter, especially those represented in Table V, are related to the material in the chapter on growth of population, one is tempted to suggest the hypothesis that when a city is growing relatively rapidly, the sex ratio will tend to be higher than when the city is increasing slowly.

Recent trends. In the decade from 1930 to 1940 the sex ratio of the total population of Atlanta decreased from 87.9 in 1930 to 85.5 in 1940; the native white population decreased from 91.6 to 88.6; the Negro population decreased from 79.6 to 78.7; but the sex ratio of the foreign-born population increased from 124.1 to 126.7.[3] From the foregoing, one is led to conclude that the female became increasingly more important in the Atlanta population during the 1930's, since the foreign-born portion of the population is so very small.

2. T. Lynn Smith, "A Demographic Study of the American Negro," *Social Forces*, 23:379-387, March, 1945.
3. *Sixteenth Census of the United States: 1940*, "Population, Vol. II, Characteristics of the Population," Part 2 (Washington: Government Printing Office, 1942), p. 198.

CHAPTER VII

MARITAL STATUS

IN A NATION SUCH AS OURS IN WHICH THE MORES DICTATE THAT A woman be married if she is to bear children, the marital condition of a population has considerable effect upon the birth rate. Furthermore, the marital status of a population is a crude measure of the prevalence and stability of the family institution.

The purpose of this chapter on marital condition is to show how the population of Atlanta compares with other large urban populations, with special reference to variations by age, although variations in the racial groups and by sex are also treated. The trend in the marital status of the population is also studied.

Although data on the marital status of the Atlanta population were available in the 1900 census, those data are of little value in this study, since they included persons of all ages; therefore, the present analysis begins with the 1910 census which eliminates those in the age groups under 15.

The most essential features of the marital condition of the Atlanta population in 1940, as revealed graphically in Figures 25 through 28, are the following: (1) that men are married in greater proportions than in the urban population of the United States and in most of the other large southern cities, and that white women are married in greater proportions at the younger ages only; (2) that both men and women of Atlanta tend to marry at an earlier age than the average of urban populations in the United States and most of the other large southern cities; (3) that in the older age groups both the Negro males and females live in the widowed state in much greater proportions than their white counterparts; and (4) that females of both races are widowed in greater proportions than the males, the Negro female in much greater proportion than the white female.

COMPARISONS WITH OTHER URBAN POPULATIONS

In view of the high proportion of females in the city of Atlanta, one is not surprised to note in Figure 25 that the Atlanta male population in the 1940 census is "more married" than the male populations of cities such as New Orleans, and even more so than the urban population of the United States.

The men of Atlanta tend to marry at an earlier age than in

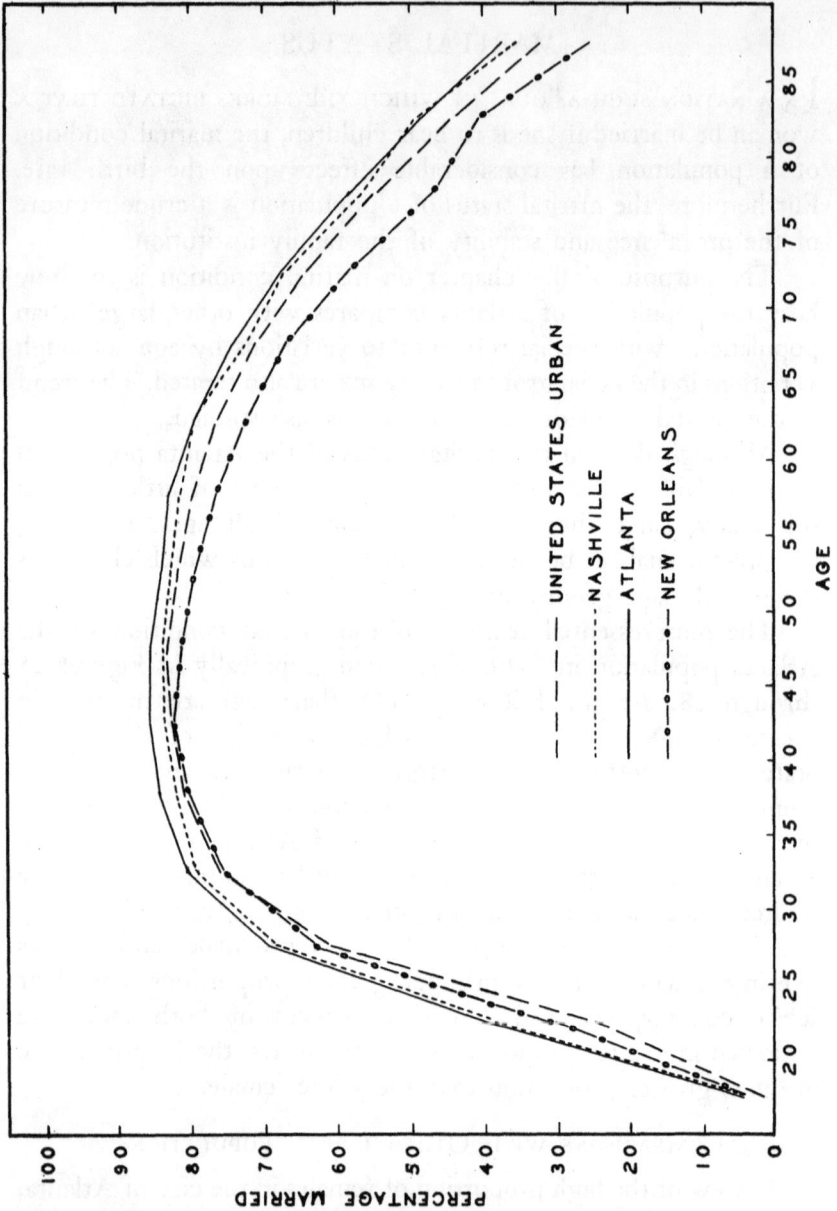

FIGURE 25. Variations in the proportions of married persons among the male populations of the United States (urban) and selected cities, by age, 1940.

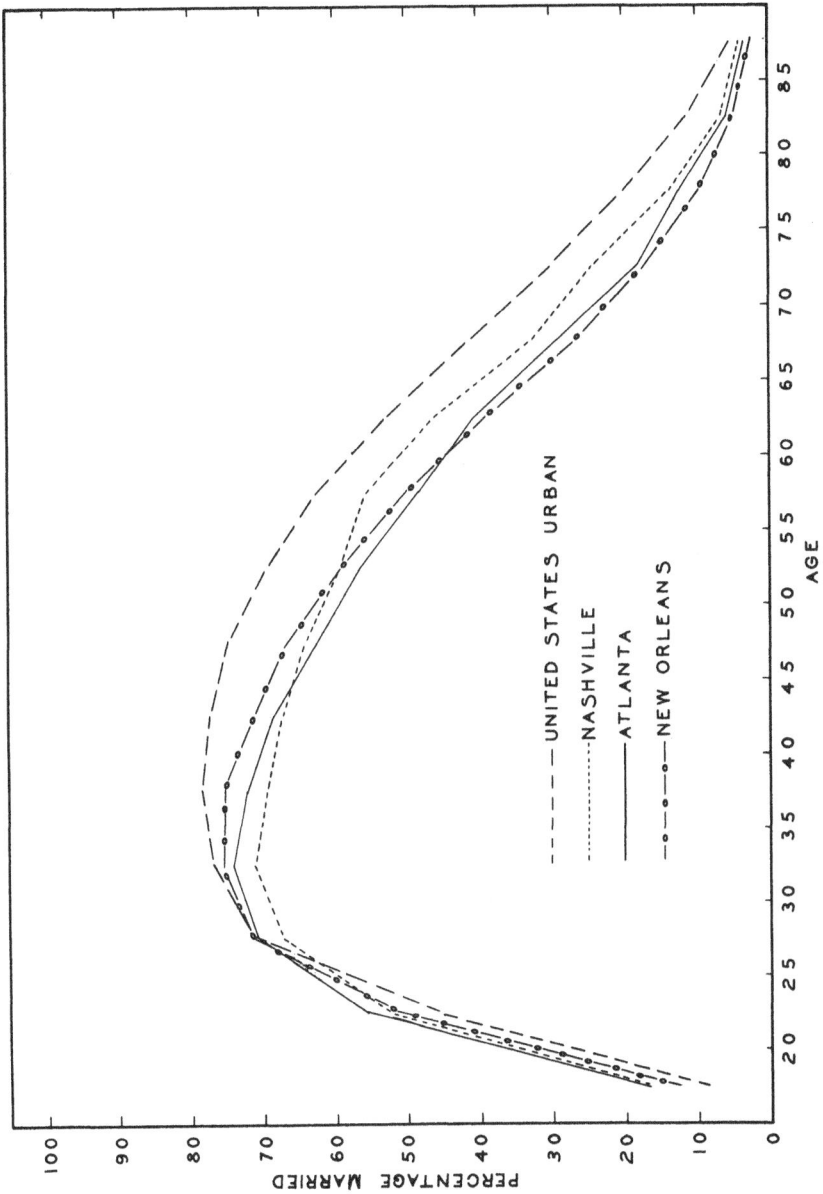

FIGURE 26. Variations in the proportions of married persons among the female populations of the United States (urban) and selected cities, by age, 1940.

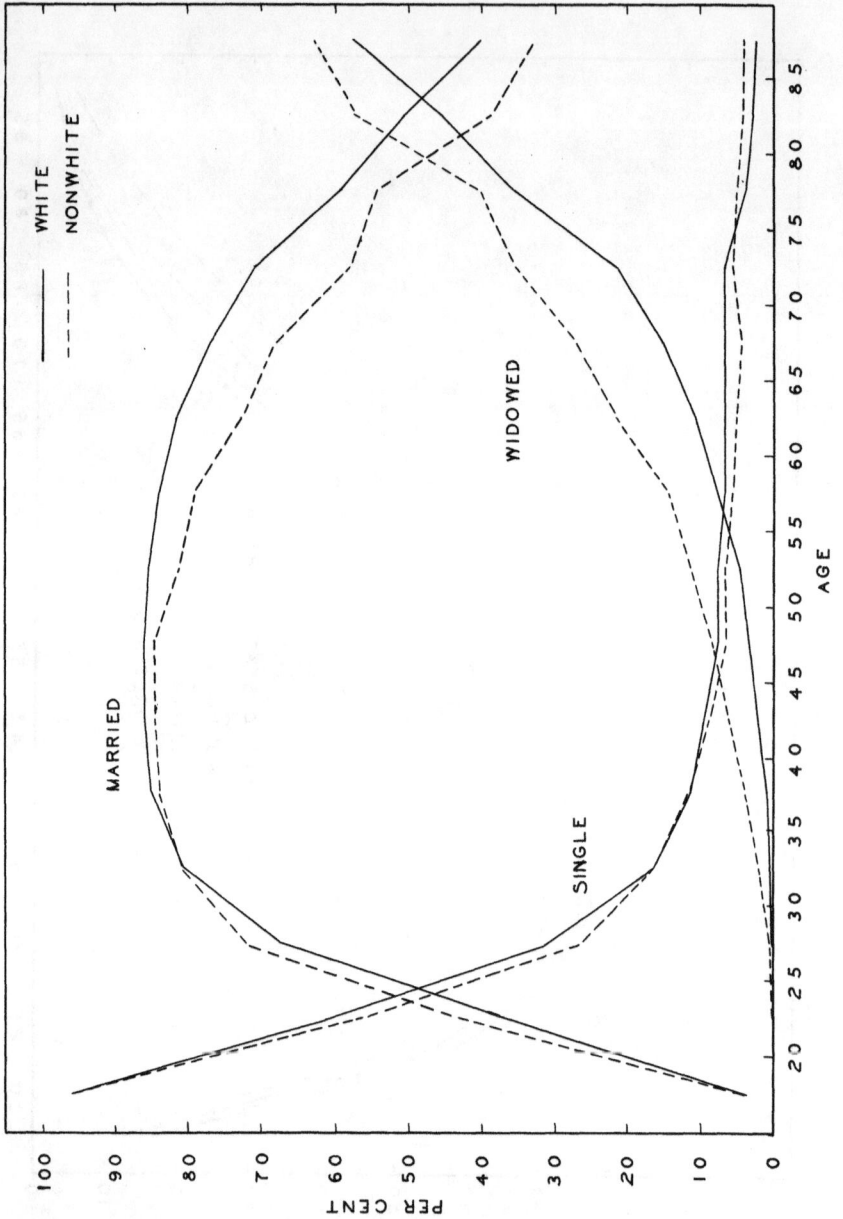

FIGURE 27.   A comparison of the marital status of white and nonwhite males in the city of Atlanta, by age, 1940.

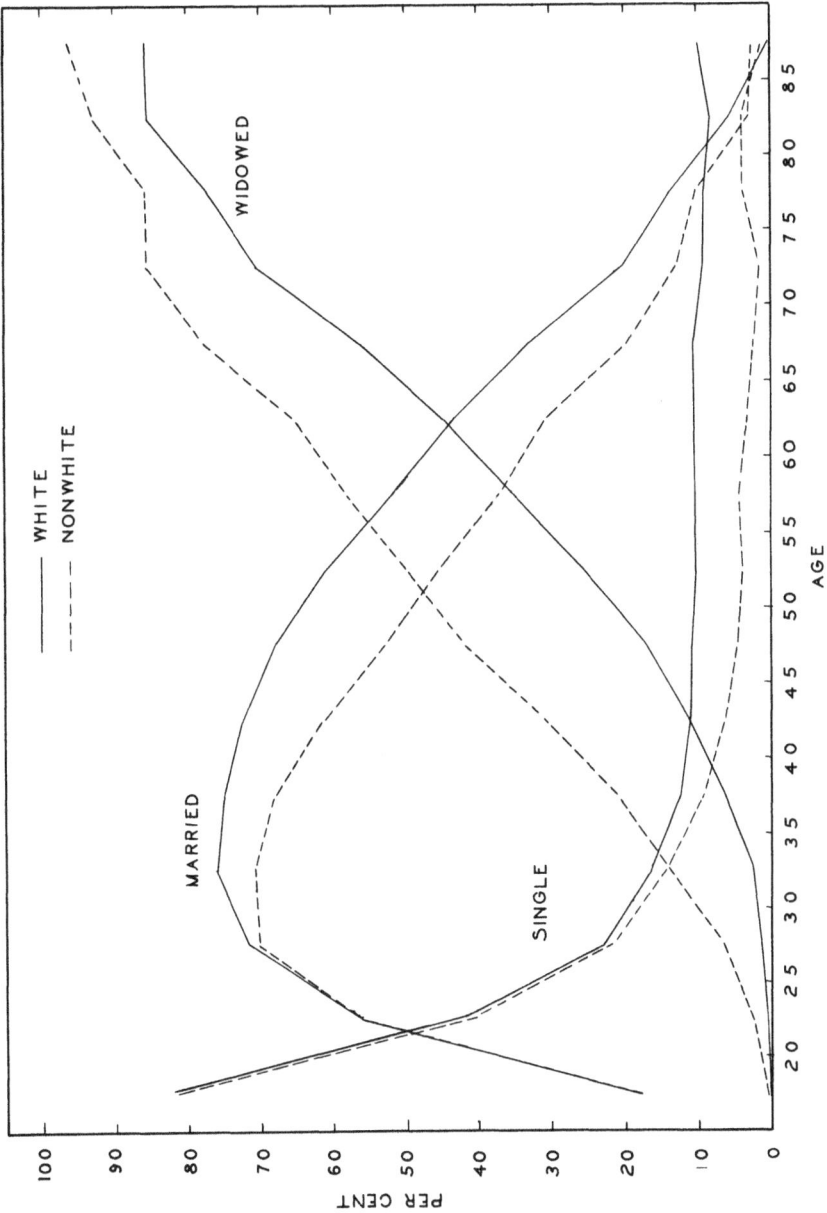

FIGURE 28. A comparison of the marital status of white and nonwhite females in the City of Atlanta, by age, 1940.

the urban United States as a whole and also than in the other southern cities with which it has been compared. There is a greater tendency for Atlanta males to be in the married category than in the urban United States, and the selected cities, at all ages except at ages 65 and 80, where Nashville males have about the same percentage in this category. For Atlanta males there is a rapid rise in the percentage in the married category between ages 20 and 35 with the peak occuring between ages 45 and 50 and a gradual decline thereafter. This curve appears to be fairly typical, since the corresponding curve for urban males in the United States runs roughly parallel to the curve for Atlanta males.

Atlanta women tend to enter marriage at an earlier age than do the women in Nashville, New Orleans, and in the urban United States. About 60 per cent of Atlanta women aged 23 are recorded in the census as married, whereas only about 50 per cent of women of this age in the urban United States are married. For the older ages, the urban women of the United States and of Nashville are married in greater proportions than the Atlanta women. At age 27, the percentage of women in the married category in the urban United States in 1940 is equal to the percentage of married women in Atlanta; and from that age on, women in the urban United States have consistently higher proportions in the married category. The curve for Atlanta women as given in Figure 26, however, is fairly characteristic of urban women in the entire country, since there is a rapid rise from the late teens to about age 25 (the 50 per cent mark is attained at age 23), and a more gradual slope from 25 to the peak at age 34 where approximately 74 per cent of women are listed as married, followed by a gradual descent in the remaining age groups.

MARITAL CONDITION AND RACE

When the nonwhite and white populations are compared, as is done in Figures 27 and 28, very little difference between the two groups up to ages 25 or 30 is noted. In the older age groups, however, the white male is found in considerably larger proportions in the married category than is the nonwhite male. The nonwhite male is much more in the widowed state in all age groups than is the white male. Nevertheless, in general, the curves

96

for the two groups are similar. The age at which the number of married males equals the number of single males comes about a year earlier for the nonwhite group. Similarly, the number of widowed males equals the number in the married category about four years earlier in the nonwhite group.

The white female is considerably more concentrated in the married category in the older age groups than her nonwhite counterpart; however, the nonwhite female far exceeds the white woman in the widowed classification. Of course these facts tend to emphasize the extreme femininity of the Negro population. It is interesting to note that by age 51, the number of widowed nonwhite females equals the number in the married group. The corresponding age for white females is age 63. The chances for the white woman to live out the later years of her life with her spouse are not very good, but are considerably better than are the chances of the nonwhite woman. At all ages above 25, there is a significantly higher percentage of single white females than of single nonwhite females.

Marital Condition and Sex

Figure 29 shows that up to the age group 35-39, the Atlanta males escaped the bonds of matrimony to a greater extent than the females; however, in the older age groups the males are in the married category to a much greater degree than the females. One should note particularly that the Atlanta female is widowed in far greater proportion than the Atlanta male (on a numerical basis, 4,213 widowers to 22,186 widows).[1]

Trends in Marital Status

When one compares the marital status of 1910 with that of 1940 (Figures 30 and 31), it is interesting to note that the Atlanta male in 1940 was married in greater proportions at all ages except the very old ones; that he married at a younger age; and in case he lived to a "ripe old age," he was much more likely to be a widower at the time of his demise.

The female of 1940 also married at a slightly younger age than did the Atlanta woman of 1910; she also helped her sister to get married to a greater extent in 1940, or in some way at least

1. *Sixteenth Census of the United States: 1940,* "Population, Vol. IV, Characteristics by Age," Part 2 (Washington: Government Printing Office, 1943), p. 12.

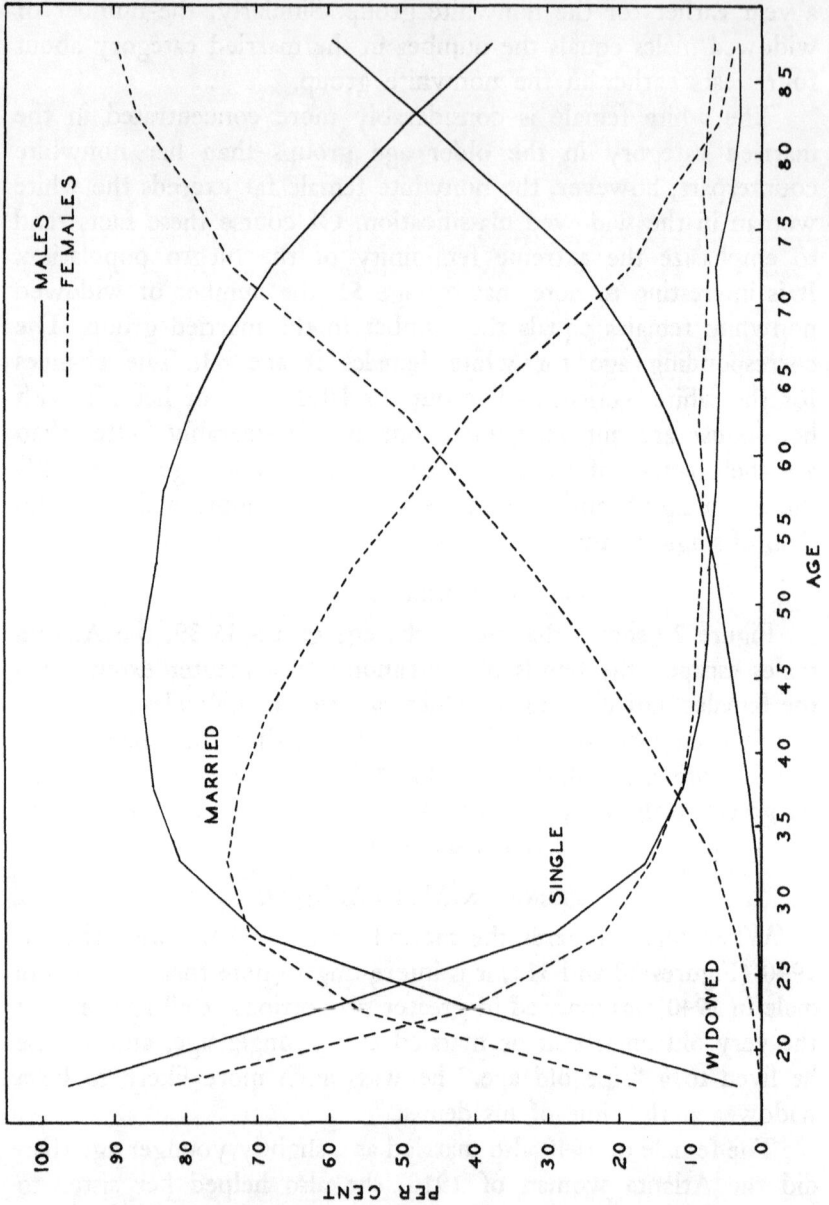

FIGURE 29. The relationship of age to marital status among the population of the city of Atlanta, by sex, 1940.

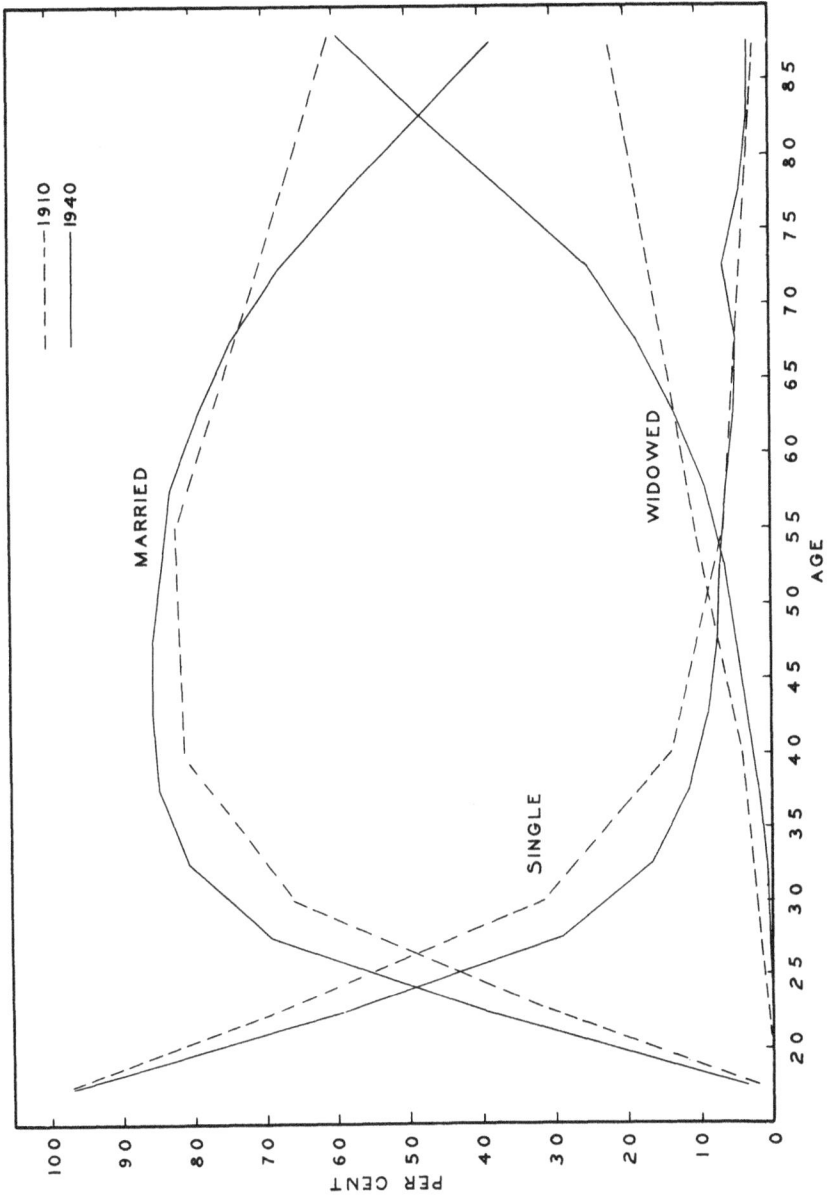

FIGURE 30. Changes in the marital status of males in the city of Atlanta, by age, 1910 to 1940.

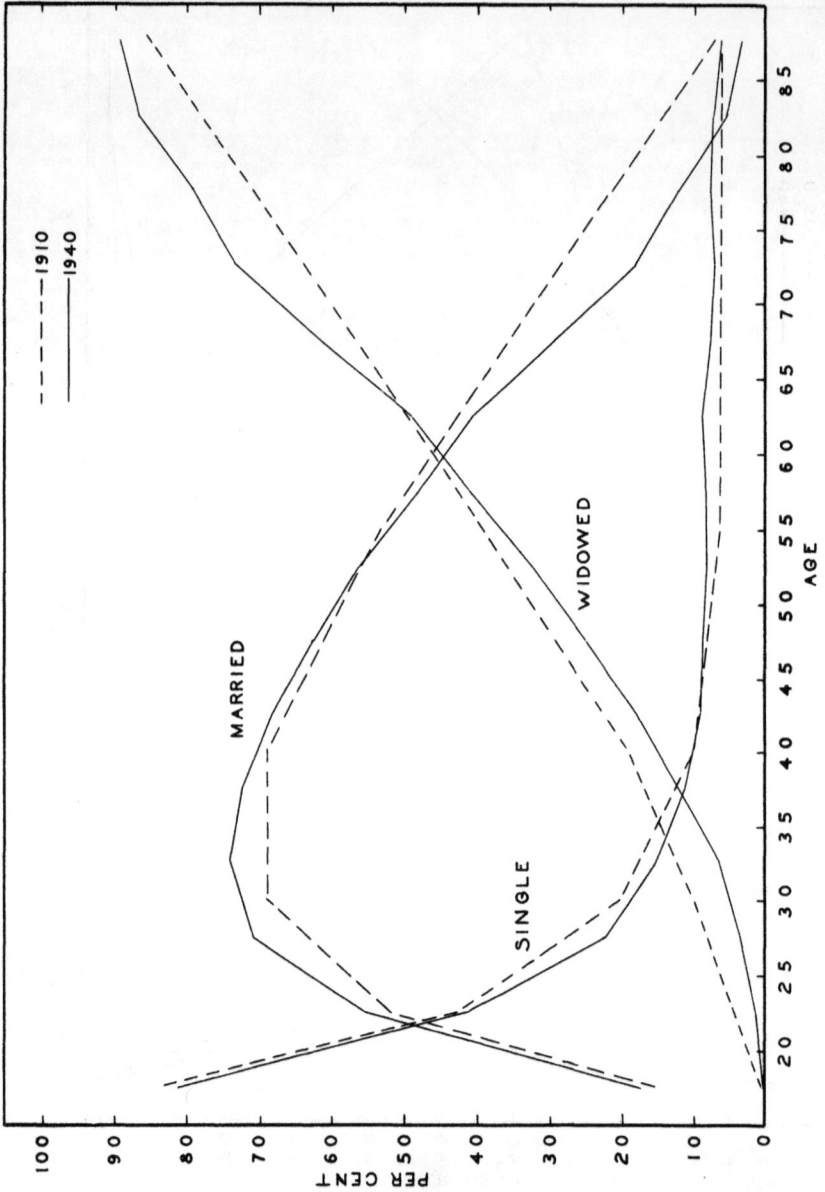

FIGURE 31. Changes in the marital status of females in the city of Atlanta, by age, 1910 to 1940.

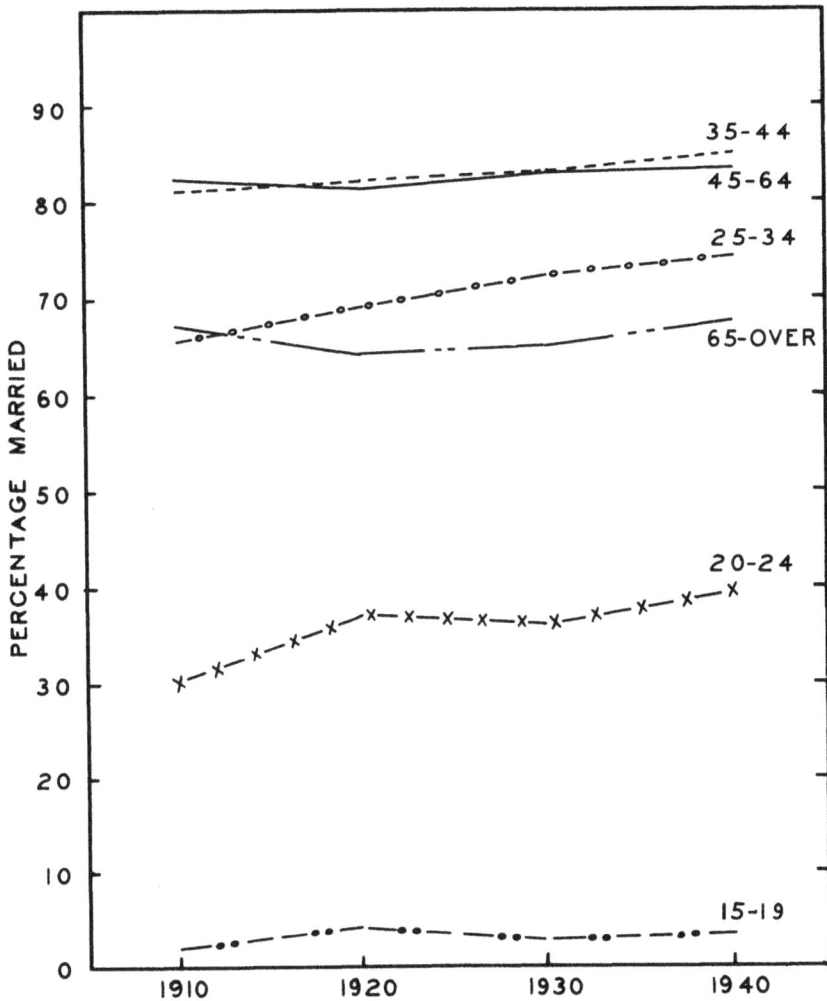

FIGURE 32. Variations in the proportions of married persons in each age group among the male population of the city of Atlanta, 1910 to 1940.

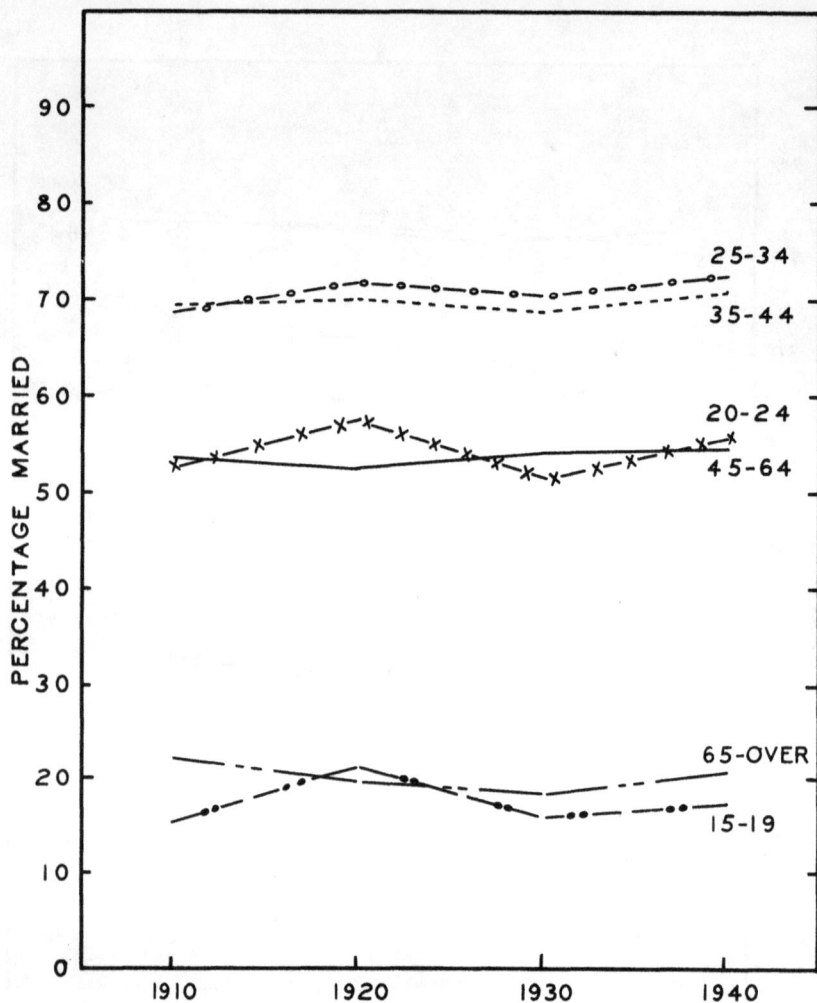

FIGURE 33. Variations in the proportions of married persons in each age group among the female population of the city of Atlanta, 1910 to 1940.

she was married in greater proportions than in 1910; and like the Atlanta male, she was just a little more likely to finish out her life span as a widow.

Figure 32 shows variations in the proportions of married persons in each of several age groups among the male population of Atlanta for each of the decennial censuses from 1910 to 1940. An analysis of this figure bears out the comments already made and indicates in general a tendency for males to prefer (at least he gets in that condition to a greater extent) the married state to a slightly greater degree as the years pass; this is especially true for the age groups 20-40. The relative stability of the percentages in the married category through this thirty-year span would tend to suggest that the institution of marriage is still about as popular as it was a generation ago and that no startling differences over this period are in evidence.

Figure 33 presents corresponding data for the female population of Atlanta in each of several age groups for each census from 1910 to 1940. Careful analysis of these data reveals only slight fluctuations in relative position of the various age groups. Thus in 1920, there were slightly higher proportions of women in the two youngest age groups (15 to 19 and 20 to 24) reported in the married category. One might offer the conjecture that this apparently unusual condition may be a result of the then recent World War I and its effect on the marriage rate of marriageable persons. The same general trend is seen in the data for Atlanta females as in the data for Atlanta males, and the percentages in each of the age groups appear to be relatively stable over this thirty-year span.

CHAPTER VIII

EDUCATIONAL STATUS

THE BENEFITS OF EDUCATION HAVE NOT BEEN EXTENDED TO people of some communities to the extent that they have been enjoyed by other populations. Thus the purpose of this chapter is to analyze the variations in the amount of schooling received by selected urban populations; to analyze particularly the educational status of the population of Atlanta by census tracts and to determine further the variations by race within these different areas; to compare the educational status of the population of suburban Atlanta with that of the central city; and to point out the trends of educational status in Atlanta and selected southern cities during the present century.

The study of the educational status of a population is significant because of the fact that educational status is one of the best indicators of the quality of the population. This is true for the following reasons: (1) The number of years of school completed measures efficiency in the use of a large portion of the family budget which is spent for advancement; (2) amount of schooling reflects the efforts of the community (parents, county, city, state, nation) toward assuring the welfare of the future; and (3) complex conditions today (complicated especially by urbanization) require aptness in calculating, reading and writing.[1]

A return of the illiterate population was made for the first time in 1840, although it included only white persons aged 20 years and over. Similar returns were made in the censuses of 1850 and 1860, but in 1870 individual returns were required for all persons 10 years of age and over.[2] Ability to write and school attendance were reported in the 1870 census publications for the then fifty principal cities, but Atlanta was not so listed.[3] The census of 1880 listed Atlanta as one of the fifty principal cities

---

1. T. Lynn Smith, *Population Analysis* (New York: McGraw-Hill Book Company, Inc., 1948), p. 153.
2. *Twelfth Census of the United States: 1900*, "Population, Vol. II," Part II (Washington: Government Printing Office, 1902), p. xcvii.
3. *Ninth Census of the United States: 1870*, "Volume I, The Statistics of the Population of the United States," (Washington: Government Printing Office, 1872), pp. 439-446.

but did not list data on educational status for the city.[4] The census of 1890 reported persons of school age by race and nativity, but, like its predecessors, did not report amount of education or per cent illiteracy among its population data.[5]

The Twelfth Census of the United States made in 1900 reported illiteracy by race and nativity for persons aged 10 years and over in cities over 25,000 which, of course, included Atlanta.[6] The test of literacy in 1900 was whether a person could read and write the language he usually spoke (not necessarily English).[7] The 1910 definition of literacy classed all persons illiterate if they were unable to write regardless of ability to read.[8]

When the much more nearly adequate data of the 1940 census are analyzed (see Table V), it is apparent that the educational status of the Atlanta population is close to the national urban average; that is, it is slightly short on median years of school completed (one-tenth of a year to be exact); a somewhat higher than average of its population has completed high school; and a less than average amount of its population has received no schooling at all. The white population ranks well above the Negro population by all the measures used.

EDUCATIONAL STATUS IN ATLANTA AND OTHER URBAN POPULATIONS

From Table V it will be seen that the educational status of the population of Dallas, Texas, is far superior to the Atlanta population or the national average or the other southern cities listed, for that matter; but Atlanta ranks ahead of both Nashville and New Orleans in median school years completed, in per cent of population graduating from high school, and in having the smallest proportion of its population with no formal schooling.

VARIATIONS IN EDUCATIONAL STATUS BY CENSUS TRACTS

When educational status of the total population in various parts of the city of Atlanta is measured by median school years completed, Figure 34, one notes that the best educated groups live

4. *Statistics of the Population of the United States at the Tenth Census* (Washington: Government Printing Office, 1893), pp. 919-925.
5. *Eleventh Census of the United States: 1890*, (Washington: Government Printing Office, 1892), p. 755.
6. *Twelfth Census of the United States: 1900*, "Population, Vol. II." Part II, pp. cxix-cxxii.
7. *Ibid.*, p. xcvii.
8. *Thirteenth Census of the United States: 1910*, "Population, Vol. I," (Washington: Government Printing Office, 1913), p. 1185.

TABLE V

EDUCATIONAL STATUS OF SELECTED URBAN POPULATIONS, 1940

	Median School Years Completed			Per Cent High School Graduates			Per Cent Completing No Formal Schooling		
	All Classes	Native White	Negroes	All Classes	Native White	Negroes	All Classes	Native White	Negroes
United States Urban Population	8.7	9.7	6.8	16.6	20.1	6.2	3.6	0.8	6.6
Atlanta	8.6	10.7	5.9	17.2	23.5	4.4	3.0	1.1	6.4
Nashville	8.4	8.9	6.6	14.5	18.5	4.5	3.2	1.6	7.1
Dallas	10.4	11.4	7.1	24.0	27.8	7.8	2.1	0.9	5.6
New Orleans	7.8	8.5	5.8	13.0	17.1	3.3	4.0	1.6	8.2

Sources: *Sixteenth Census of the United States: 1940,* "Population, Vol. II Characteristics of the Population," Part 1 (Washington: Government Printing Office, 1943), p. 40; *Sixteenth Census of the United States: 1940,* "Population, Vol. II, Characteristics of the Population," Part 2 (Washington: Government Printing Office, 1943), p. 377; *Sixteenth Census of the United States: 1940,* "Population," Part 3 (Washington: Government Printing Office, 1943), p. 429; and *Sixteenth Census of the United States: 1940,* "Population, Vol. II, Characteristics of the Population," Part 6 (Washington: Government Printing Office, 1943), pp. 721 and 1029.

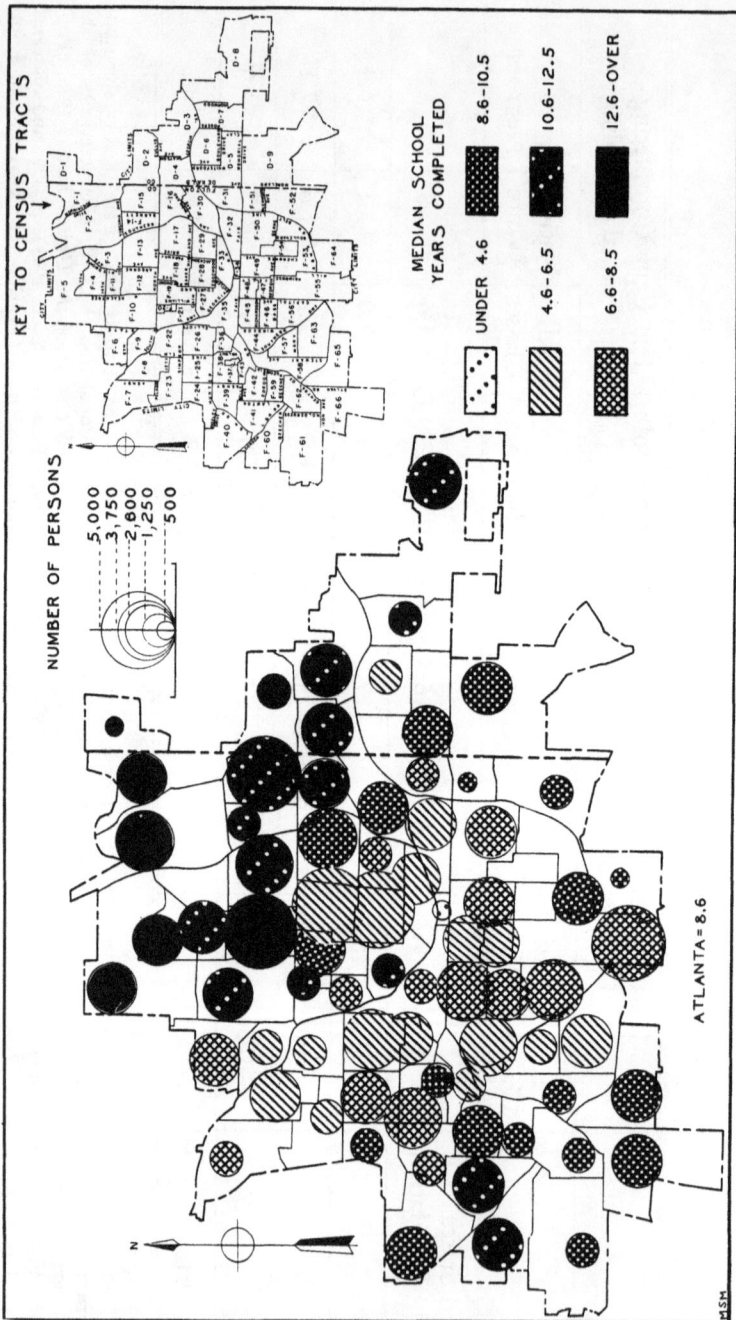

FIGURE 34. Variations in the median number of years of schooling received by the Atlanta population aged 25 years and over, by census tracts, 1940.

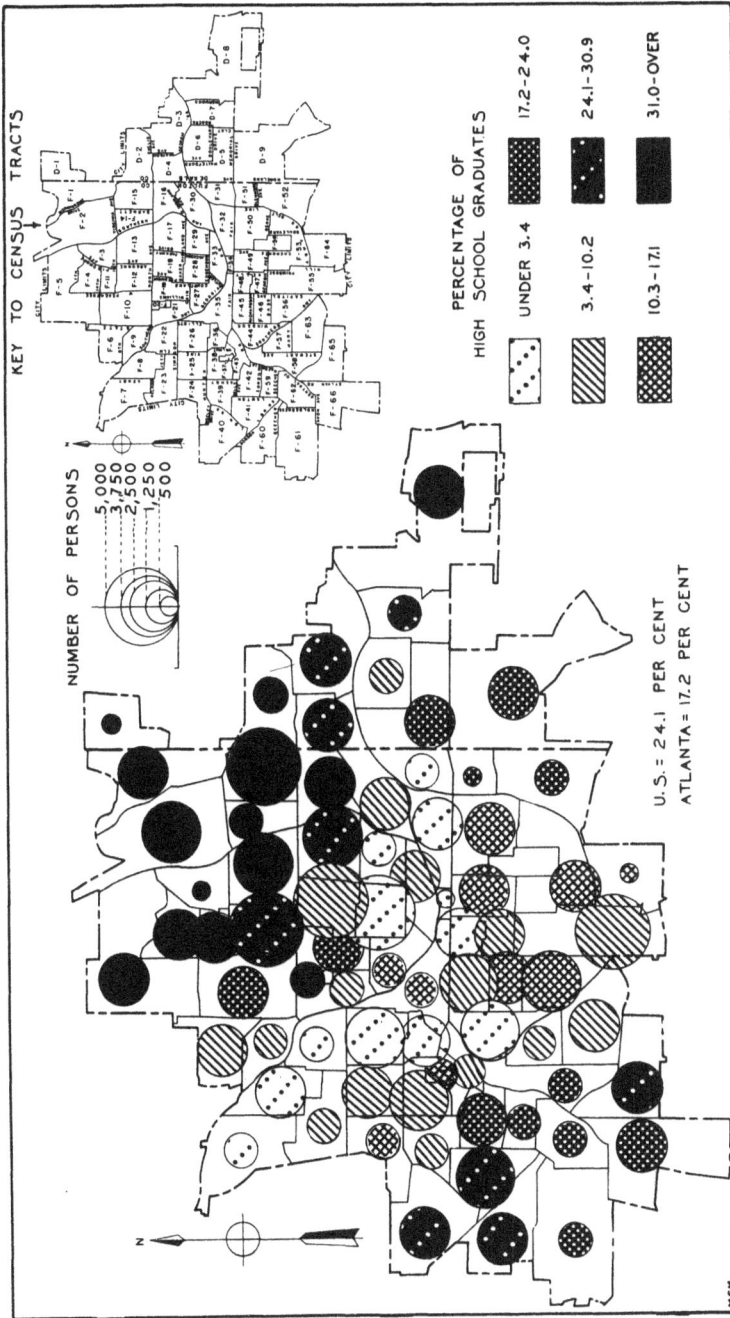

FIGURE 35. Variations in the proportions of the Atlanta population aged 25 years and over who had completed high school, by census tracts, 1940.

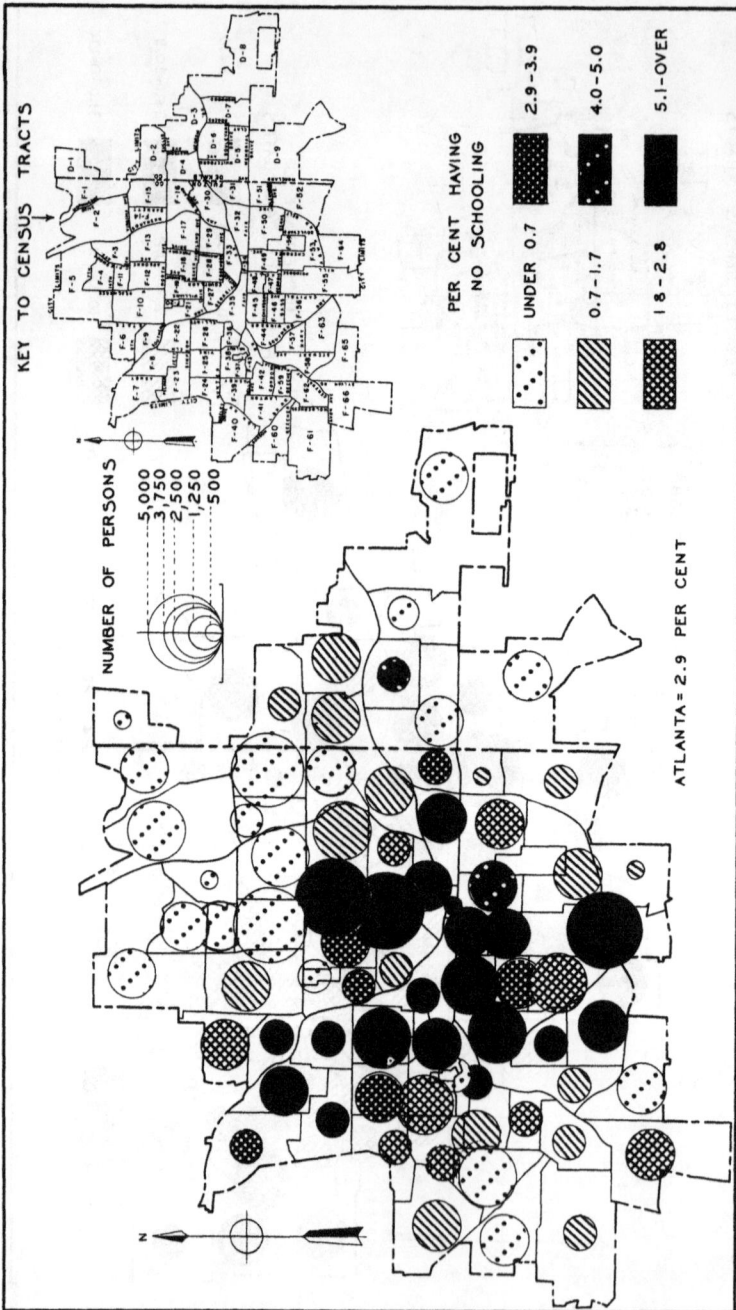

FIGURE 36. Variations in the proportions of the Atlanta population (all classes) aged 25 years and over who received no formal schooling, by census tracts, 1940.

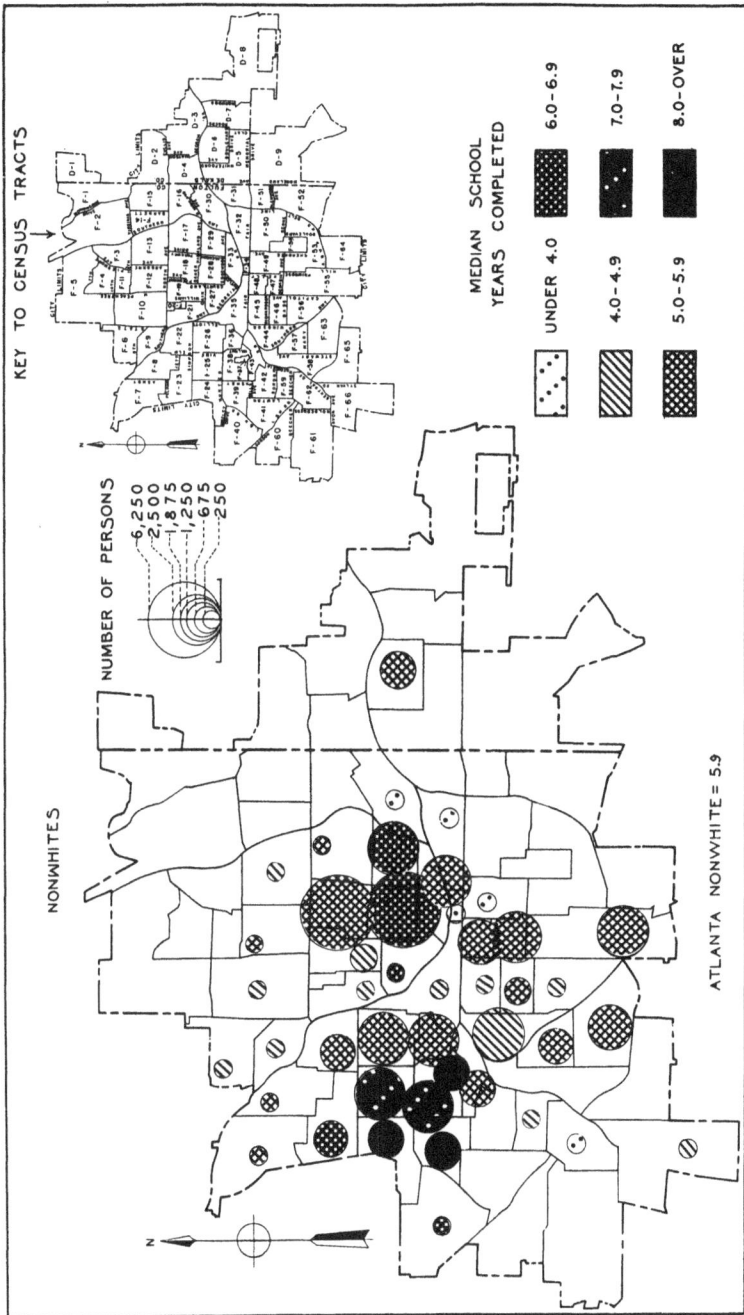

FIGURE 37. Variations in the amount of schooling received by the Atlanta nonwhite population aged 25 years and over, by census tracts, 1940.

at the periphery of the city, and that the northern and eastern portions of the city seem to contain those with most education. Only one tract (F-34 near the center of the city) reports a median schooling of less than 4.6 years.

The highest percentage of high school graduates is found in the northeastern and southwestern portions of the city (see Figure 35).

In Figure 36, it is emphasized that the persons who have not been exposed to formal schooling are concentrated in the census tracts in the central area of the city with only one exception, that being those people who live in Tract D-6.

RACIAL VARIATIONS IN EDUCATIONAL STATUS BY CENSUS TRACTS

Figure 37 shows that the most highly educated portion of the Negro population is in tracts F-24, F-39, F-25, F-38, and F-37, even though these tracts are only average or below average, relative to the total population as shown in Figure 34. The presence in this western part of the city of a university center composed of six Negro colleges may be an important and responsible factor.

In a manner similar to the foregoing, the highest percentage of high school graduates is found in the northeastern and the southwestern portions of the city (see Figure 35); the educational status of the white population is the determining factor as is borne out by Figure 38. The highest percentages of high school graduates in the nonwhite population are found in about the same areas as those possessing the highest number of years of schooling; but in addition, tract F-29 stands out rather sharply in Figure 39. After referring to Figures 40 and 41, it is interesting to note that the highest percentage of persons with no schooling, particularly among the nonwhites, is located in tracts of comparatively small population (Negro).

COMPARISON OF CITY AND SUBURBAN EDUCATIONAL STATUS

When the Atlanta suburban population is compared to the city population with regard to median years of school completed, one is impressed by the fact, in Figure 42 particularly, that there is a lack of the lighter shadings, which indicates that this population stands well; but likewise, one is impressed by the lack of the very dark shades of the figure in regard to the nonwhite population (see Figure 43). It seems, then, in general, that the Atlanta

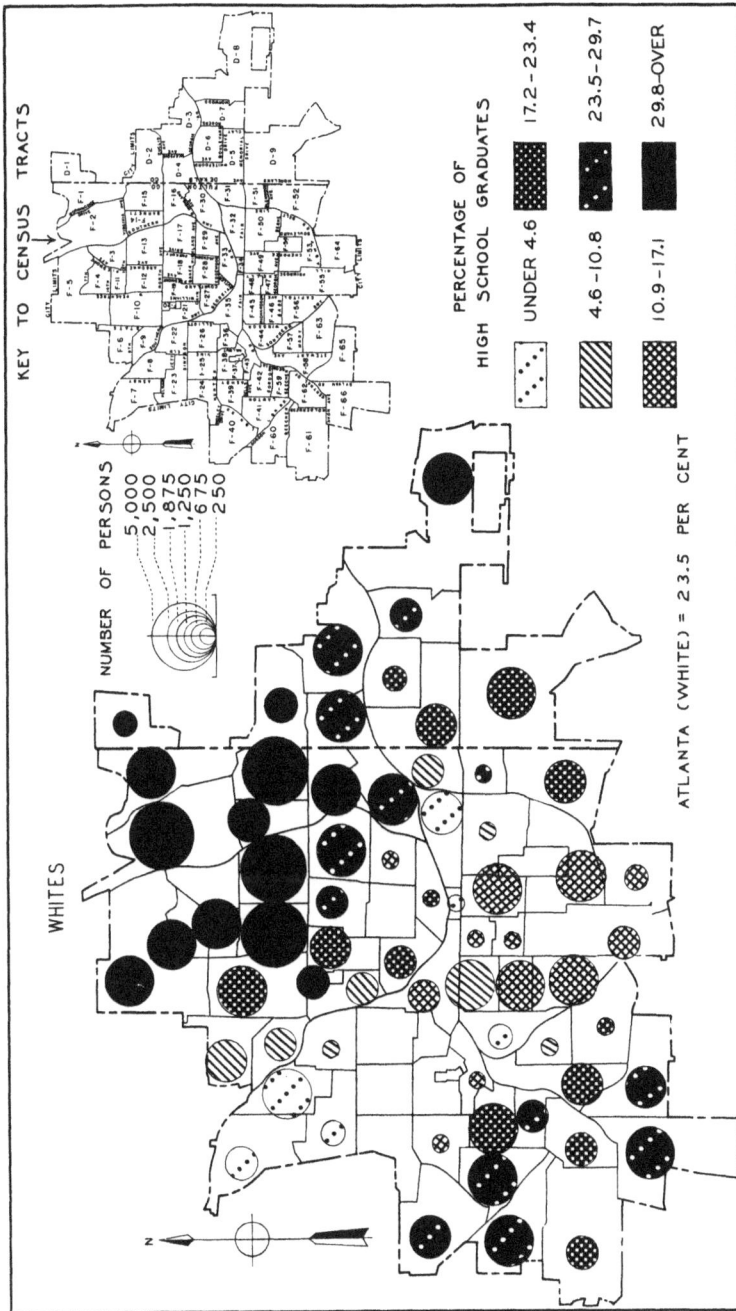

FIGURE 38. Variations in the proportions of the Atlanta white population aged 25 years and over, who had completed high school, by census tracts, 1940.

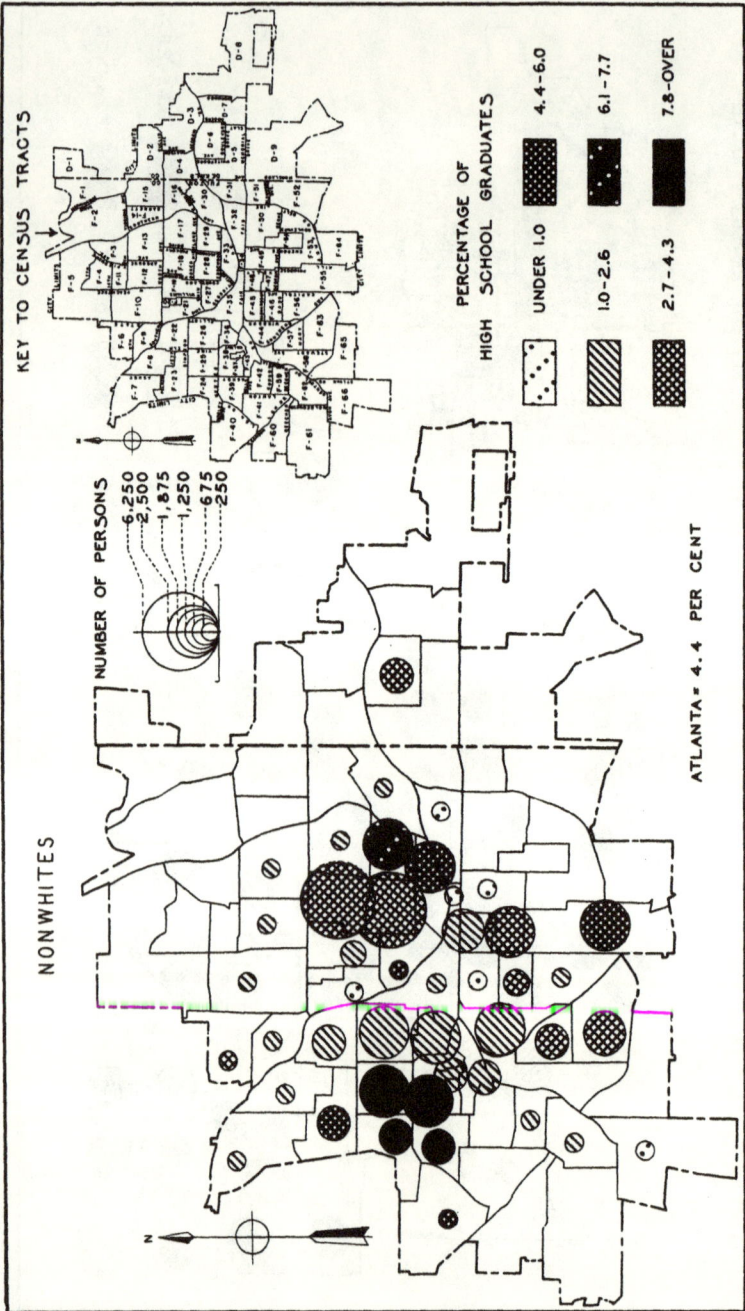

FIGURE 39. Variations in the proportions of the Atlanta nonwhite population aged 25 years and over who had completed high school, by census tracts, 1940.

114

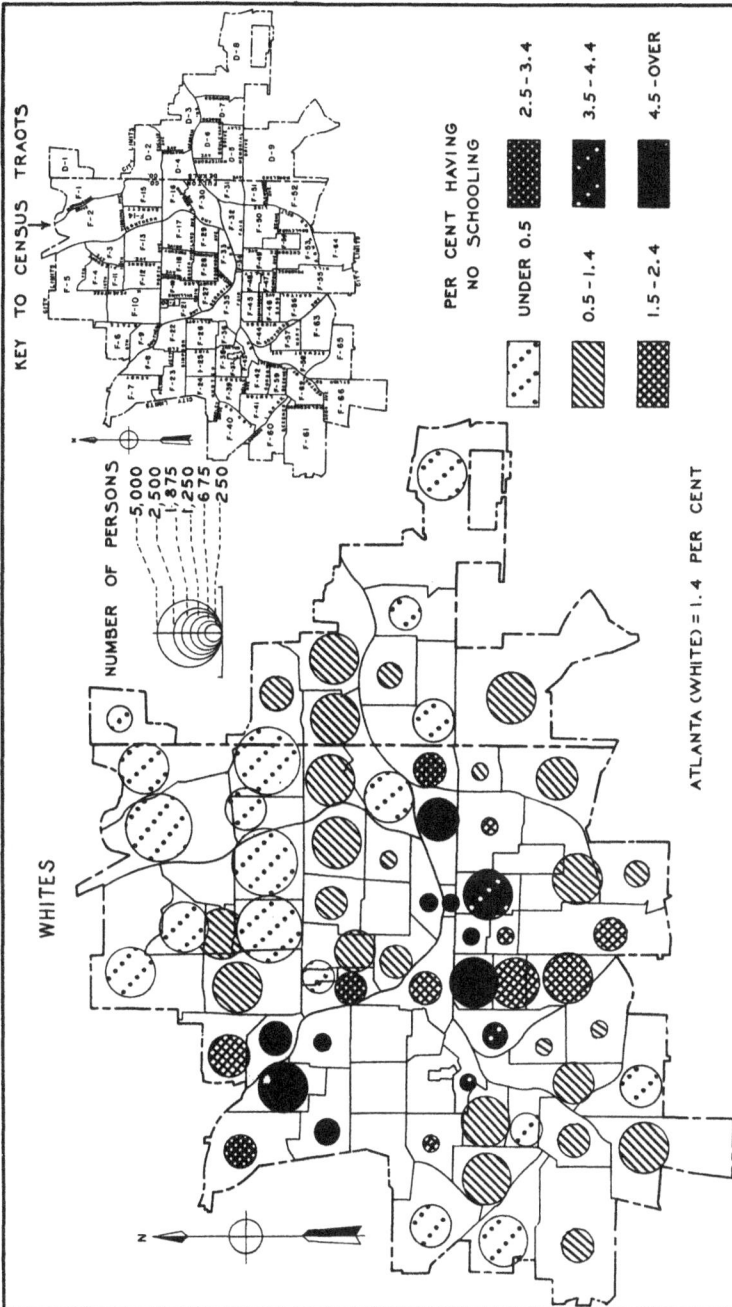

FIGURE 40. Variations in the proportions of the Atlanta white population aged 25 years and over, who received no formal schooling, by census tracts, 1940.

115

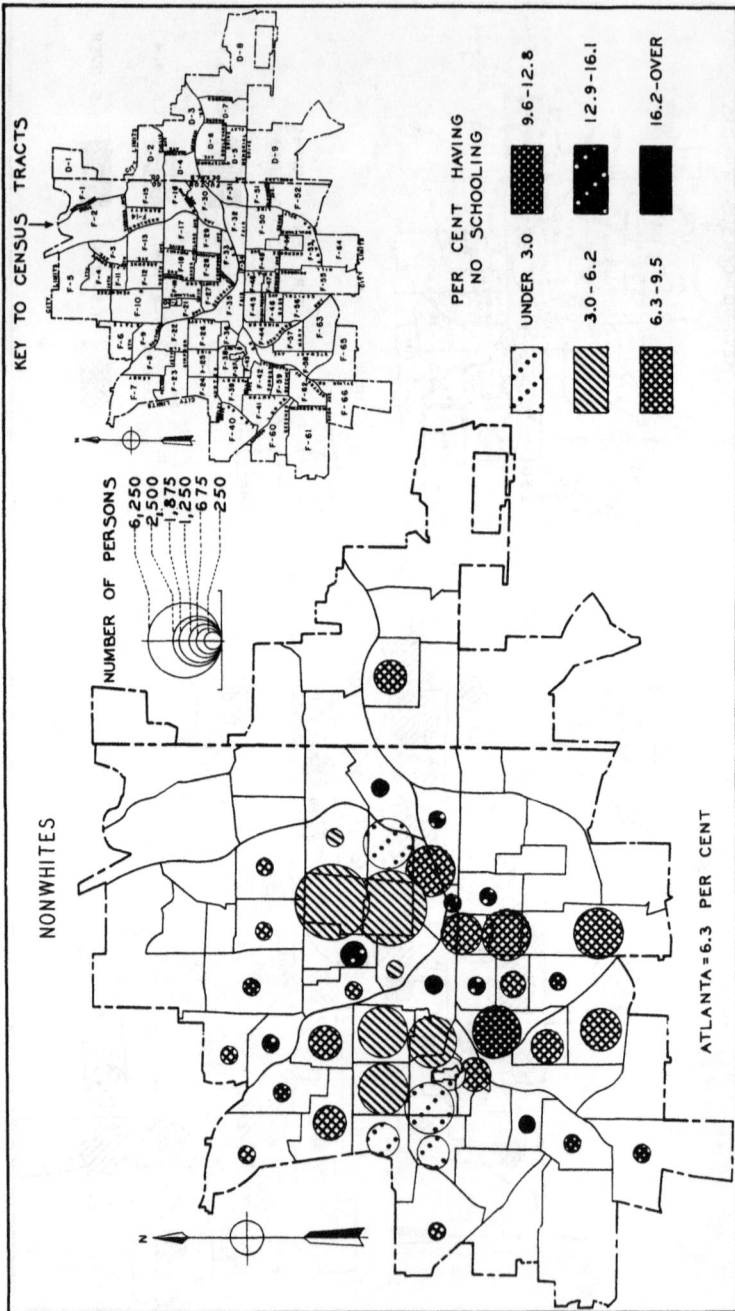

FIGURE 41. Variations in the proportions of the Atlanta nonwhite population aged 25 years and over who received no formal schooling, by census tracts, 1940.

116

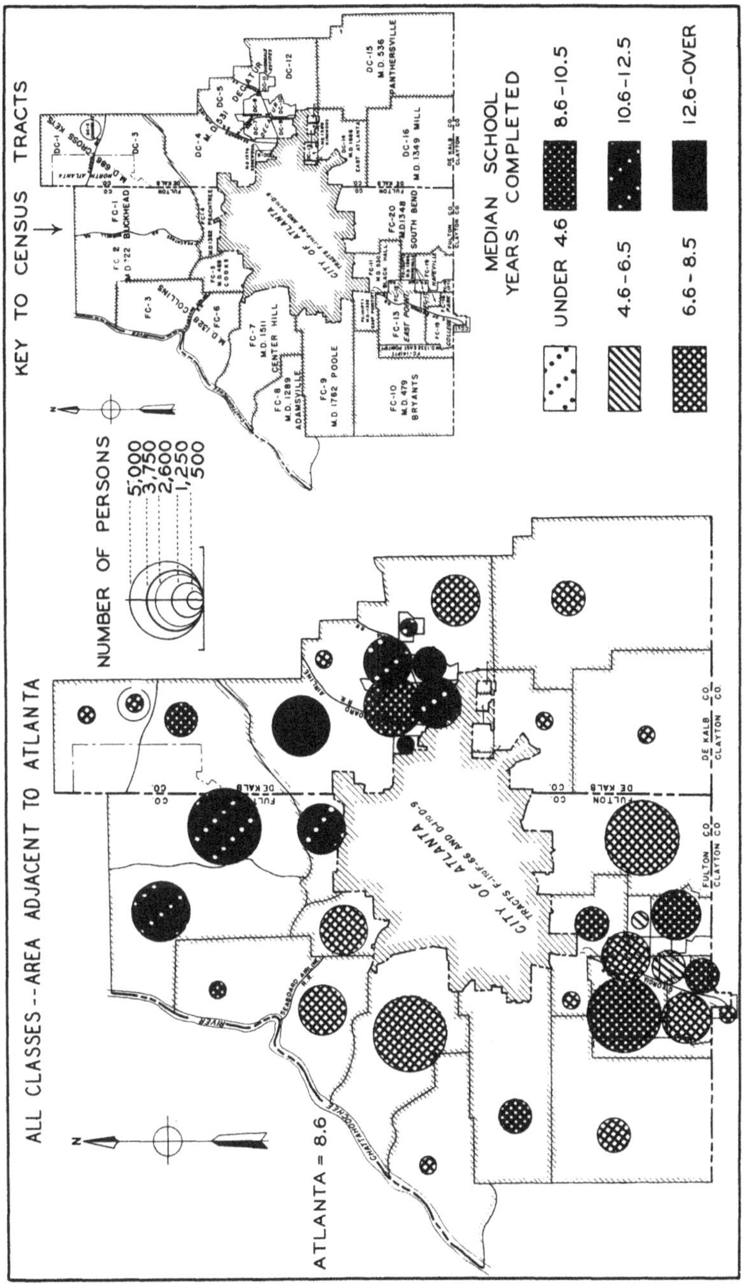

FIGURE 42. Variations in the median number of years of schooling received by the Atlanta suburban population aged 25 years and over, by census tracts, 1940.

117

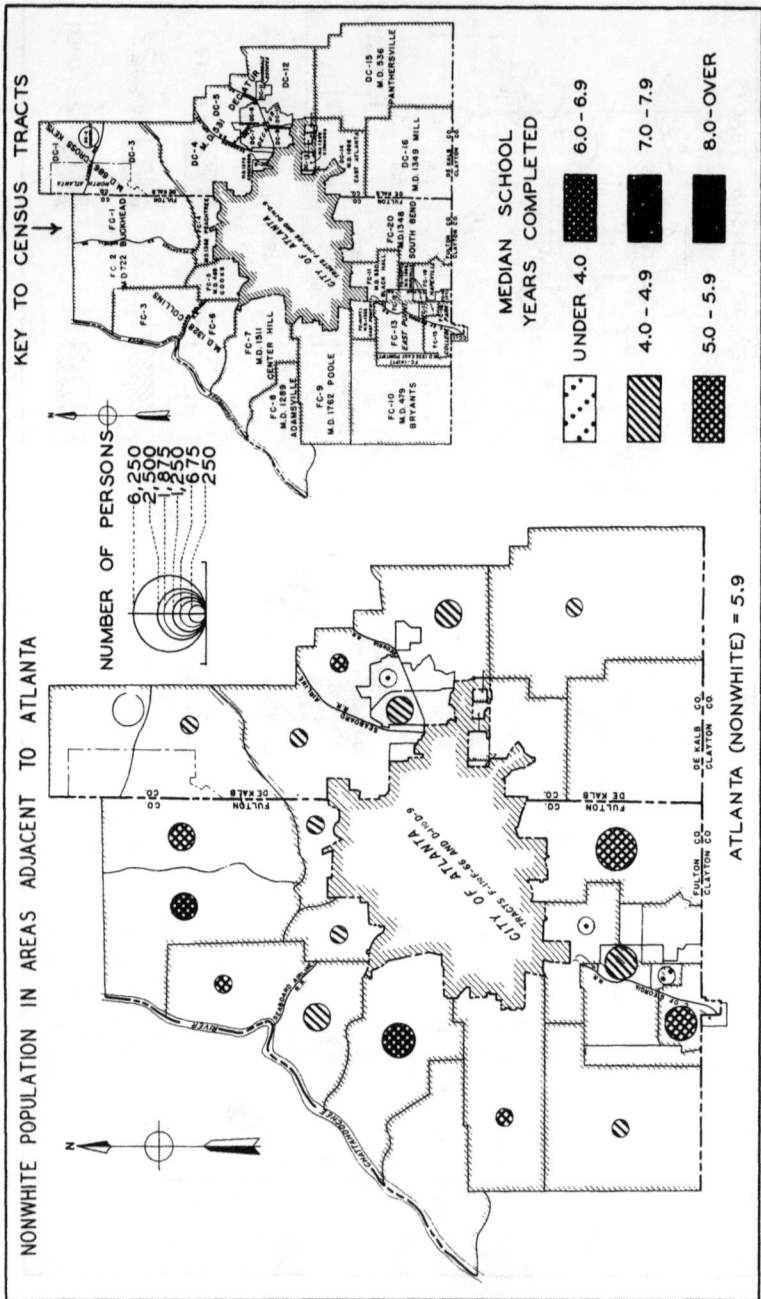

FIGURE 43. Variations in the amount of schooling received by the nonwhite population aged 25 years and over, in areas adjacent to Atlanta, by census tracts, 1940.

118

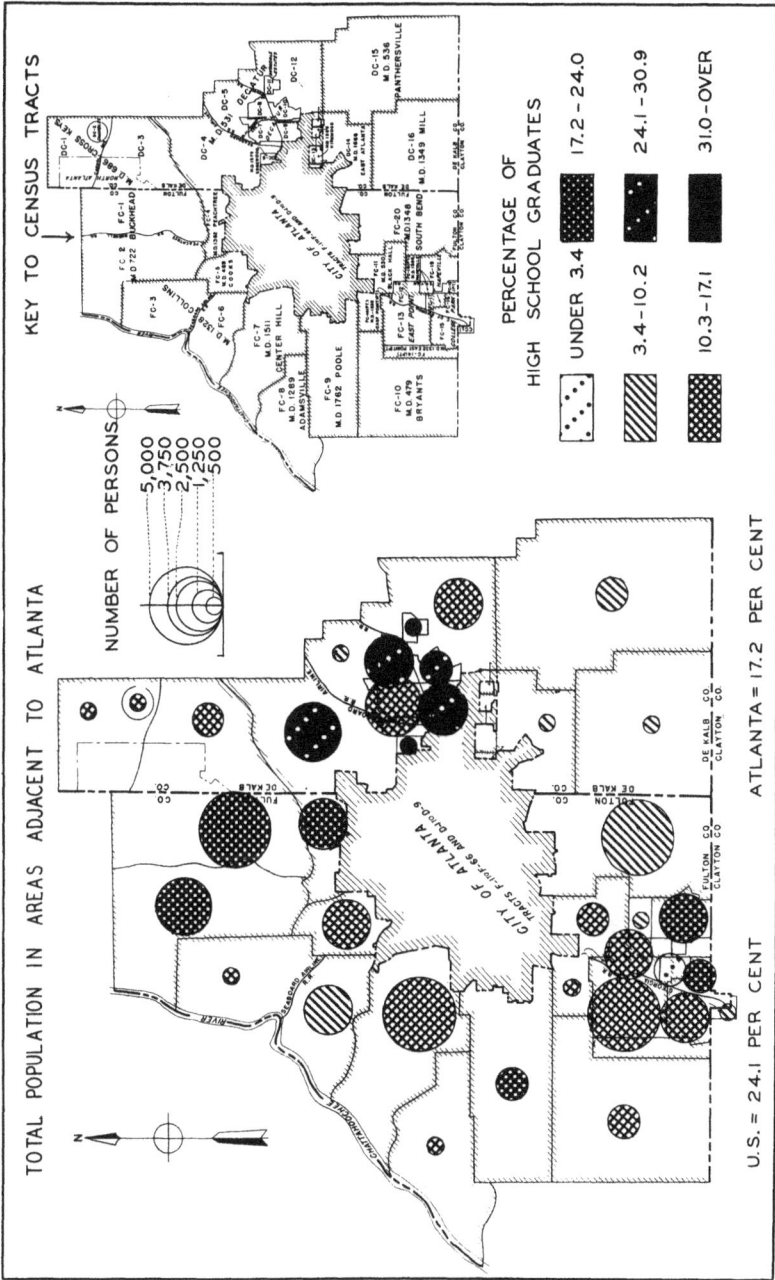

FIGURE 44. Variations in the proportions of the population aged 25 years and over, in areas adjacent to Atlanta, who had completed high school, by census tracts, 1940.

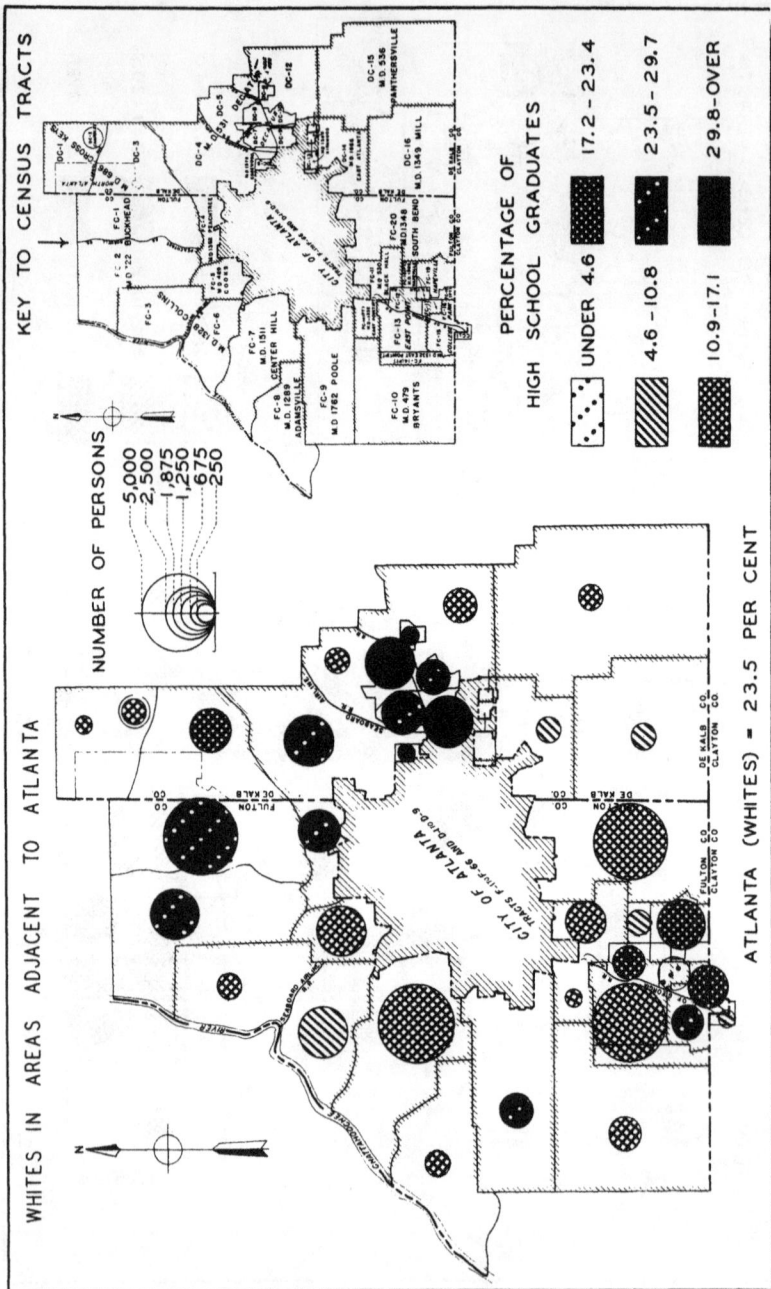

FIGURE 45. Variations in the proportions of the white population aged 25 years and over, in areas adjacent to Atlanta, who had completed high school, by census tracts, 1940.

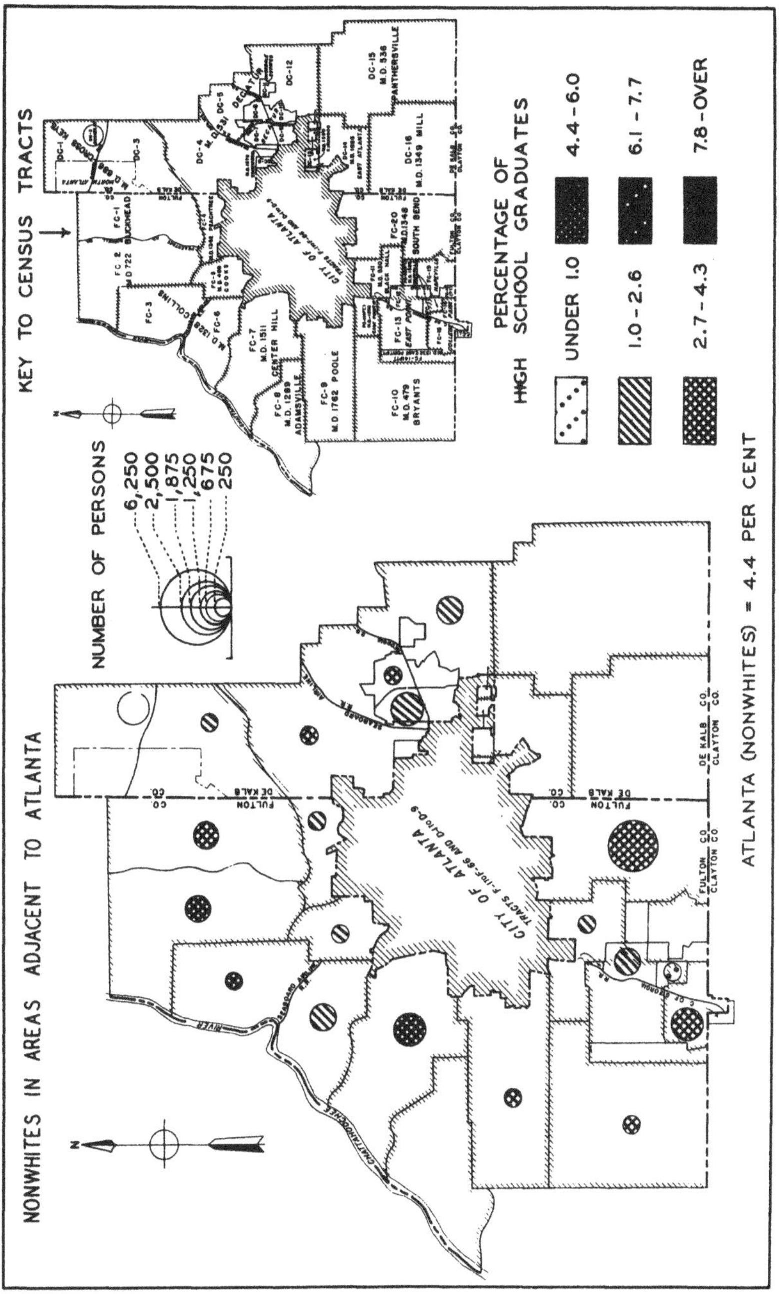

FIGURE 46. Variations in the proportions of the nonwhite population aged 25 years and over, in areas adjacent to Atlanta, who had completed high school, by census tracts, 1940.

121

suburban population is better educated than the urban population, which is due largely to the presence of small proportions of Negroes; but that the Negro population is better educated in the city than in the suburban area.

Considerable effort, time, and study have been expended on the analysis of the percentage of high school graduates in the suburban population and these data are presented in Figures 44, 45, and 46; nevertheless, it is impossible at this time to make a valid generalization between the suburban and the city population.

When the percentage of the white suburban population having no schooling (Figure 47) is compared with the white city population, it is noted that the percentages seem to be higher for the suburban population; the suburban Negro population seems likewise to have higher percentages with no formal schooling (Figure 48).

TRENDS IN EDUCATIONAL STATUS

As was pointed out previously in this work, the percentage of illiteracy is a very poor measure of the educational status of a population as well as being rather useless as a comparative index. Since this was the best criterion available until 1940, however, Table VI has been prepared to throw some light on the relative educational status of the Atlanta population previous to 1940.

Data on percentage of illiteracy are provided for Atlanta and three southern cities for the four censuses prior to 1940, i.e., 1900 to 1930, inclusive, for the total population and for each of the three subgroups: native whites, foreign-born whites, and Negroes. For the total populations, there has been a steadily downward trend in percentage of illiteracy in each city. It is of interest to note that Atlanta improved its relative position among the cities during this period. From the lowest in 1900 among the southern cities studied, Atlanta moved to third (ahead of Nashville) in 1910 and 1930. Nashville, however, which ranked fourth in 1910 and 1920, moved up to second rank in 1930, displacing New Orleans, which slipped from second to fourth in a single decade. The general picture as reflected in these data is for the proportion of illiteracy among native whites to be lowest, followed in order by the foreign-born whites and Negroes. For Atlanta, the proportion of illiterates in the total population was by 1930 reduced to nearly one-fourth of the proportion reported

122

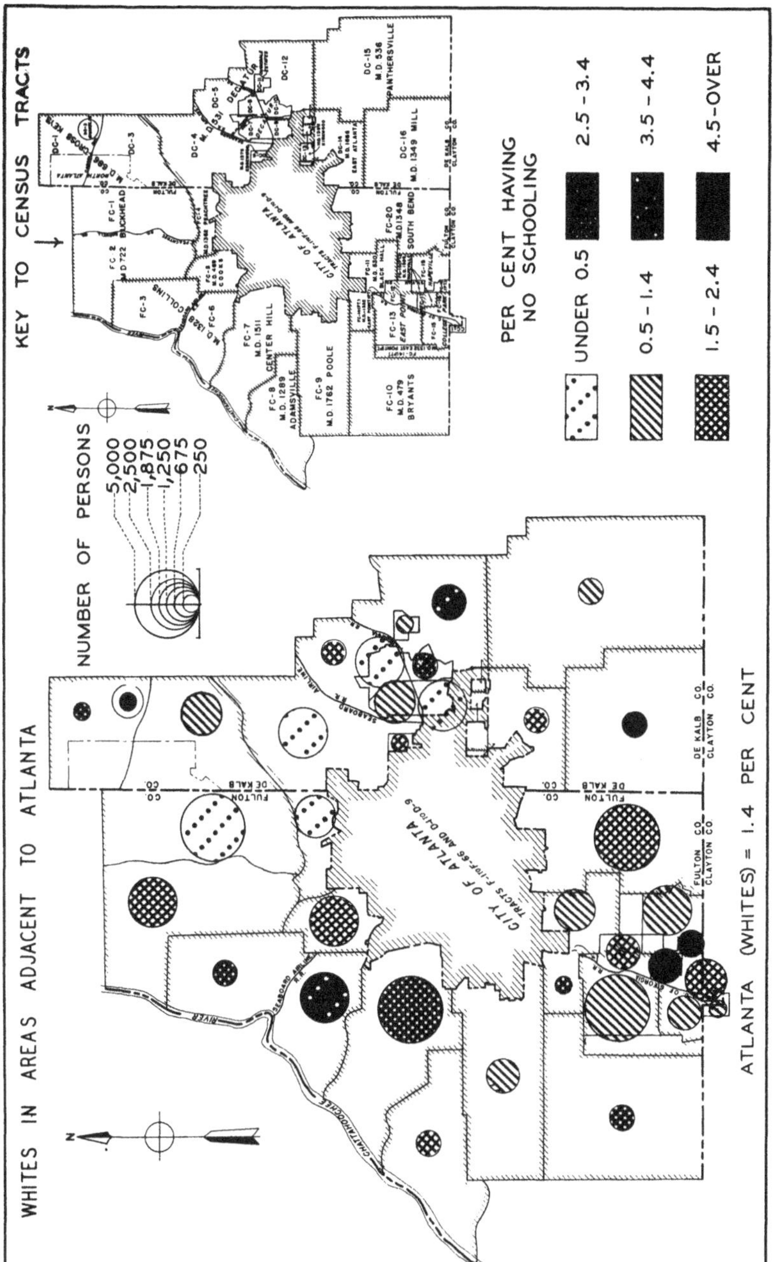

FIGURE 47. Variations in the proportions of the white population aged 25 years and over, in areas adjacent to Atlanta, who received no formal schooling, by census tracts, 1940.

TABLE VI

Per Cent Illiteracy in the Population Aged 10 Years and Over in Selected Cities, 1900 to 1930

CITY	1900				1910				1920				1930			
	Total Pop.	Native Whites	Foreign-born Whites	Negroes	Total Pop.	Native Whites	Foreign-born Whites	Negroes	Total Pop.	Native Whites	Foreign-born Whites	Negroes	Total Pop.	Native Whites	Foreign-born Whites	Negroes
Atlanta	15.8	2.6	8.6	35.1	8.1	1.7	4.4	21.7	6.6	1.2	4.8	17.8	4.1	0.9	4.5	10.4
Nashville	14.4	2.9	9.9	32.4	9.4	1.9	4.6	25.3	7.2	2.0	7.4	18.4	3.6	1.0	4.1	9.9
Dallas	7.2	1.4	8.0	25.2	4.0	0.6	6.1	15.4	3.2	0.5	16.4	11.3	2.3	0.5	5.2	6.6
New Orleans	13.6	2.0	18.3	36.1	6.5	0.9	9.8	17.1	5.9	1.0	13.9	15.7	5.4	1.3	14.8	13.4

Sources: *Twelfth Census of the United States: 1900*, "Population, Vol. II, PartII (Washington: Government Printing Office, 1902), pp. cxix-cxii.
Thirteenth Census of the United States: 1910, "Population, Vol. I," (Washington: Government Printing Office, 1913), pp. 1251, and 1260-1261.
Fourteenth Census of the United States: 1920, "Population, Vol. III," (Washington: Government Printing Office, 1922), pp. 222, 399, 970, and 1015.
Fifteenth Census of the United States: 1930, "Population, Vol. III" Part I (Washington: Government Printing Office 1932), p. 69.

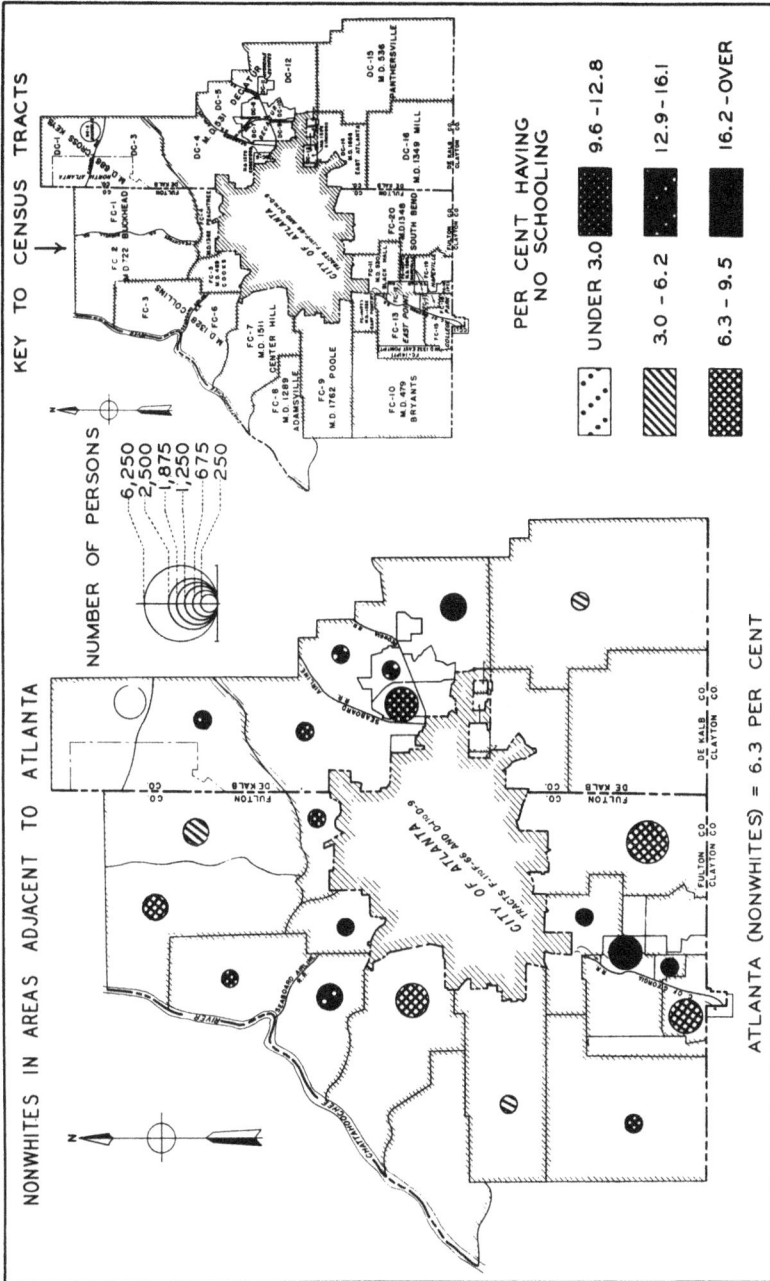

FIGURE 48. Variations in the proportions of the nonwhite population aged 25 years and over, in areas adjacent to Atlanta, who received no formal schooling, by census tracts, 1940.

in 1900. For Negroes, the proportion of illiterates during this period was reduced from 35 per cent to 10 per cent. Although criteria of illiteracy vary somewhat and the data are crude and not susceptible to complete analysis, this reduction in percentage of illiteracy reflects the emphasis during this century on improvement in the educational status of the people.

CHAPTER IX

OCCUPATIONAL STATUS

IMMENSE QUANTITIES OF DATA CONCERNING THE OCCUPATIONS OF the people of Atlanta have been gathered by the Bureau of the Census. This chapter is an attempt to extract from that mass of data the significant characteristics of the occupational structure of the Atlanta population, especially as to class of worker, distribution by major occupational groups, distribution by industry, changes in occupations from 1890 to 1930, and analysis of the foregoing as far as possible by race and sex.

It is important to study occupational status of a population because one's relationships with his fellows are strongly conditioned by his vocation; one's occupation is an important factor producing individual differences.[1] Occupation also effects fundamentally such demographic phenomena as life expectancy, rates of reproduction, and marital status.[2]

OUTSTANDING FEATURES OF
ATLANTA'S OCCUPATIONAL STRUCTURE

The most outstanding features of the population of Atlanta from an occupational standpoint are as follows: (1) A greater proportion of Atlanta males works for wages and salaries than most other large southern cities or for the average of all large cities in the nation; (2) the male of Atlanta is much less likely to be an employer or self-employed than the male in other large urban populations in the South; (3) the nonwhite worker in Atlanta works for wages to a greater extent than the white and owns his own business to a lesser extent; (4) the Atlanta nonwhite female is an employer or self-employed to a much greater extent than is the white female; (5) a very high proportion of males in Atlanta is engaged as service workers, while an excessively high proportion of Atlanta women (largely Negroes) is engaged in domestic service work; and (6) the Atlanta occupational structure has not changed radically since 1890.

1. Kimball Young, *Personality and Problems of Adjustment* (New York: F. S. Crofts & Co., 1940), p. 299.
2. T. Lynn Smith, *Population Analysis* (New York: McGraw-Hill Book Company, Inc., 1948), p. 164.

Occupational Status by Sex in Atlanta and
Other Large Urban Populations

In 1940 Atlanta had 78,437 males employed (excepting emergency work) of whom 63,543 were private wage or salary workers; 6,233 were government workers; 8,509 were employers and own account workers; and 152 persons were unpaid family laborers.[3] In order to understand how this distribution compares to other urban populations, Table VII has been prepared. It will be noted that a greater proportion of Atlanta males works for wages and salaries than of any of the other cities cited or for the average of the large cities; that the male of Atlanta is much less likely to be an employer or self-employed than the other comparative urban populations; that only Dallas has a larger proportion of its women working as employers and own account workers than Atlanta; and that like the male population, only Dallas has a smaller proportion of its women in government work than Atlanta.

In order to provide a more detailed analysis of the data and to clarify the concept of "class of worker," Table VIII is presented. This table gives the percentage distribution of employed persons (excepting emergency workers) by class of worker and by sex for the urban United States, the urban South, Atlanta, and New Orleans; and for the two cities named, distribution is shown for the two main racial groups. From this table it may be noted that in general a greater proportion of Atlanta workers is working for private salaries and wages than in other large urban populations (the only exception being the New Orleans nonwhite female).

The data provided in the 1940 census permit a further breakdown of the population over 14 in the labor force by major occupational groups. Table D, Appendix, presents data of this type for male workers for the urban United States and four selected southern cities. Table E, Appendix, presents similar data for female workers.

Among the urban male population of the United States, it may be noted that operatives and kindred workers make up the largest category; however, among the southern cities studied, only Nashville has the largest percentage of its males falling into this classification. The other three cities, Atlanta, Dallas, and New

3. *Sixteenth Census of the United States: 1940*, "Population, Vol. III, The Labor Force," Part 2 (Washington: Government Printing Office, 1943), pp. 735-738.

TABLE VII

Per Cent Distribution of Employed Persons (Except on Public Emergency Work), By Class of Worker, By Sex, For Selected Urban Populations of 100,000 or More, 1940

Population	Male				Female			
	Private wage or salary workers	Government workers	Employers and own account	Unpaid family workers	Private wage or salary workers	Government workers	Employers and own account	Unpaid family workers
Total all cities of the United States of 100,000 or more in 1940	77.7	8.8	13.3	0.3	83.0	9.2	6.2	1.6
Atlanta	81.0	7.9	10.8	0.2	82.2	8.4	8.2	1.2
Dallas	78.0	5.8	15.9	0.2	82.3	6.7	9.2	1.9
Nashville	79.4	8.4	12.0	0.2	83.0	9.2	6.9	0.9
New Orleans	75.4	10.6	13.6	0.4	80.7	9.2	8.0	2.2

Source: *Sixteenth Census of the United States: 1940*, "Population, Vol. III, The Labor Force," Part 1 (Washington: Government Printing Office, 1943), p. 60.

Orleans, have the largest percentage of males classified under clerical, sales, and kindred workers. All the southern cities seem to have a smaller proportion of males in the professional group than the national average, and Atlanta stands out only by having a larger proportion of males engaged as service workers.

In analyzing Table E, Appendix, an excessively high proportion of Atlanta women is found to be engaged in domestic service work (a high proportion of whom is Negroes); it may be noted also that the proportion of southern females classified as professional workers is lower than the urban national average; and among professional workers one must note that Atlanta women are least represented in comparison to other southern female populations.

By examining closely the figures given in Table F, Appendix, and comparing those for Atlanta and for the urban United States, it is possible to secure a picture of the general economic base or structure of Atlanta. For males, Atlanta has a proportion less than the national average in the following categories: agriculture, forestry, and fishing; mining; and manufacturing. In the categories of business and repair services, amusement and related services, recreation and related services, professional and related services, and government Atlanta males rank within one per cent of the national average. In the areas of construction; transportation, communication, and other public utilities; wholesale and retail trade; finance, insurance, and real estate; and personal services Atlanta men rank proportionately higher than the national average. This picture coincides with the conventional representation of Atlanta as a transportation, trade, and distribution center.

OCCUPATIONAL STATUS OF THE WHITE AND NONWHITE POPULATION

It will be noted in Table VIII that the data bear out what is generally known: that the nonwhite works for wages to a greater extent than the white and owns his own business to a lesser extent. One striking deviation is the fact that the Atlanta nonwhite female is an employer or self-employed worker to a much greater extent than is the white female.

The high percentage (Table E, Appendix), of domestic service workers found in Atlanta is very significant; in this category, Atlanta females have nearly twice as great a proportion (31.2 to 16.4 per cent) as the national average. Other southern

TABLE VIII

Per Cent Distribution of Employed Persons (Except Those Engaged in Emergency Work), By Class of Worker, Color, and Sex, For Selected Urban Populations of 250,000 or More, 1940

Population		Private wage or salary workers	Government workers	Employers and own account	Unpaid family workers
Urban United States:	Total	78.0	9.2	12.0	0.7
	Males	76.8	8.8	14.2	0.3
	Females	80.8	10.4	7.1	1.7
Urban South:	Total	75.0	11.2	13.0	0.8
	Males	74.4	10.7	14.6	0.3
	Females	76.1	12.2	9.9	1.7
Atlanta (All Classes):	Males	81.0	7.9	10.8	0.2
	Females	82.2	8.4	8.2	1.1
(White)	Males	77.7	9.4	12.7	0.2
	Females	79.0	11.7	7.4	1.9
(Nonwhite)	Males	89.1	4.5	6.3	0.1
	Females	86.2	4.3	9.2	0.3
New Orleans (All Classes):	Males	75.4	10.6	13.6	0.4
	Females	80.7	9.2	8.0	2.2
(White)	Males	71.6	12.7	15.2	0.5
	Females	74.7	12.8	9.2	3.3
(Nonwhite)	Males	87.6	3.8	8.4	0.2
	Females	90.3	3.4	5.9	0.3

Sources: *Sixteenth Census of the United States: 1940*, "Population, Vol. III, The Labor Force," Parts 1, 2, 3 (Washington: Government Printing Office, 1943).

cities have greater proportions in this category than the national average but not so high as does Atlanta. Since about 67 per cent of employed Negro females are engaged in rendering personal services, and since the Negro population of Atlanta has a much lower sex ratio than does the white population, these facts together may account for the fact that Atlanta women are not so well represented in other categories and also for the lower than average sex ratio of the total population.

TRENDS IN OCCUPATIONAL STATUS OF THE ATLANTA POPULATION

Figures 49 and 50 vividly point out the shifts in occupations for the half-century from 1880 to 1930. The 1880 data included a heterogeneous grouping in the professional classification and no refinement was attempted until 1890. Male workers in agriculture have consistently declined, while female workers in the professional and clerical classes have consistently increased. The general occupational structure of Atlanta, however, has not changed radically during this period, as the generally straight lines in the figures (particularly that for males) indicate.

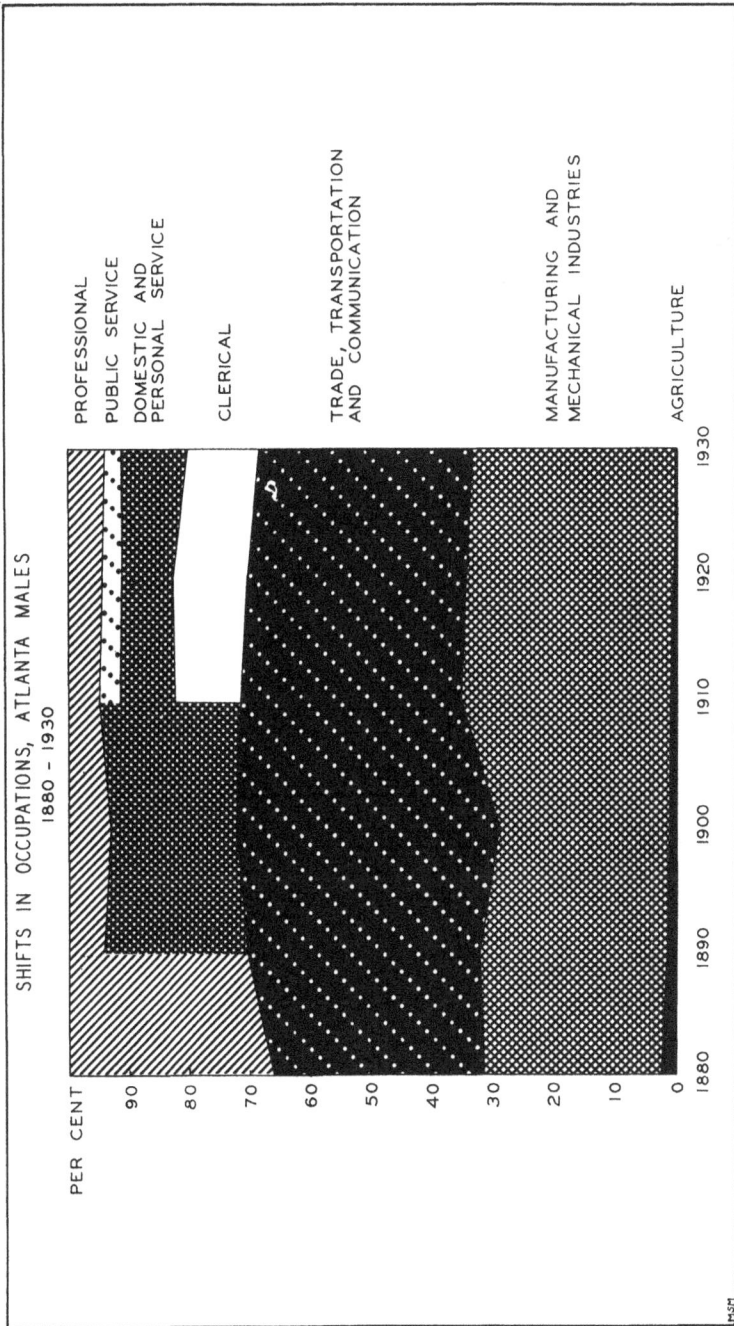

FIGURE 49. Changes in the occupational structure of the
male population of Atlanta, 1880-1930.

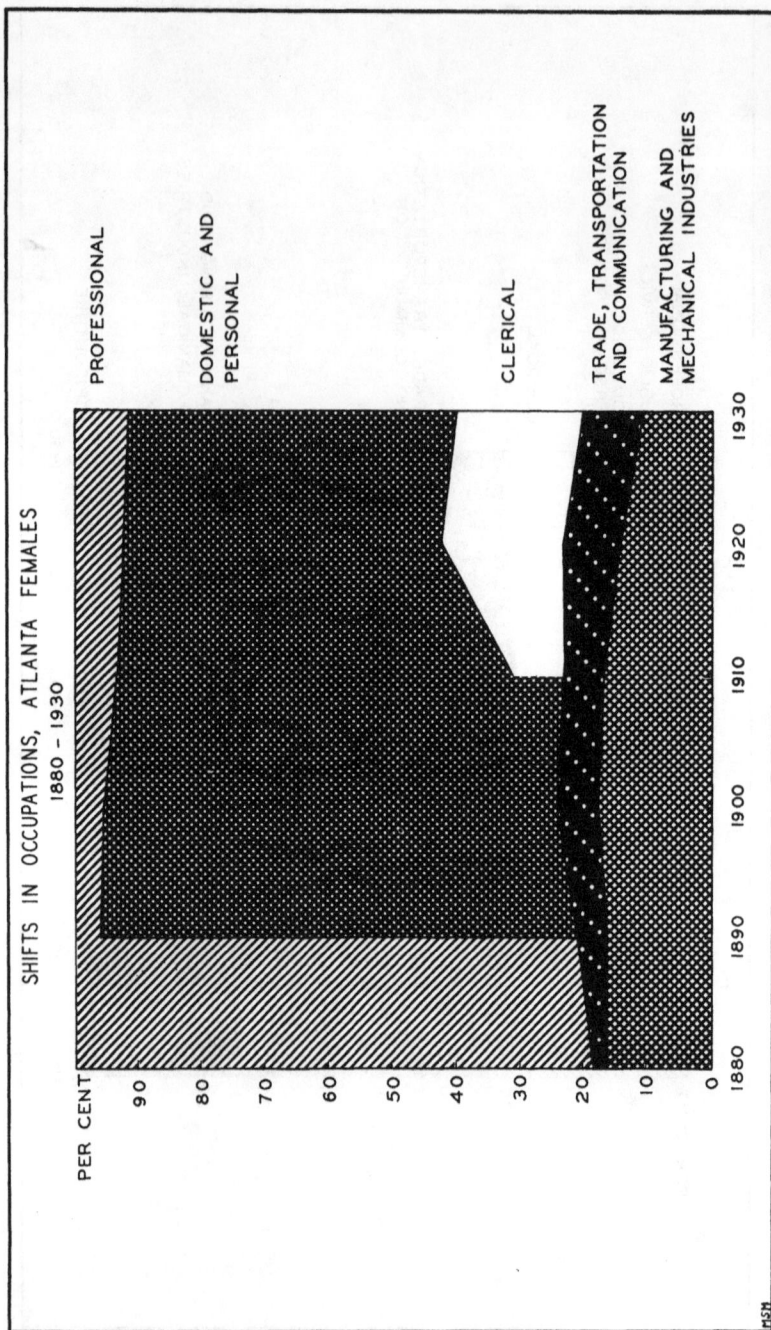

FIGURE 50. Changes in the occupational structure of the female population of the city of Atlanta, 1880-1930.

CHAPTER X

RELIGIOUS COMPOSITION

R ELIGIOUS COMPOSITION IS SIGNIFICANT IN THE STUDY OF POPULA-
tion because distinct differences of a demographic nature are
found between different religious groups. This is not to say that
these differences are due to religious factors *per se,* for along with
religious differences often go variations in economic and social
status of the members of the various religious bodies. In spite of
these involved relationships, however, distinct differences exist in
the birth rates and the death rates among different religious
groups.[1] It is important that an attempt be made to determine the
religious composition of the population under consideration so
that in the total analysis of the Atlanta population as many
variables as possible may be isolated.

The purpose of this chapter is to determine the degree of
religious differentiation, the percentage of church membership in
leading denominations, the sex ratios within church memberships,
and the trend of growth of church memberships.

In the United States, religious tolerance, religious freedom,
and religious differentiation have progressed far beyond that of
any other large country; this is true particularly in reference to
the number and varieties of religious denominations.[2] For instance,
there were 256 denominations (including independent and feder-
ated churches) listed in the 1936 report of religious bodies.[3] Within the city of Atlanta there were 49 different religious bodies listed
for 1936.[4]

The outstanding feature of the religious composition of Atlanta
in 1936 was the fact that it was 87 per cent Protestant of which
a high proportion was Baptist. All Baptists combined represented
nearly 40 per cent of the total church membership. The Methodists
stood in second place with about 27 per cent of the total membership. Members professing the Jewish religion stood third
(7.9 per cent); Presbyterians ranked fourth (6.6 per cent); and

1. Warren S. Thompson, *Population Problems* (New York: McGraw-Hill Book
   Company, Inc., 1942), pp. 118-119.
2. T. Lynn Smith, *Population Analysis* (New York: McGraw-Hill Book
   Company, Inc., 1948), pp. 176-177.
3. *Census of Religious Bodies: 1936,* Vol. 1 (Washington: Government Printing Office, 1941), p. 9.
4. *Ibid.,* pp. 450-451.

the Catholics ranked fifth (5.5 per cent). One other feature of the religious composition should be mentioned; namely, the extent to which the female dominated the church membership in Atlanta. The sex ratio among the church membership in Atlanta was 66; only Dallas, of the cities studied, had a lower sex ratio in its membership and that by one-tenth of one point.

THE RELIGIOUS COMPOSITION OF THE POPULATION OF ATLANTA AND OTHER LARGE URBAN POPULATIONS

Religious differentiation. Specific data with reference to religious differentiation in the entire United States as well as in Atlanta and other selected cities covering each decennial census from 1906 through 1936 are provided in Table G, Appendix.

Examination of this table reveals that religious differentiation in the total United States has continued from 188 denominations in 1906 to more than 250 denominations in 1936. If this rate of differentiation seems to be rapid, the increase has been taking place even more rapidly in the urban communities under consideration. The number of denominations has increased more than two-fold in Atlanta, Dallas, and New Orleans. For Nashville the number of denominations has nearly doubled. One should particularly note that the greatest increase came for all the cities during the decade 1916 to 1926, while for this same decade the increase for the United States as a whole was comparatively slow (from 202 to 213).

The larger denominations. Table IX has been prepared to show the relative rank of various denominations in selected cities; it should be pointed out that the writer is aware of the limitations of his data of the regional variations in denominations; particularly, that Atlanta is in the Baptist belt. One notes immediately that New York City has three of the great religious faiths of the world, ranked one (Jewish), two (Catholic), three (Protestant Episcopal); likewise, the first three ranks of the church members of New Orleans are filled in the order: Catholic, Protestant (Negro Baptist), and Jewish.

Referring to the other cities under consideration, the three leading denominations are all Protestant, with the Negro Baptist ranking first in all three cities, followed by the Baptist and Methodist in Atlanta, and the Methodist and Baptist in that order in Birmingham and Dallas.

TABLE IX

Denominations Ranking First, Second, and Third, Respectively, According to Number of Church Members, in Selected Cities, 1936

City	Total Number of Members	First Rank		Second Rank		Third Rank	
		Denomination	Number of Members	Denomination	Number of Members	Denomination	Number of Members
New York	4,245,907	Jewish Congregations	2,035,000	Roman Catholic Church	1,551,296	Protestant Episcopal Church	133,435
Atlanta	152,083	Negro Baptists	32,044	Southern Baptist Convention	28,358	Methodist Episcopal Church South	24,832
Birmingham	109,945	Negro Baptists	28,609	Methodist Episcopal Church South	22,689	Southern Baptist Convention	13,262
Dallas	119,446	Negro Baptists	21,170	Methodist Episcopal Church	18,953	Southern Baptist Convention	16,458
New Orleans	264,370	Roman Catholic Church	191,933	Negro Baptists	18,822	Jewish Congregations	8,700

Source: *Census of Religious Bodies: 1936*, Vol. I (Washington: Government Printing Office, 1941), pp. 70-71.

Table H, Appendix, provides a breakdown for four selected southern cities of the major religious faiths (1,000 members or more). A study of this table reveals that New Orleans, long recognized as a Catholic stronghold, has nearly three-fourths of its church members in that group. The other three cities have 80 per cent or more of their members in the Protestant group, Atlanta being the most dominantly Protestant with 87 per cent of its members in this broad category embracing most of the non-Catholic Christian churches.

One is also impressed, especially, by the large church membership in New Orleans. New Orleans has more than 100,000 church members in excess of any other southern city; this is probably due to the influence of the Catholic church and to the practice of including children under 13 as members in greater proportions than do other faiths (particularly many Protestant).

Since there were so many very small denominations, Table I, Appendix, was constructed to determine the outstanding affiliations of church members. Table J, Appendix, merely presents the Atlanta church membership in detail.

Figure 51, though subject to limitations as previously pointed out, shows rather plainly the distribution of the membership of the five largest religious groups in Atlanta, Dallas, Nashville, and New Orleans.

SEX RATIOS AMONG CHURCH MEMBERS

In consideration of the sex ratio of church members, it will be observed in Table X that the church membership in all the southern cities under consideration has sex ratios lower than the national average; this probably reflects the presence of the extremely feminine Negro population (see Chapter VI, Sex Composition). Only Dallas had a sex ratio among church members lower than Atlanta, and that by one-tenth of one point. It should be recalled that southern cities generally have lower sex ratios than the national average for urban communities. On a nationwide basis, church memberships are generally made up of a greater number of women than men; i.e., sex ratios are usually below 100.[5] These factors would appear to account for the unusually low sex ratios of the church memberships of the southern cities.

5. Smith, *op. cit.*, p. 186.

TABLE X

Sex Ratios Among Church Membership
in Selected Urban Populations
(Cities of 25,000 or More), 1936

Population	Sex Ratios
Total for Cities of 25,000 or More in 1930	79.0
Atlanta	66.0
Birmingham	71.1
Nashville	69.7
New Orleans	78.5
Dallas	65.9

Source: *Census of Religious Bodies: 1936*, Vol. I (Washington: Government Printing Office, 1941), pp. 424-436.

RECENT TRENDS IN CHURCH MEMBERSHIP

Table XI presents the total church membership of Atlanta and four other selected urban populations in 1936 and 1926, and the number and percentage of increase or decrease from 1926 to 1936. Examination of the table reveals that the church membership of Atlanta increased by nearly one-fourth in the decade 1926-1936; Dallas had an increase of about 16 per cent; but both Birmingham and New Orleans lost membership. New York had a slight gain of 4.1 per cent. It would be of interest to discover

TABLE XI

NUMBER OF CHURCH MEMBERS IN SELECTED CITIES, 1926-1936

City	Total Number of Members 1936	Total Number of Members 1926	Increase or Decrease 1926 - 1936	
			Number	Per Cent
New York	4,245,907	4,079,501	166,406	4.1
Atlanta	152,083	122,855	29,228	23.8
Birmingham	109,945	125,253	-15,308	-12.2
Dallas	119,446	102,631	16,815	16.4
New Orleans	264,370	276,490	-12,120	-4.4

Source: *Census of Religious Bodies: 1936*, Vol. I (Washington: Government Printing Office, 1941), p. 72.

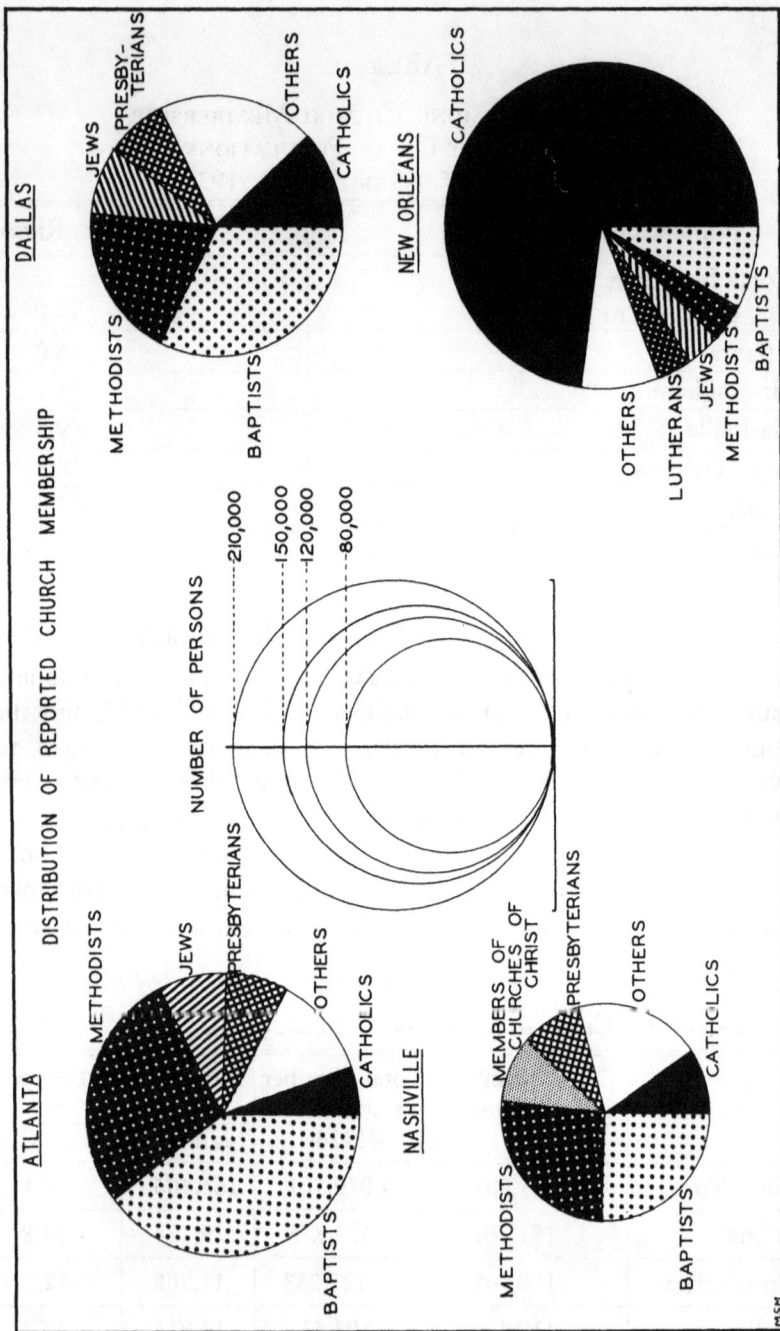

FIGURE 51. Distribution of reported church membership, by major religious groupings, in selected southern cities, 1936.

the extent to which these gains and losses are affected by the corresponding increase or decrease of the total population of these cities during the decade from 1926 to 1936. These figures are not available, however, and the census data for 1930 and 1940 do not reflect in every case the status which existed four years previously. In addition, it has been previously pointed out (see Chapter I, Introduction) that data on the religious composition of the population of groups in the United States cannot reliably be compared with data in other areas under study, for reasons outlined therein. It is, however, of interest to note that the church membership of Atlanta appears to be increasing more rapidly, at least in the present decade, than the total population of the city. Growth in church membership may, however, bear a closer relationship to growth of population in the metropolitan area than to the city proper, which is known to have a relatively smaller rate of growth.

Equitable Building (Now Trust Company of Georgia Building)
Atlanta's First "Modern" Skyscraper—First Occupied in 1892.

The Carnegie Library (About 1902).

Candler Building (About 1906)—Beginning of the Business Move
To the Present North Area.

Administration Building, Georgia School of Technology.

Courtesy Georgia Power Company.

Roosevelt High School, Formerly Girls High School of Atlanta.

Courtesy of the Atlanta Chamber of Commerce.

Intersection of Peachtree Street and Broad Street Looking South (About 1940.)

Atlanta Terminal Station (1940's).

Peachtree Road Methodist Church (1949).

CHAPTER XI

FERTILITY

THE PURPOSE OF THIS CHAPTER IS TO ANALYZE THE RAPIDITY AND extent to which the population of Atlanta reproduces itself. In order to do this, it is necessary to study rather thoroughly the crude birth rate, the fertility ratio, the net reproduction rate, and the indexes of net reproduction of the Atlanta population. Furthermore, in order that the true picture may be determined, the data are broken down by race and these results related to the ecological pattern of the city. Finally, in order that the results may be as meaningful as possible, they are compared to the urban population of the United States, the South, and other large southern cities. To the analysis of these data and these factors this chapter is devoted.

The study of fertility in the analysis of a population is significant because only when data on fertility are related to mortality can there be an accurate basis for much governmental legislation and the planning of programs of public health and education; furthermore, these data provide guidance in the planning of programs in industry. There is a great deal of popular interest in fertility; in addition many individuals who have written about the "problems of population" have done considerable speculating about the rapidity of human reproduction.

OUTSTANDING FEATURES OF FERTILITY IN ATLANTA

Five outstanding features of fertility in Atlanta can be readily listed: (1) The Atlanta population fails to reproduce itself by at least one-third each generation; this is true even though the white population replaces itself to a greater extent than the Negro population; (2) since 1890 the trends in fertility have been generally downward in the Atlanta population; (3) in general the fertility rates in the Atlanta population decrease as socio-economic status rises; (4) the fertility rates in Atlanta are considerably lower than among the average urban population of the United States; and (5) as late as the decade between 1930 and 1940 the rates of reproduction decreased in Atlanta.

FERTILITY IN ATLANTA AND OTHER URBAN POPULATIONS IN 1940

Crude birth rates. In Table K, Appendix, data are presented showing the number of births and the crude birth rates for selected urban populations in the South, and for cities of 100,000 or more in the United States for 1940. When the crude birth rate is used as a measure of fertility, it is noted that the four southern cities studied have higher rates than the national average of cities of 100,000 or more inhabitants. Nashville is the only southern city studied which has a higher crude birth rate than Atlanta, and it is higher by only one-tenth of a point. The same observation can be made for the white population of these cities, but Nashville's superiority in this instance is greater. In the classification of "all other races" (which is primarily Negro in southern cities) it will be noted that the birth rate is higher for all cities except Nashville. Particularly noteworthy is the fact that New Orleans has the lowest crude birth rate for its white population and the highest crude birth rate for those of other races.

Fertility ratios. In 1940 the fertility ratio for the population of Atlanta was 224 (see Table L, Appendix); Dallas had a fertility ratio of 215, which made it the only large southern city studied which had a lower fertility ratio than Atlanta. The average fertility ratio of all urban populations in the United States in 1940 was 257. It will also be noted that all the southern cities studied were below the national urban average; and as pointed out elsewhere, this finding is to be expected in view of the high degree of urbanity in the cities studied in comparison to the urban population of the United States.

Among the Negro populations of the southern cities in 1940 with the exception of New Orleans, the fertility ratios were all lower than the national urban average. Dallas had the lowest fertility ratio with 189; Nashville was next lowest with 210; and Atlanta with a fertility ratio of 218 stood next to New Orleans.[1]

The fertility ratios of the native white populations were all higher than the Negro populations with the exception again of New Orleans. Dallas stood at the bottom with a fertility ratio of 226 and then followed New Orleans and Atlanta; Nashville stood highest with 262 children under 5 per 1,000 women aged 15 to 44.

1. For some limitations of the fertility ratio in measuring rates of reproduction among Negroes, see Louise Kemp, "A Note on the Use of the Fertility Ratio in the Study of Rural-Urban Differences in Fertility," *Rural Sociology*, 10:312-313, September, 1945.

Net reproduction rate and indexes of net reproduction. The net reproduction rate of the city of Atlanta was calculated by combining birth data and the data found by means of the life table (which is shown in the chapter on mortality). These data are subject to the following severe limitations: (1) No corrections were made for underenumeration in the census data or for under-registration of births and deaths for the data pertaining to Atlanta; and (2) death rates for the ages 75 and over in the life tables are based on urban Mississippi persons rather than on Atlanta persons (some correction has been made in regard to these data by the authors).[2] With these limitations it was found that the net re-production rate for the white population of Atlanta was 93.6 and for the Negro population it was 71.4 (see Tables M and N, Appendix). These findings are exceptionally high in comparison to net reproduction rates computed by other investigators and even high in comparison to indexes of net reproduction computed by methods in this study.

To check the high rates of reproduction found, the data on mortality were related to census data and the indexes of net reproduction computed as shown in Table O, Appendix. There it is noted that the indexes are not out of line but agree very closely with data from other sources in that the index of net reproduction varies between .53 and .64.

VARIATIONS IN FERTILITY IN ATLANTA AND SUBURBAN ATLANTA

Variations in the crude birth rate by census tracts, 1930. The crude birth rate by census tracts is shown in Figure 52 for 1930. One notes that in 1930, census tracts F-23, F-32, F-64, and F-66 had the highest crude birth rates. The lowest crude birth rates occurred in the populous northern part of the city which had a heavy adult population and a fairly high level of living; in addition, low rates were recorded in the downtown district of census tract F-27. It would have been desirable to show the crude birth rate for 1940 here; but those data were not immediately available (according to the statistician of the Atlanta City Health Department, Mr. Charles C. Turner).

Racial variations in fertility ratios by census tracts. Rates of reproduction are closely related to race (not necessarily race

2. Vernon Davis and John C. Belcher, *Mississippi Life Tables by Sex, Race and Residence: 1940* (Jackson, Mississippi: Mississippi Comission on Hospital Care, 1948), p. 2.

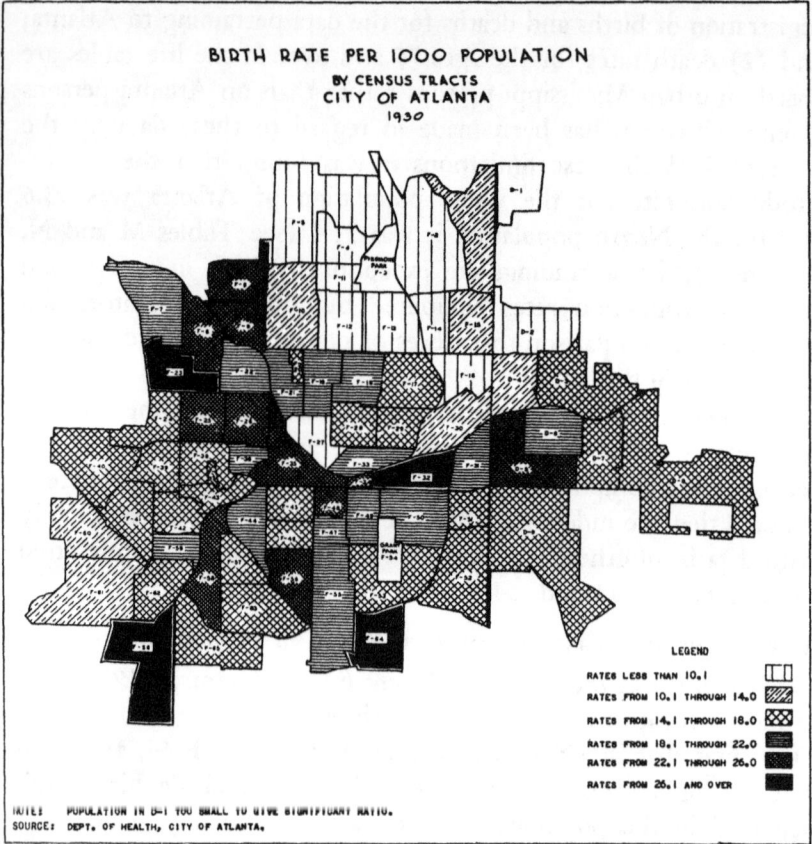

FIGURE 52. Crude birth rate of the Atlanta population, by census tracts, 1930. (Reproduced from WPA of Georgia official project 465-34-3-4.)

per se but certainly the socio-economic aspects of race).

(1) *Whites.* Figures 53 and 54 present fertility ratios in Atlanta for all classes and for native whites, by census tracts. In analyzing the reproduction rate of the city of Atlanta by means of the fertility ratio, these figures indicate that the lowest fertility ratios for the white population occur in census tracts F-4, F-12, and F-27. The first two of these tracts are in the northern residential section, a densely populated area containing a fairly high proportion of rooming-houses and small apartments for business girls and childless couples. The third census tract, F-27, is a downtown district having a small population, much of which is concentrated in hotels and small apartments.

The highest fertility ratios for whites are found in census tracts F-6, F-8, F-9, F-21, and F-23 in the northwest portion of the city; and in F-32, F-34, F-47, F-48, F-44, and F-57 in the south central portion. In the first group of tracts there are several large textile mills and a concentration of small "light" industries. In census tracts F-20 and F-21, there are two large federal housing projects (Techwood and Clark Howell), which have a dense population dominated by small-income families usually with one or more small children per family. Similarly, the areas contained in the census tracts in the south central part of town are dominated by industrial development including textile mills, paper mills, railroad shops, automobile assembly plant, and numerous others. In tracts F-35 and F-48 there is a large federal housing project (Capitol Homes) in which the small-income family with children is the predominant type. Tract F-32, a highly industrialized area, contains many persons employed in the textile industry.

(2) *Negroes.* For the Negro population, as shown in Figure 55, the lowest fertility ratio occurs in tract F-27, which contains a very small population. This tract is a downtown tract and contains very few one-family dwelling units. Another very low ratio occurs in tract F-12, which is a densely populated area in the northern part of the city, but which contains few Negroes. It seems reasonable to assume that many of these Negroes are house-servants who are residing at the domicile of their employers. The highest fertility ratios for Negroes occur in tracts F-32, F-62, and F-66, all of which have small Negro populations. Two of these (F-62 and F-66) are on the outer fringe of the city, and are largely residential areas dominated by the one-family and

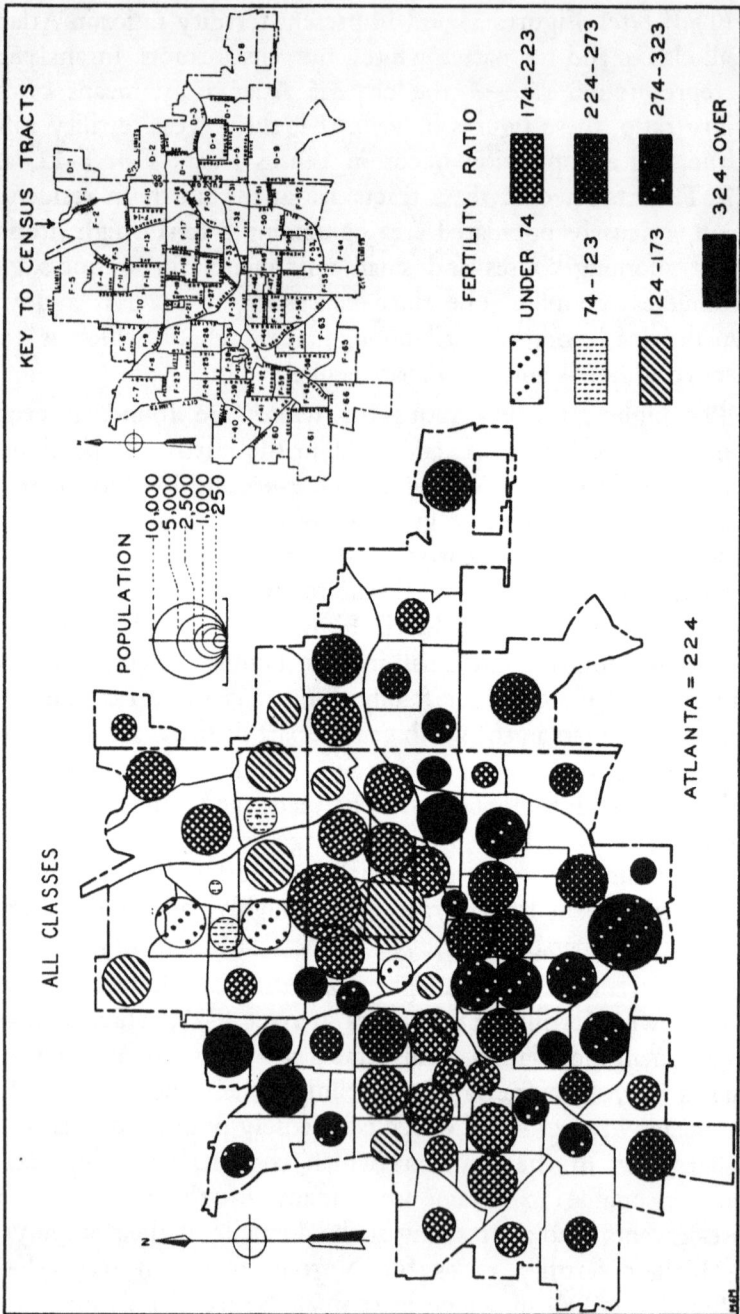

FIGURE 53. Fertility ratios of the population (all classes) of Atlanta, by census tracts, 1940.

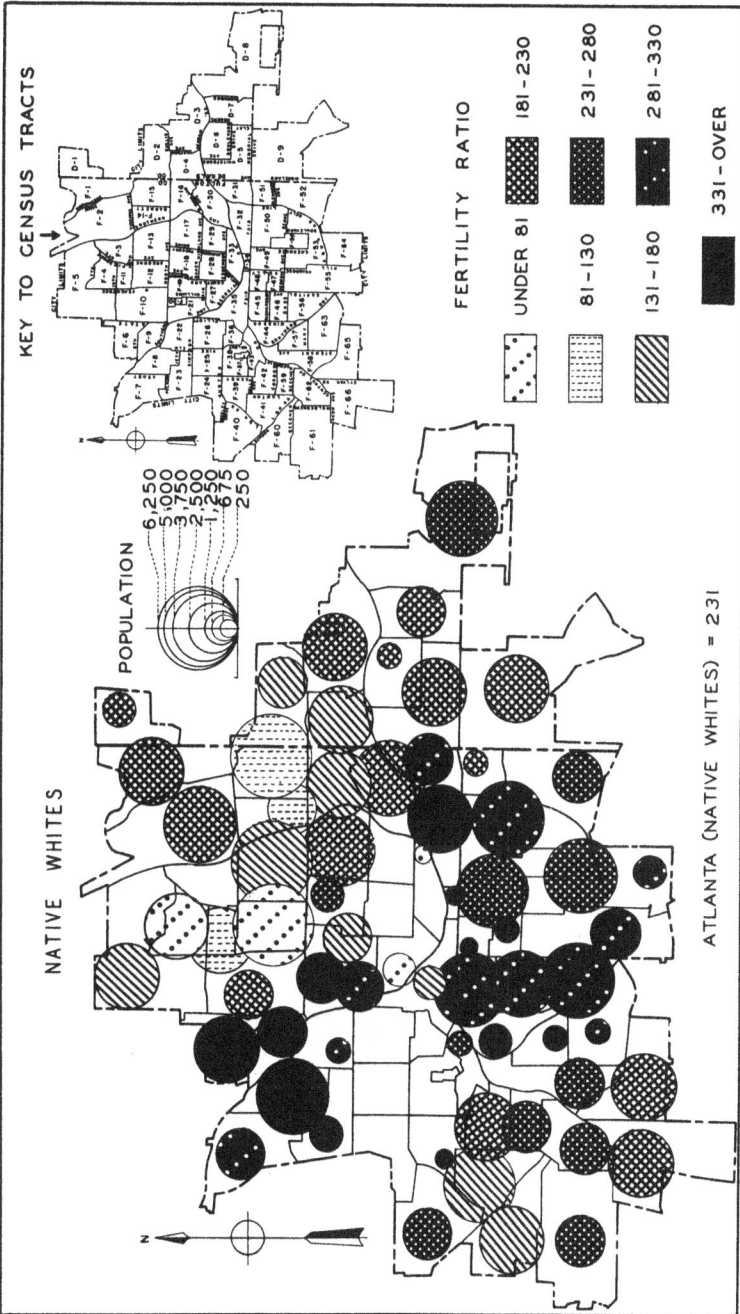

FIGURE 54. Fertility ratios of the native white population of Atlanta, by census tracts, 1940.

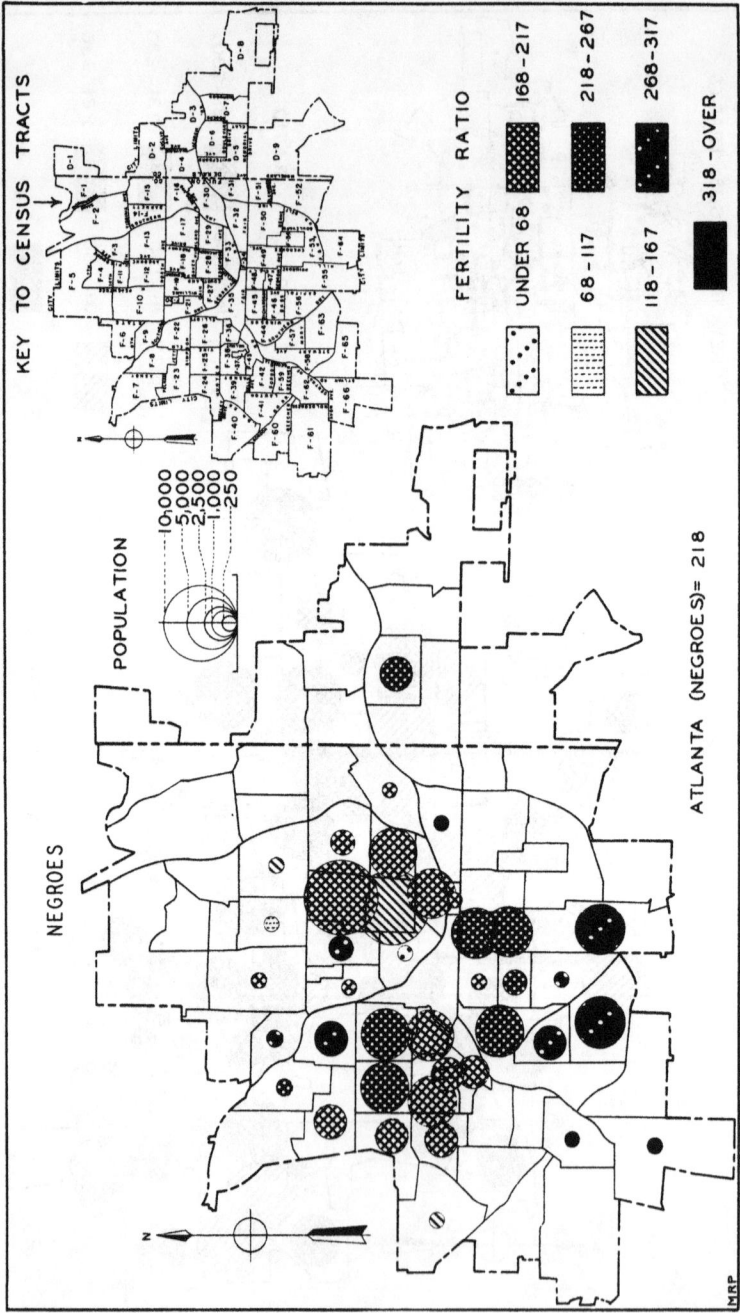

FIGURE 55. Fertility ratios of the Negro population of Atlanta, by census tracts, 1940.

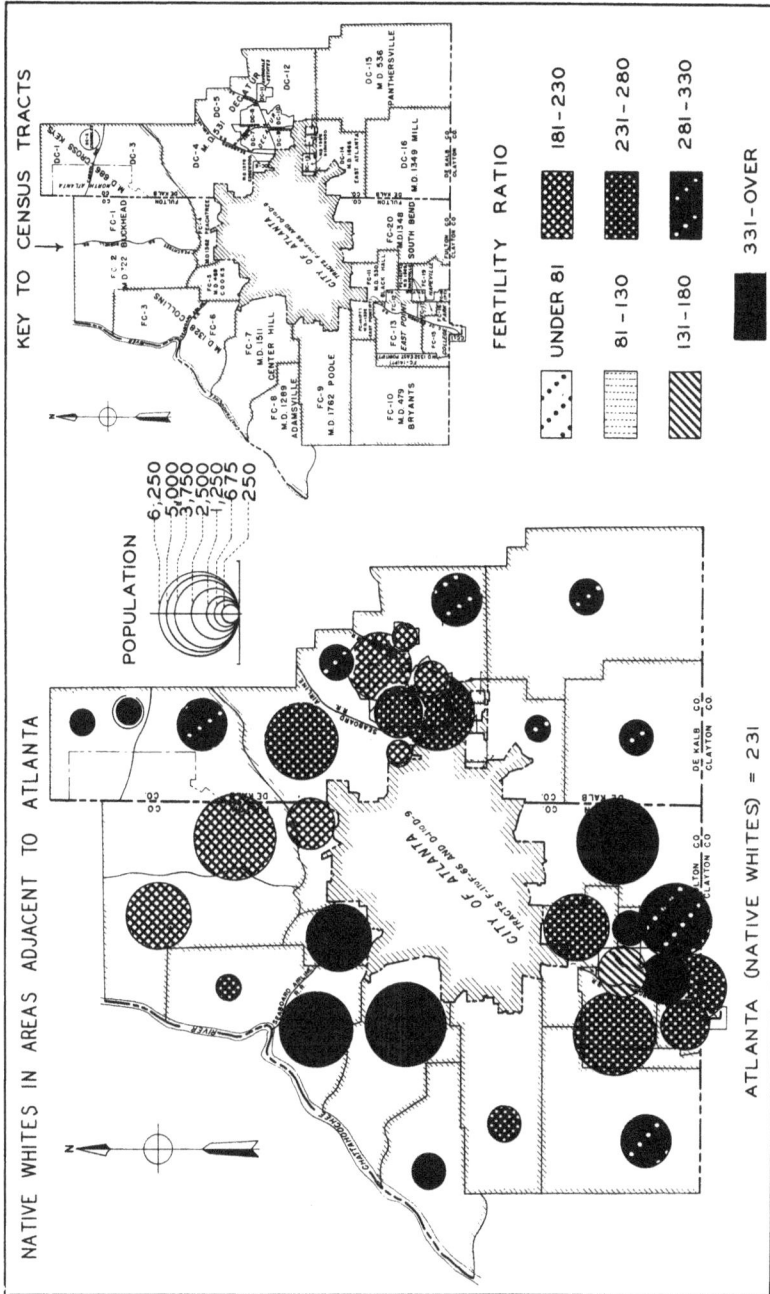

FIGURE 56. Fertility ratios of the native white population in areas adjacent to Atlanta, by census tracts, 1940.

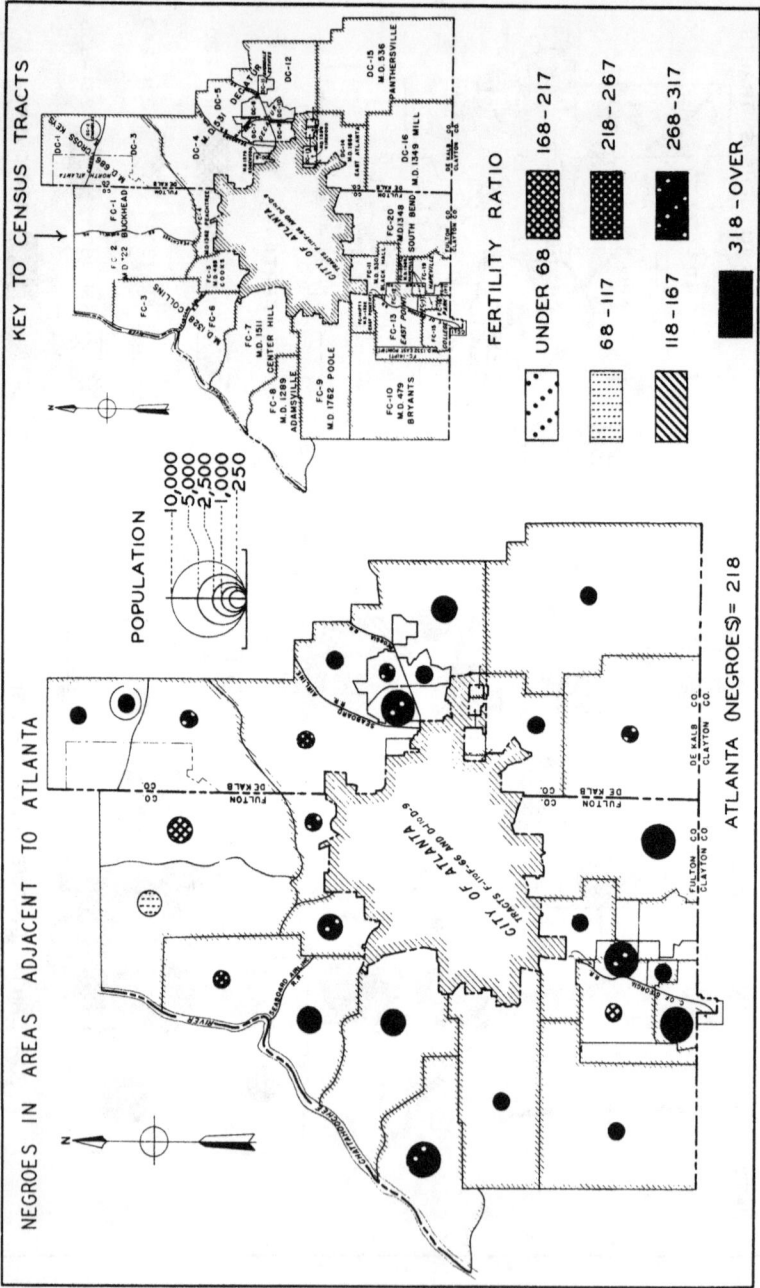

FIGURE 57. Fertility ratios of the Negro population in areas adjacent to Atlanta, by census tracts, 1940.

152

two-family dwelling types. These findings tend to support Notestein's conclusion that fertility rates fall off as socio-economic status increases; i.e., the highest fertility rates are found among families living in the poorer residential areas.[3]

Fertility ratios in suburban Atlanta. Figures 56 and 57 present the fertility ratios for the population residing immediately adjacent to Atlanta. In general the shadings are darker, indicating higher fertility rates; thus these findings support the general hypothesis that as urbanity increases, fertility seems to decrease.[4]

TRENDS IN ATLANTA'S FERTILITY FOR HALF A CENTURY

Table L, Appendix, which presents the number of children under 5 per 1,000 women aged 15 to 44 by race and nativity for selected urban populations, 1890 to 1940, is useful for further study and analysis. There are several generalizations which can be made about the data presented therein, but the writer has been unable to account for some of the findings.

First of all, for the period 1890 to 1940 the trends of the fertility ratios have been downward, although not consistently so, for all groups in each of the urban populations studied. This finding is consistent with the general decline of rates of reproduction in western European countries and in the United States. Many reasons have been suggested to account for this decline; among these reasons are the more extensive use of more effective contraceptive devices, abortion, changes in age at marriage and proportions of married women, ambition to change status and therefore voluntary childlessness or limitation of family size, and a host of other reasons or possibilities.[5] Smith summarizes the matter by stating that we are able to demonstrate that urbanization is the cause of the falling rates of reproduction although we are not able to point out the particular city traits responsible. Of course he would include in, or as a concomitant of, urbanization the attitudes on the part of parents which cause them to limit the number of offspring.[6]

Secondly, one notes that with only one exception the fertility

---

3. Frank W. Notestein, "The Differential Rate of Increase Among the Social Classes of the American Population," *Social Forces*, 12:17-33, October, 1933.
4. T. Lynn Smith, *Population Analysis* (New York: McGraw-Hill Book Company, Inc., 1948), p. 232.
5. Warren S. Thompson, *Population Problems* (New York: McGraw-Hill Book Company, Inc., 1942), pp. 188-215.
6. *Population Analysis*, pp. 228-232.

ratios for the Negro population are lower than the other classifications; i.e., all classes and native whites. The exception noted is the 1940 data for New Orleans, which show the fertility ratio for the Negro population to be higher than either for the whites or for the city as a whole. These findings tend to confirm further the hypothesis "that urban life dries up the reproductive springs of the Negro population even more rapidly than it leads to race suicide among whites."[7]

A third generalization that can be made from these data is that the differential in fertility has become less in the last half century; that is, in 1940 the fertility ratios varied between 189 and 267, while in 1890 the extremes were 307 and 436. In view of the tremendous Catholic influence in New Orleans, one is somewhat surprised that the ratios are not higher for that city; apparently "urbanization" is more powerful than religious affiliation in this case.

As a result of the analysis of Table L, Appendix, a rather basic question has been raised in the mind of the investigator. This question concerns the validity of the index (fertility ratio) as a measure of fertility. Without trying to answer it completely, it seems that recency of migration into a city, particularly of females, would have a severe depressing effect on this index.

Although it has been impossible to corroborate the fact, it seems that the low fertility ratios found in the Negro population for the first two or three decades under consideration might possibly be accounted for by the failure of the enumerator to count the Negro children in the same proportion that white children were counted.

Among the several urban populations studied, it may be noted that between 1890 and 1940, the most severe drop in the fertility ratio for all classes was in Dallas from 417 to 215. Atlanta sustained the next greatest decrease in ratio, followed in order by New Orleans and Nashville. In considering the decrease in ratios for whites from 1890 to 1940, Dallas again had the most severe drop, followed in order by New Orleans, Atlanta, and Nashville. For Negroes, the situation is somewhat similar, with Dallas leading in amount of decrease, followed by Atlanta, New Orleans, and Nashville. One might conclude therefore, that in comparison

7. T. Lynn Smith, "A Demographic Study of the American Negro," *Social Forces*, 23:384, March, 1945.

with the three urban populations considered, the fertility ratio of Atlanta's population is decreasing more rapidly than that of Nashville, and less rapidly than that of Dallas. Atlanta's status in this respect as compared with New Orleans is less definite. All four southern urban populations report smaller ratios for each decade since 1910 than that of the urban United States.

Indexes of net reproduction. In order to determine the trend between 1930 and 1940 of the extent to which the Atlanta population was replacing itself and to compare further this replacement rate to other urban populations, Table XII was prepared. The indexes obtained are extremely crude and are presented to determine only in a very general way the replacement rate. The data headed "permanent replacement quota" show the "ratio of children under 5 per 1,000 women aged 20 to 44 years inclusive, in the stationary population, computed for native whites in 1929-31."[8] These data are for total populations and do not strictly apply to the urban segment of the population. A further inadequacy of the table is the fact that in 1940 fertility rates are related to data for 1929-1931 even though fertility rates and mortality rates had changed considerably since that time.

In comparing the replacement rates calculated in Table XII with those published by the Census Bureau, it was interesting to note that the adjusted net reproduction rate for white women of Atlanta for 1935 to 1940 was 622 as compared to 620 calculated by the very crude method of this work. When the data for New Orleans were compared, the rate furnished by the Census Bureau was 608 in comparison to 630 in this work. Thus these data are in surprisingly close agreement.[9]

In order to show the trend of the net reproduction rate over a longer period of time, Table P, Appendix, was constructed. The replacement rates referred to above are in general agreement with the trends shown in the data published by the Census Bureau for the white population; i.e., the fertility rates of the white population have generally declined; however, the net reproduction rate for nonwhites of southern cities has increased since 1905 although the fertility ratios for the southern cities have declined. It is realized

8. Rupert B. Vance, *All These People* (Chapel Hill: The University of North Carolina Press, 1945), p. 92.
9. *Sixteenth Census of the United States: 1940,* "Population, Differential Fertility, 1940 and 1910, Standardized Fertility Rates and Reproduction Rates," (Washington: Government Printing Office, 1944), p. 29.

TABLE XII

APPROXIMATE NET REPRODUCTION INDEX OF THE NATIVE WHITE POPULATION
URBAN UNITED STATES, AND FOUR SELECTED SOUTHERN CITIES, 1930 AND 1940

Population	Ratio of Children Under 5 to Women 20-44		Permanent Replacement Quota (1929-1931)	Index of Reproduction per Generation	
	1930	1940		1930	1940
Urban United States	471	348	444[1]	1.06	.78
Atlanta	326	276	444[2]	.73	.62
Dallas	323	267	455[3]	.71	.59
Nashville	373	316	449[4]	.83	.70
New Orleans	392	278	442[5]	.89	.63

1 Total United States.
2 Georgia.
3 Texas.
4 Tennessee.
5 Louisiana.

Sources: National Resources Committee, *Population Statistics, 1, National Data* (Washington: Government Printing Office, 1937), p. 50; *Fifteenth Census of the United States: 1930,* "Population, Vol. II, General Report, Statistics by Subjects," (Washington: Government Printing Office, 1933), pp. 587, 757, 789, and 790; *Sixteenth Census of the United States: 1940,* "Population, Vol. II, Characteristics of the Population," Part 1 (Washington: Government Printing Office, 1943), pp. 23, 119, 125, 135, and 136.

that these data are not exactly comparable in view of the extremely large degree of urbanity of the cities under consideration in comparison to the urban population in general. Furthermore, it would easily be possible for the fertility ratios to decrease and yet the net reproduction rate to increase if the death rates were reduced considerably, as well as for other reasons. Actually the data are not adequate to determine the true net reproduction rate of the Negro population for the southern cities under consideration.

FERTILITY TRENDS DURING WORLD WAR II

The data on number of births occurring to residents of Atlanta and urban places of 100,000 or more support generally the hypothesis that fertility rates drop during war years and rise again immediately after demobilization.[10]

In Table Q, Appendix, it is shown that Atlanta births for the total population dropped from a high in 1942 to a low in 1943 and remained low for 1944 and 1945 only to exceed any previous record in 1946. The high for large urban places was reached in 1943; and a lower number of births was registered in 1944 and in 1945, with a tremendous increase coming in 1946. It is probable that the drop may have been much greater had it not been for the

10. Smith, *Population Analysis,* pp. 94-97.

fact that the "bumper baby crop" which came immediately after the First World War was in the ages of highest reproductivity during the Second World War.[11]

FERTILITY DATA SUMMARIZED

In spite of the many limitations that have been pointed out in this chapter, it is felt that some rather definite conclusions can be drawn from the data, since the several sources are in rather close agreement with one exception. The findings of this chapter indicate: (1) that the native white urban populations of 1940 were failing to reproduce themselves to a greater extent than they were in 1930; (2) that the native white populations of southern cities were failing to reproduce themselves to a much greater extent than the national urban average (this is as one would expect, since these cities represent the extremely urbanized portion of the urban population); (3) that the native white populations of Dallas and Atlanta have the lowest replacement indexes of the southern cities; (4) that the native white population of New Orleans had the greatest decline in its replacement rate during the decade 1930 to 1940 of any of the southern cities; (5) that in general the nonwhite populations of southern cities are failing to replace themselves to a greater extent than the white populations; and (6) that the Atlanta population lacks replacement by at least one-third each generation, the white population replacing itself to a greater extent than the Negro population.

11. *Ibid.*, p. 223-228.

CHAPTER XII

MORTALITY

THIS CHAPTER IS PRESENTED TO DETERMINE AND ANALYZE BY BOTH race and sex the death rate and the expectation of life of the Atlanta population; to determine the infant mortality rate of the white and Negro populations of Atlanta; to determine the leading causes of death of the Atlanta population; to determine the trends in the death rates as well as the trends in infant mortality rates and causes of death; and finally to present the data in a meaningful manner by comparing them to other urban populations, particularly other large southern cities.

If for no other reason than general public interest, a study of mortality would be worthwhile, for almost all people are interested in life expectancy, trends in causes of death (especially in control of specific causes), changes in the risks of maternity, and similar phenomena related to mortality. Over and above general public interest, there are many reasons why the study of mortality is significant. Life insurance companies depend upon life tables as the basis for their operations, and of course life tables represent only one arrangement of mortality data. Mortality is one of the three basic factors that influence the number of inhabitants of any given area. Longevity affords an excellent index of the quality of a population as likewise does the infant mortality rate; and in view of generally incomplete data on morbidity, mortality rates afford a measure of the health of a population.

OUTSTANDING FEATURES OF MORTALITY IN ATLANTA

When the mortality data for Atlanta are analyzed, several outstanding features are revealed. The crude death rate for the white population is lower than the national average and lower than most of the large southern cities; on the other hand, the death rate for nonwhites is more than 25 per cent higher than the national average and exceeds the average of cities of 100,000 or more in all the states containing cities of 100,000 or more with the exception of Kentucky and Utah. The females of both races have longer life expectancy than males, but there is a marked differential between the races; however, in comparison to other populations, the Atlanta population stands well. The infant mortality rate for all classes and for whites is below the national

159

average, and the nonwhite rate is approaching the average although there is a large differential between the whites and nonwhites.

Tuberculosis is still one of the five leading causes of death in Atlanta.

MORTALITY IN ATLANTA AND OTHER URBAN POPULATIONS

Crude death rates. In order to compare the death rates of other cities of 100,000 in certain southern states with that of Atlanta, Table R, Appendix, was prepared. This table presents specific death rates by age and race for cities of 100,000 or larger for the United States and for cities of this size in Georgia, Louisiana, Tennessee, and Texas. Figure 58 shows the relationship of age to the death rate among the white and Negro populations of Atlanta in 1940.

It will be noted that the crude death rate for the "all ages" group of Atlanta exceeds the other urban populations under consideration with the exception of New Orleans.

The death rate for persons under one year of age for Atlanta is considerably above the national average, but it is exceeded by New Orleans and the average of the Texas cities of over 100,000 inhabitants. The specific death rate for Atlanta persons aged 1-4 is lower than the rate for the same age group in other large southern cities.

(1) *Whites.* It will also be noted that among the urban populations selected for study, Atlanta has the lowest death rate for its white population; i.e., lower than the national average or any of the other large southern populations listed. The populations of cities of 100,000 of the following states, however, had lower crude death rates for the white populations than did Atlanta; i.e., had a crude death rate below 10.1: Alabama, Kansas, Michigan, Minnesota, North Carolina, Oklahoma, Utah, and Wisconsin.[1]

(2) *"All other races."* The death rate for the "all other races" (primarily Negro) population of Atlanta is about 27 per cent higher than the national average of cities over 100,000, and stands well above the death rate of the same category in other southern cities. In fact, of all the states containing cities

1. Forrest E. Linder and Robert D. Grove, *Vital Statistics Rates in the United States: 1900-1940* (Washington: Government Printing Office, 1947), pp. 198-209.

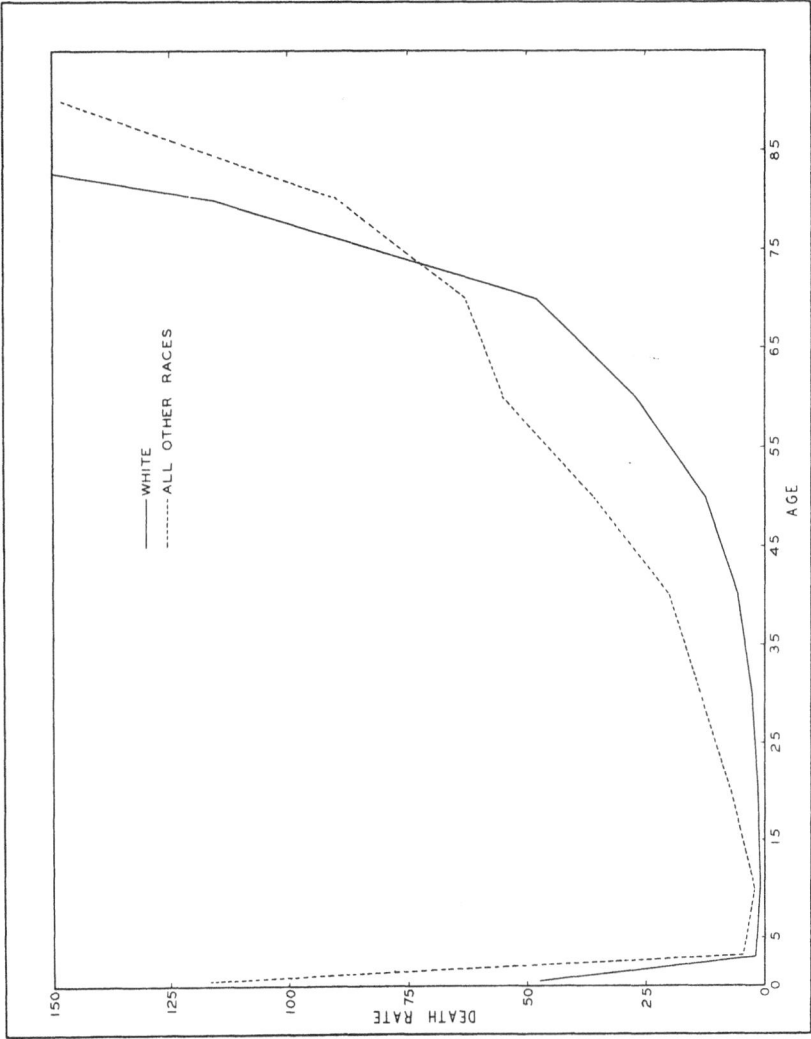

FIGURE 58.   Relationship of age to the death rate among the white and Negro populations of Atlanta, 1940.

161

of 100,000 or more, only Kentucky and Utah had higher crude death rates for "all other races" than Georgia (City of Atlanta).[2] In the "all other races" classifications, it will be noted that the Atlanta specific death rates are higher at every age than the national average or the average of other southern cities from age 5 to 60.

Generalizations concerning death rates. From the foregoing data, the generalization may be made that for Atlanta and other large southern urban populations at all ages with the exception of the very old age groups, the age-specific death rates are higher for the "all other race" classification than for the white population; in all cases, the crude death rate based on all ages is lower for whites than for those of other races. The foregoing findings are in general agreement with other findings, but it must be pointed out that one must not infer from these differences in the death rates of the white and colored populations that "these rates are the result of inherent race differences."[3] In regard to to racial differential, Thompson states:

> . . . until the conditions of life in the two groups approximate one another rather closely, the presumption is that differences in death rates arise out of differences in sanitary and medical care and in economic status rather than out of inherent biological differences.[4]

Expectation of life. In order to show how the expectation of life of the Atlanta population compares with the expectation of life of other populations, Table XIII is presented.

This table (XIII) presents the expectation of life in selected populations by race and sex at various ages; i.e., at birth, and at ages 20, 50, and 70. It should be pointed out that for urban Mississippi and Atlanta, data cover the intervals 20-24, 50-55, and 70-75, rather than the exact ages 20, 50, and 70. It will be noted that Atlanta females in both races have a longer expectation of life than males. This is in accordance with most mortality data with the notable exception of India at certain ages.[5] Secondly, the data

2. *Ibid.*, pp. 198-209.
3. Warren S. Thompson, *Population Problems* (New York: McGraw-Hill Book Company, Inc., 1942), pp. 239-240.
4. *Ibid.*, p. 240. (From *Population Problems*, by Warren S. Thompson. Copyright 1942. Courtesy of McGraw-Hill Book Co.)
5. T. Lynn Smith, *Population Analysis* (New York: McGraw-Hill Book Company, Inc., 1948), pp. 250-256.

on the Atlanta population correspond very closely to the expectation of life in urban Mississippi (it may be recalled that a portion of the data for Atlanta life tables depends upon Mississippi data); however, the Atlanta white child has a considerably longer life expectation at birth than the white child born in urban Mississippi. In comparison with the other populations listed, the Atlanta population stands well, since the data for Mississippi and Atlanta represent the situation about two-and-one-half years later than the other data (except at birth). In fact, at ages 50 and 70, the life expectancy for Atlanta residents goes well ahead of the United States urban population, especially for females. Even at age 20, Atlanta white females can expect to live six years longer on the average than the city-dwelling woman in the United States and about two years longer than the average for the South Atlantic States.

The life expectancy at birth of the white male and the white female in the United States in 1939-1941 was 62.8 and 67.3, respectively; for the same period the Negro males had an expectation of life of 52.3, while the Negro female could expect to live 55.6 years.[6] In comparison to these data, life expectancy of the Atlanta population is lower than the national average, although this is not a comparison with the national urban average

The stationary populations shown in Table S and Table T, Appendix, were prepared from the life tables to be used in connection with the study of fertility.

VARIATIONS IN MORTALITY WITHIN THE CITY OF ATLANTA

Crude death rates. Figure 59 is presented to show the areas with the highest and lowest crude death rates within the city of Atlanta in 1930. In general, the highest death rates were in the central portion of the city. The lowest death rates were in the northern, eastern, and a few southwestern tracts. Many of these last mentioned areas are residential areas ranging from fairly substantial to wealthy income levels.

Data on crude death rates were not available for census tracts in 1940.

Expectation of life. In order to gain some idea of the expecta-

6. Metropolitan Life Insurance Company, *State and Regional Life Tables: 1939-1941* (Washington: Government Printing Office, 1948), pp. 44-45 and 106-109.

TABLE XIII

EXPECTATION OF LIFE IN SELECTED POPULATIONS, 1939-1941

	United States Urban Population 1930	South Atlantic States 1939-41	Georgia 1939-41	Urban Mississippi 1940	Atlanta 1939-41
At birth:					
white males	56.73	61.71	61.72	57.2	59.38
white females	61.05	67.03	67.46	65.1	66.63
Negro males	-------	-------	-------	46.7	43.02
Negro females	-------	-------	-------	51.7	48.87
At age 20 (20-25):					
white males	44.20*	47.13*	47.04*	44.4	44.95
white females	47.35*	51.59*	51.96*	51.3	51.24
Negro males	-------	-------	-------	36.4	30.63
Negro females	-------	-------	-------	39.8	36.74
At age 50 (50-55):					
white males	19.78*	21.77*	21.64*	19.8	19.63
white females	22.40*	24.99*	25.43*	24.5	24.69
Negro males	-------	-------	-------	17.0	14.19
Negro females	-------	-------	-------	19.3	17.17
At age 70 (70-75):					
white males	8.50*	9.32*	9.19*	8.3	8.33
white females	9.70*	10.49*	10.68*	10.1	10.50
Negro males	-------	-------	-------	7.7	7.73
Negro females	-------	-------	-------	9.4	9.50

* At exact ages 20, 50, and 70 instead of midpoint of five-year interval.

Sources: Metropolitan Life Insurance Company, *Statistical Bulletin*, 116, July, 1935; Metropolitan Life Insurance Company, *State and Regional Life Tables: 1939-1941* (Washington: Government Printing Office, 1948), pp. 44-45, and 106-109; Vernon Davies and John C. Belcher, *Mississippi Life Tables by Sex, Race and Residence: 1940* (Jackson, Mississippi: Mississippi Commission on Hospital Care, 1948), pp. 4-5, and 8-9; and life tables this study.

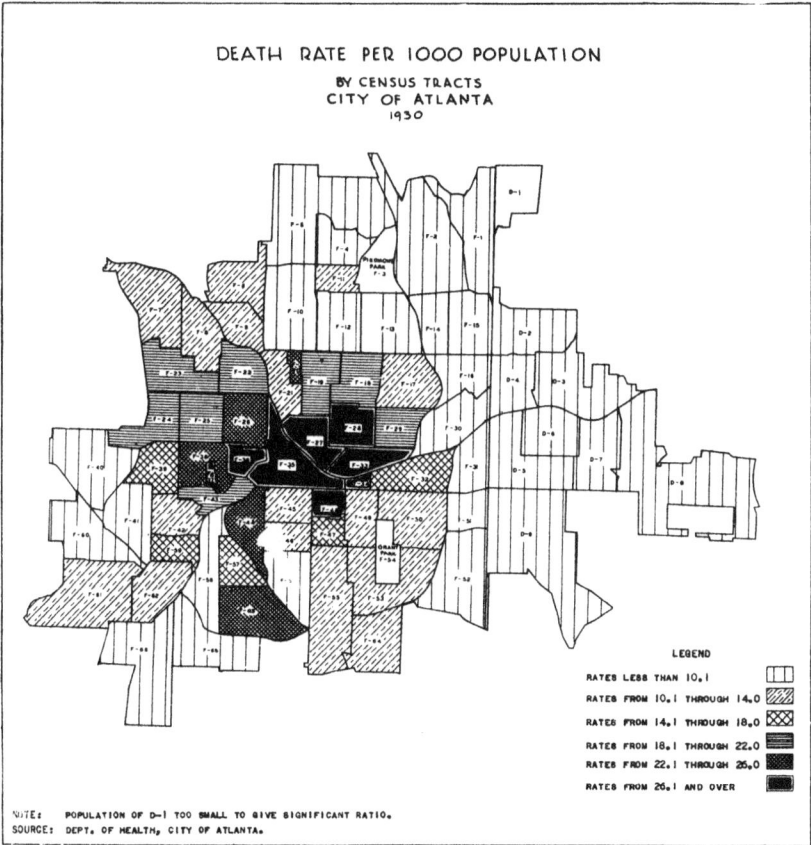

FIGURE 59. Crude death rate of the Atlanta population, by census tracts, 1930. (Reproduced from WPA of Georgia official project 465-34-3-4.)

tion of life of the Atlanta population, abridged life tables have been constructed (subject to limitations pointed out in methodology) and are shown in Tables XIV to XVII. These tables present, respectively, the abridged life tables covering the period 1939-1941 for white males, white females, Negro males, and Negro females. Inspection of these tables reveals that women of both groups have higher life expectancies at all ages except the extremely old (95-99) Negro group, and both white groups exceed the respective Negro groups by significant margins.

Infant mortality. In Figure 60, the infant mortality of Atlanta per 1,000 population during the period 1928-1936 is presented. This shows that highest rates of infant mortality were in the central, western, and southern portions of the city; the lowest rates were in the northeastern section of the city (a residential area of generally higher than average socio-economic status). Figures 61 and 62 present infant mortality rates by race by census tracts for 1947 only. It was necessary to limit this presentation to the more populous tracts, but the areas of high infant mortality are essentially the areas that were high for the period 1928 to 1936. It would have been much better to present an average infant mortality over many years, but these data were not immediately available from the Atlanta statistician.

Leading Causes of Death in Atlanta

The five leading causes of death in 1944 in the United States were (excluding "congenital malformations and diseases peculiar to the first year" and "other accidents"): diseases of the heart, cancer and other malignant tumors, intracranial lesions of vascular origin, nephritis, and pneumonia (all forms) and influenza.[7] In Table U, Appendix, using the above five causes as a basis, the number of deaths caused by each of these diseases is shown as well as the relation by percentage to the total number of deaths in selected cities. The first exception noted is that tuberculosis (all forms) is the fifth cause of death in Atlanta and New Orleans; otherwise, the causes of death rank in the same order as "killers" in southern cities as in the whole United States. About one-fourth of the people of Atlanta die of heart disease, while

7. Bureau of the Census, "Deaths and Death Rates for Selected Causes, by Age, Race, and Sex United States, 1944," *Vital Statistics—Special Reports,* 25:286-299, November, 1946.

TABLE XIV

(Constructed by Reed-Merrell Method)

Age Interval x to x + n	Number surviving to exact age x out of 100,000 born alive	Probability of a person of exact age x dying within the interval x to x + n	Number dying during year of age	Number of years lived by cohort between age x and age x + n	Total years of life remaining to survivors at age x	Average number of years of life remaining at the beginning of year of age
	l_x	$_nq_x$	d_x	L_x	T_x	e_x
(1)	(2)	(3)	(4)	(5)	(6)	(7)
0-	100,000	.05544	5,544	95,986	5,937,509	59.38
1-4	94,456	.01124	1,062	375,058	5,841,523	61.84
5-9	93,394	.00772	721	464,959	5,466,465	58.53
10-14	92,673	.00837	776	461,496	5,001,506	53.97
15-19	91,897	.01154	1,060	456,850	4,540,010	49.40
20-24	90,837	.00936	850	452,125	4,083,160	44.95
25-29	89,987	.01524	1,371	446,612	3,631,035	40.35
30-34	88,616	.01524	1,351	439,891	3,184,423	35.94
35-39	87,265	.02613	2,280	431,085	2,744,532	31.45
40-44	84,985	.04187	3,558	416,584	2,313,447	27.22
45-49	81,427	.06064	4,938	395,343	1,896,863	23.30
50-54	76,489	.08120	6,211	367,820	1,501,520	19.63
55-59	70,278	.13189	9,269	329,296	1,133,700	16.13
60-64	61,009	.18668	11,389	277,228	804,404	13.19
65-69	49,620	.25019	12,414	217,203	527,176	10.62
70-74	37,206	.32396	12,053	155,883	309,973	8.33
75-79	25,153	.49076*	12,344	94,008	154,090	6.13
80-84	12,809	.60506*	7,750	42,916	60,082	4.69
85-89	5,059	.77578*	3,925	14,057	17,166	3.39
90-94	1,134	.79721*	904	2,635	3,109	2.74
95-99	230	.88534*	204	474	474	2.06
100 and over	26	---------	--------	--------	--------	--------

* Based on rates of Mississippi urban white males.

Sources: *Sixteenth Census of the United States: 1940*, "Population and Housing, Atlanta, Georgia," (Washington: Government Printing Office, 1942), p. 4; *Vital Statistics of the United States, Supplement: 1939-1940*, Part III (Washington: Government Printing Office, 1943), p. 477; *Vital Statistics of the United States: 1941*, Part II (Washington: Government Printing Office, 1943), pp. 196-197; Vernon Davies and John C. Belcher, *Mississippi Life Tables, by Sex, Race, and Residence: 1940* (Jackson, Mississippi: Mississippi Commission on Hospital Care, 1948), pp. 4-5 and 8-9.

TABLE XV

ABRIDGED LIFE TABLE FOR WHITE FEMALES, ATLANTA, GEORGIA, 1939-1941
(Constructed by Reed-Merrell Method)

Age Interval x to x + n	Number surviving to exact age x out of 100,000 born alive	Probability of a person of exact age x dying within the interval x to x + n	Number dying during year of age	Number of years lived by cohort between age x and age x + n	Total years of life remaining to survivors at age x	Average number of years of life remaining at the beginning of year of age
	l_x	$_nq_x$	d_x	L_x	T_x	e_x
(1)	(2)	(3)	(4)	(5)	(6)	(7)
0-	100,000	.04615	4,615	96,659	6,662,539	66.63
1-4	95,385	.00905	863	379,296	6,565,880	68.84
5-9	94,522	.00464	439	471,381	6,186,584	65.45
10-14	94,083	.00349	328	469,609	5,715,203	60.75
15-19	93,755	.00544	510	467,576	5,245,594	55.95
20-24	93,245	.00742	692	464,571	4,778,018	51.24
25-29	92,553	.00941	871	460,703	4,313,447	46.61
30-34	91,682	.01356	1,243	455,449	3,852,744	42.02
35-39	90,439	.01746	1,579	448,360	3,397,295	37.56
40-44	88,860	.02006	1,783	440,102	2,948,935	33.19
45-49	87,077	.03245	2,826	428,756	2,508,833	28.81
50-54	84,251	.04599	3,875	412,098	2,080,077	24.69
55-59	80,376	.06680	5,369	389,231	1,667,979	20.75
60-64	75,007	.10120	7,591	356,934	1,278,748	17.05
65-69	67,416	.14206	9,577	314,327	921,814	13.67
70-74	57,839	.22989	13,297	257,162	607,487	10.50
75-79	44,542	.34531*	15,381	184,592	350,325	7.87
80-84	29,161	.51128*	14,909	107,369	165,733	5.68
85-89	14,252	.68729*	9,795	44,443	58,364	4.10
90-94	4,457	.83631*	3,727	10,999	13,921	3.12
95-99	730	.46666*	341	2,922	2,922	4.00
100 and over	....	....	....	....	....	....

* Based on rates of Mississippi urban white females.

Sources: *Sixteenth Census of the United States: 1940*, "Population and Housing, Atlanta, Georgia," (Washington: Government Printing Office, 1942), p. 4; *Vital Statistics of the United States, Supplement: 1939-1940*, Part III (Washington: Government Printing Office, 1943), p. 477; *Vital Statistics of the United States: 1941*, Part II (Washington: Government Printing Office, 1943), pp. 196-197; Vernon Davies and John C. Belcher, *Mississippi Life Tables, by Sex, Race, and Residence: 1940* (Jackson, Mississippi: Mississippi Commission on Hospital Care, 1948), pp. 4-5 and 8-9.

TABLE XVI

ABRIDGED LIFE TABLE FOR NEGRO MALES, ATLANTA, GEORGIA, 1939-1941
(Constructed by Reed-Merrell Method)

Age Interval x to x + n	Number surviving to exact age x out of 100,000 born alive	Probability of a person of exact age x dying within the interval x to x + n	Number dying during year of age	Number of years lived by cohort between age x and age x + n	Total years of life remaining to survivors at age x	Average number of years of life remaining at the beginning of year of age
	l_x	$_nq_x$	d_x	L_x	T_x	e_x
(1)	(2)	(3)	(4)	(5)	(6)	(7)
0-	100,000	.10313	10,313	92,533	4,302,328	43.02
1-4	89,687	.02338	2,097	353,264	4,209,795	46.94
5-9	87,590	.00742	650	436,118	3,856,531	44.03
10-14	86,940	.01055	917	432,761	3,420,413	39.34
15-19	86,023	.02735	2,353	424,967	2,987,652	34.73
20-24	83,670	.05306	4,440	407,929	2,562,685	30.63
25-29	79,230	.07083	5,612	382,612	2,154,756	27.20
30-34	73,618	.09237	6,800	351,348	1,772,144	24.07
35-39	66,818	.10256	6,853	317,323	1,420,796	21.26
40-44	59,965	.14267	8,555	279,035	1,103,473	18.40
45-49	51,410	.18899	9,716	232,902	824,438	16.04
50-54	41,694	.22164	9,241	185,053	591,536	14.19
55-59	32,453	.25291	8,208	141,462	406,483	12.53
60-64	24,245	.32514	7,883	100,689	265,021	10.93
65-69	16,362	.25844	4,229	70,496	164,332	10.04
70-74	12,133	.35638	4,324	49,835	93,836	7.73
75-79	7,809	.52938*	4,134	28,306	44,001	5.63
80-84	3,675	.64803*	2,382	11,779	15,695	4.27
85-89	1,293	.81639*	1,056	3,369	3,916	3.03
90-94	237	.84434*	200	472	547	2.31
95-99	37	.83098*	31	75	75	203
100 and over	6	--------	--------	--------	--------	------

* Based on rates of Mississippi urban Negro males.

Sources: *Sixteenth Census of the United States: 1940*, "Population and Housing, Atlanta, Georgia," (Washington: Government Printing Office, 1942), p. 4; *Vital Statistics of the United States, Supplement: 1939-1940*, Part III (Washington: Government Printing Office, 1943), p. 477; *Vital Statistics of the United States: 1941*, Part II (Washington: Government Printing Office, 1943), pp. 196-197; Vernon Davies and John C. Belcher, *Mississippi Life Tables, by Sex, Race, and Residence: 1940* (Jackson, Mississippi: Mississippi Commission on Hospital Care, 1948), pp. 4-5 and 8-9.

TABLE XVII

ABRIDGED LIFE TABLE FOR NEGRO FEMALES, ATLANTA, GEORGIA, 1939-1941
(Constructed by Reed-Merrell Method)

Age Interval x to x + n	Number surviving to exact age x out of 100,000 born alive	Probability of a person of exact age x dying within the interval x to x + n	Number dying during year of age	Number of years lived by cohort between age x and age x + n	Total years of life remaining to survivors at age x	Average number of years of life remaining at the beginning of year of age
	l_x	$_nq_x$	d_x	L_x	T_x	e_x
(1)	(2)	(3)	(4)	(5)	(6)	(7)
0-	100,000	.08940	8,940	93,527	4,887,100	48.87
1-4	91,060	.01974	1,798	359,542	4,793,573	52.64
5-9	89,262	.01089	972	443,594	4,434,031	49.67
10-14	88,290	.00653	577	440,397	3,990,437	45.20
15-19	87,713	.03245	2,846	431,905	3,550,040	40.47
20-24	84,867	.03255	2,762	417,672	3,118,135	36.74
25-29	82,105	.04882	4,008	400,842	2,700,463	32.89
30-34	78,097	.05605	4,377	379,664	2,299,621	29.45
35-39	73,720	.06224	4,588	357,725	1,919,957	26.04
40-44	69,132	.10464	7,234	328,088	1,562,232	22.60
45-49	61,898	.11395	7,053	292,350	1,234,144	19.94
50-54	54,845	.17503	9,600	250,661	941,794	17.17
55-59	45,245	.20208	9,143	203,168	691,133	15.28
60-64	36,102	.23935	8,641	158,181	487,965	13.52
65-69	27,461	.20605	5,658	122,637	329,784	12.01
70-74	21,803	.28118	6,131	93,749	207,147	9.50
75-79	15,672	.37982*	5,953	63,326	113,398	7.24
80-84	9,719	.55588*	5,403	34,507	50,072	5.15
85-89	4,316	.73301*	3,164	12,753	15,565	3.61
90-94	1,152	.87228*	1,005	2,616	2,812	2.44
95-99	147	.91105*	134	196	196	1.33
100 and over	13	----------	--------	--------	--------	--------

* Based on rates of Mississippi urban Negro females.

Sources: *Sixteenth Census of the United States: 1940*, "Population and Housing, Atlanta, Georgia," (Washington: Government Printing Office, 1942), p. 4; *Vital Statistics of the United States, Supplement: 1939-1940*, Part III (Washington: Government Printing Office, 1943), p. 477; *Vital Statistics of the United States: 1941*, Part II (Washington: Government Printing Office, 1943), pp. 196-197; Vernon Davies and John C. Belcher, *Mississippi Life Tables, by Sex, Race, and Residence: 1940* (Jackson, Mississippi: Mississippi Commission on Hospital Care, 1948), pp. 4-5 and 8-9.

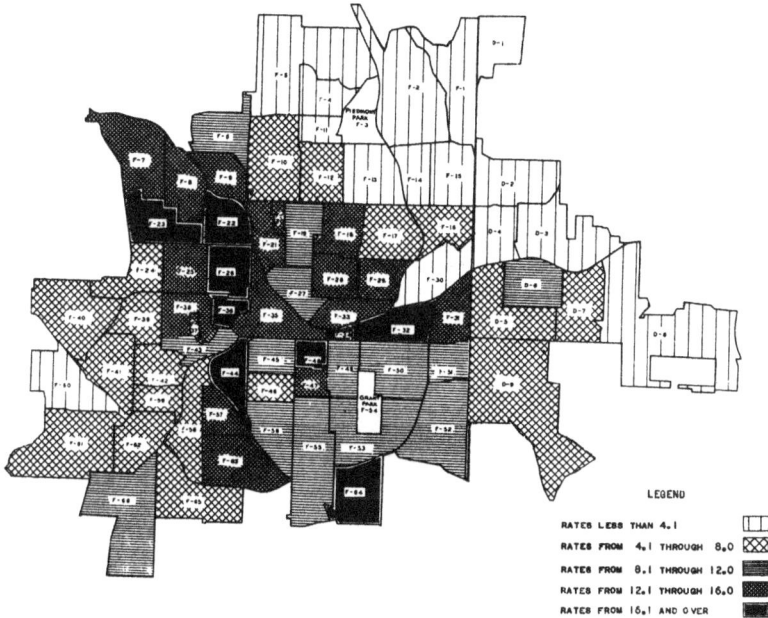

INFANT MORTALITY PER 1000 POPULATION
BY CENSUS TRACTS
CITY OF ATLANTA
FOR AN EIGHT YEAR PERIOD, 1928-1936

LEGEND

RATES LESS THAN 4.1
RATES FROM 4.1 THROUGH 8.0
RATES FROM 8.1 THROUGH 12.0
RATES FROM 12.1 THROUGH 16.0
RATES FROM 16.1 AND OVER

NOTE: POPULATION OF D-1 TOO SMALL TO GIVE SIGNIFICANT RATIO.
SOURCE: DEPT. OF HEALTH, CITY OF ATLANTA.

FIGURE 60.   Infant mortality rate per 1000 population, city
of Atlanta, by census tracts, 1928-1936. (Reproduced from WPA
of Georgia official project 465-34-3-4.)

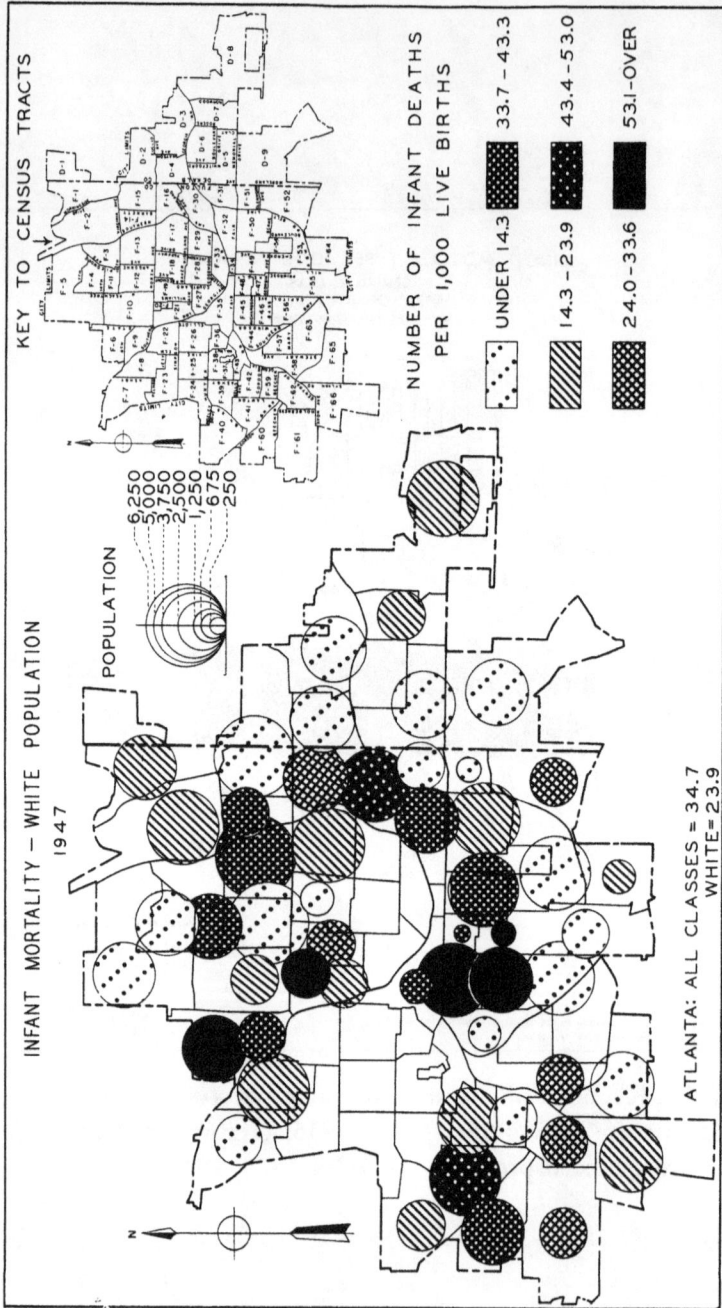

FIGURE 61. Infant mortality rates of the white population of Atlanta, by census tracts, 1947.

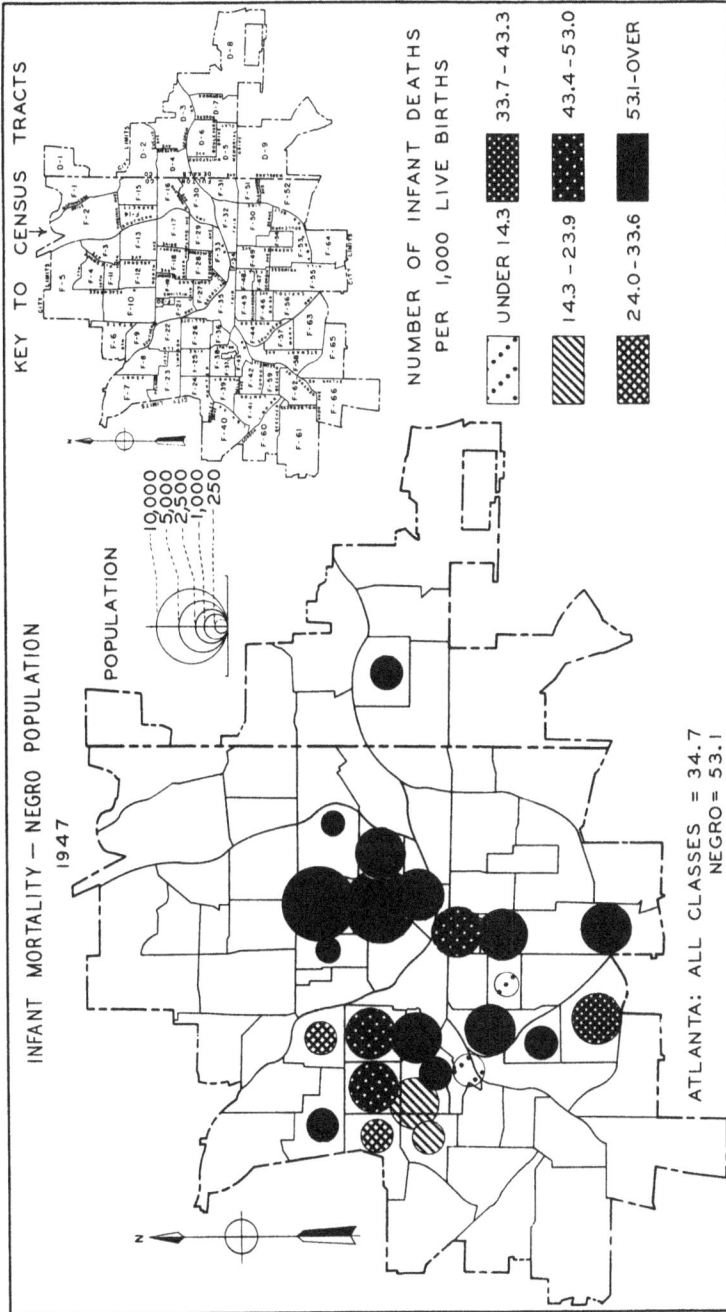

FIGURE 62. Infant mortality rates of the Negro population of Atlanta, by census tracts, 1947.

nearly a third die from the same disease in New Orleans. Nephritis is by far a greater cause of death in Atlanta than in the other populations studied. Even though the above differences have been noted, the differences are very slight; and since the data are for one year only, it is likely that there might be some chance variations.

Seasonal Variations of Mortality in Atlanta

Linder and Grove present data that show at the present time (1940) in the United States the crude death rates reach a maximum in the winter months and decline rather consistently until they reach a low in August and/or September.[8] The total number of deaths in Atlanta follows generally this same pattern.

Trends in Mortality in Atlanta

Crude death rates. In Table XVIII the crude death rates for the population of Atlanta are presented by race from 1896 to 1947; the deaths since 1930 have been adjusted to residents only. There has been a gradual but not consistent decline in the death rate for both races for the last fifty years. It should be pointed out, however, that the very low death rates since 1940 cannot long continue; for even with a crude death rate of 10, the average expectation of life would be 100 years. Now it is known that the average expectation of life in Atlanta is below 70 years, and the only reason such crude death rates as 8.7 exist in 1947 is that the average age of the population of Atlanta is rising. Before too many years the crude death rate of the Atlanta population will again rise and no one should become alarmed about such an increase; it is inevitable unless a "fountain of youth" is discovered. Even at the present time, based on life tables calculated in this study, the stationary death rates for the Atlanta population are as follows: white males, 16.8; white females, 15.0; Negro males, 23.2; and Negro females, 20.5.

Expectation of life. Since, as far as the writer has been able to discover, no life tables have been previously constructed for Atlanta, it is impossible to show trends in life expectancy; besides, reliable data necessary for life table construction have been available only for recent years for the city of Atlanta.

Infant mortality. In Table V, Appendix, are presented infant

8. *Op. cit.,* p. 125.

TABLE XVIII

CRUDE DEATH RATES IN ATLANTA, BY RACE, 1896-1947

Year	White	Negro	Total
1896	18.4	33.4	24.0
1897	15.3	27.8	20.4
1898	15.3	27.8	20.3
1899	18.6	30.9	23.7
1900	15.9	25.1	19.7
1901	14.3	29.0	20.5
1902	17.3	28.6	21.7
1903	13.5	25.0	17.7
1904	13.9	29.4	20.0
1905	14.2	27.5	19.1
1906	14.2	28.6	19.2
1907	14.4	26.7	18.8
1908	10.6	21.1	14.9
1909	11.1	20.1	14.2
1910	14.0	25.2	17.7
1911	14.1	28.1	18.8
1912	13.3	25.8	17.4
1913	12.0	27.7	17.2
1914	13.6	24.8	17.3
1915	11.9	24.1	15.9
1916	11.9	23.9	15.8
1917	13.6	24.0	16.9
1918	15.6	27.0	19.2
1919	13.5	21.5	16.1
1920	14.7	23.8	17.6
1921	12.5	20.6	15.5
1922	12.9	23.9	16.4
1923	13.7	27.0	18.0
1924	13.4	28.5	18.3
1925	12.6	25.1	16.7
1926	11.9	25.3	16.3
1927	11.9	22.4	15.3
1928	12.5	23.7	16.2
1929	12.1	24.2	16.1
1930	9.3	22.4	13.5

1931	9.3	20.7	13.1
1932	8.8	18.2	11.9
1933	8.7	19.4	12.2
1934	9.6	21.2	13.5
1935	9.3	19.8	12.9
1936	10.2	22.3	14.3
1937	9.2	20.2	12.5
1938	9.2	18.6	12.4
1939	8.5	18.0	11.8
1940	8.2	17.9	11.6
1941	7.5	17.8	11.1
1942	7.7	15.2	10.3
1943	8.4	15.4	10.8
1944	7.5	13.5	9.6
1945	8.1	14.1	10.2
1946	7.2	12.6	9.1
1947	6.9	12.1	8.7

Note: Rates in years 1930-1947 inclusive adjusted to resident only.
Source: J. F. Hackney, *City of Atlanta Health Department, Annual Report 1947* (Atlanta: City of Atlanta, Department of Health, 1948), p. 16.

mortality rates (per 1,000 live births), by race, for cities of 100,000 or larger for the United States and for Georgia, Louisiana, Tennessee, and Texas. As will be seen from this table, in 1928 Atlanta had a higher infant mortality rate than the large cities in Louisiana or Tennessee and a much higher rate than the national average of large cities (100,000 or more). By 1940, although Atlanta was still well above the national average for "all races" and much above the average for "other races," the infant mortality rate was lower for all classifications (except "all other races" in Tennessee) than New Orleans, the large cities of Tennessee, and the large cities of Texas. In fact, the infant mortality rate for the Atlanta white population was lower than the average of the white population of all cities over 100,000 in the nation; Atlanta's rate of 32.1 was 4 points lower than the 36.1 recorded for the white population of large cities throughout the nation. For "all races" Atlanta passed New Orleans in reducing infant mortality rates, never again to be overtaken, in 1935; was ahead of Tennessee cities from 1929 to 1940, with the exception of

1939; and led the Texas cities every year from 1932 on, excepting 1938.

In order to bring the study of mortality a little more up to date, Table W, Appendix, was prepared. This table presents infant deaths per 1,000 live births, by color, for cities of the United States of 100,000 or more and the cities of Atlanta, Dallas, Nashville, and New Orleans from 1941 through 1946. The same general trends are noted as have been previously pointed out although they are not quite so consistent. It should be noted that the infant mortality rates for all classes of the population and the white population of Atlanta are lower than the national average. Also by 1946, the white infant mortality rate was considerably below the national average and the nonwhite rate was approaching the average. Of the southern cities only New Orleans in 1946 had a lower nonwhite infant mortality rate than did Atlanta.

The trend of infant mortality rates in Atlanta is presented in Table X, Appendix. It should be noted that by 1947 the infant mortality rate of the white population was more than 50 per cent less than the rate in 1930; the infant mortality rate for Negroes had been reduced by a still greater amount during the same period. There is a tremendous differential between whites and Negroes for each year during the period. Although the population of Atlanta is only one-third Negro, in every year except two during the 17-year period, there were more Negro infant deaths than white infant deaths.[9] On the average, the infant mortality rate of the Negro population is nearly twice as great as that of the white population.

9. J. F. Hackney, *City of Atlanta Health Department, Annual Report: 1947* (Atlanta, Georgia: City of Atlanta, Department of Health, 1948), p. 18.

CHAPTER XIII

MIGRATION

THIS CHAPTER IS DEVOTED TO THE STUDY OF MIGRATION IN ORDER to determine the amount of movement of people into the city of Atlanta, the source of those people, and the selectivity of that movement as to age, sex, and race. The analysis is limited to data for 1940.

Migration has been important throughout human history but from the point of view of this study, it is important for the following reasons: (1) Movement of people *per se* is extremely significant socially; (2) other demographic phenomena are enormously affected by stability or lack of stability of residence of the population; (3) migration puts a strain upon individual personalities who are required to adjust to both the breaking of old ties and habits and the forming of new ones (this applies to migrants as well as nonmigrants); (4) migration affects societal institutions which are left unsupported or which are over-burdened; and (5) there is a close relationship between migration and the growth and replacement of urban populations. The latter is particularly important, for as is well known, the rural areas of our country grow and more than repopulate themselves by natural increase; that is, by an excess of births over deaths; while the urban and industrial areas which do not even repopulate themselves, depend upon migration for growth and even for maintenance of existing population.

In 1940 about 18 per cent of the native population of Atlanta had been born in states other than Georgia; however, most of these people had come to Atlanta from other southern states and particularly those adjacent to Georgia. One might say then that Atlanta does not qualify as a cosmopolitan city but can be classified as a provincial city. The extent of migration to Atlanta from other areas of Georgia cannot be exactly determined in this manner. It is known, however, that there is considerable migration into the city, particularly during the ages 15 to 50.

To show the source of the Atlanta population and to provide a comparison with other southern cities, Figures 63 through 70 were prepared. The most outstanding characteristics noted here are the similarities; that is, all the southern cities studied are

179

similar in that they have recruited their populations largely from adjacent areas. This is in striking contrast to many American cities; e.g., Los Angeles, which recruits its population throughout the United States.[1]

By using these figures to compare the white population with the nonwhite population, it is noted that the nonwhite migrant usually travels much shorter distances than the white migrants to southern cities. This, too, sharply contrasts with the movement of nonwhites to northern cities; northern cities receive their Negro populations from long distances and particularly the "black belt" of the South.[2] For example, in 1930 there were more Negroes in Chicago who were born in Mississippi than there were Negroes in New Orleans who were born in Mississippi.[3]

Immigration to Atlanta of persons born in foreign countries has been relatively unimportant, for in 1940 there were only 4,293 foreign-born white persons in Atlanta.[4] About one-fourth of these people was born in Russia (U.S.S.R.); 440 came from Greece; 386 came from Germany; 360 were born in Poland; 318 came from England and Wales; and the remainder came largely from Europe, only 290 coming from Asia.[5]

In order to determine whether the migration processes were selective of age, sex, and race Figures 71 and 72 were prepared. Figure 71 shows the percentages of the native white population of Georgia who resided in Atlanta, by age and sex, 1940. Figure 72 shows the same phenomena for the Negro population. If the age distribution of the Atlanta population were a result only of the effects of births and deaths, the lines would hover around the heavy line between 9 and 10 per cent.

It is noted that the Negro population is concentrated in Atlanta during the productive years of life to a much greater extent than the white population. Females of both races concentrate in the city to a much greater extent than males; the white female remains in the city in greater proportions much longer

1. T. Lynn Smith, *Population Analysis* (New York: McGraw-Hill Book Company, Inc., 1948), p. 330.
2. *Ibid.*, pp. 335-337.
3. *Ibid.*, pp. 336-337.
4. *Sixteenth Census of the United States: 1940*, "Population and Housing, Atlanta, Georgia," (Washington: Government Printing Office, 1942), p. 19.
5. *Ibid*, p. 19.

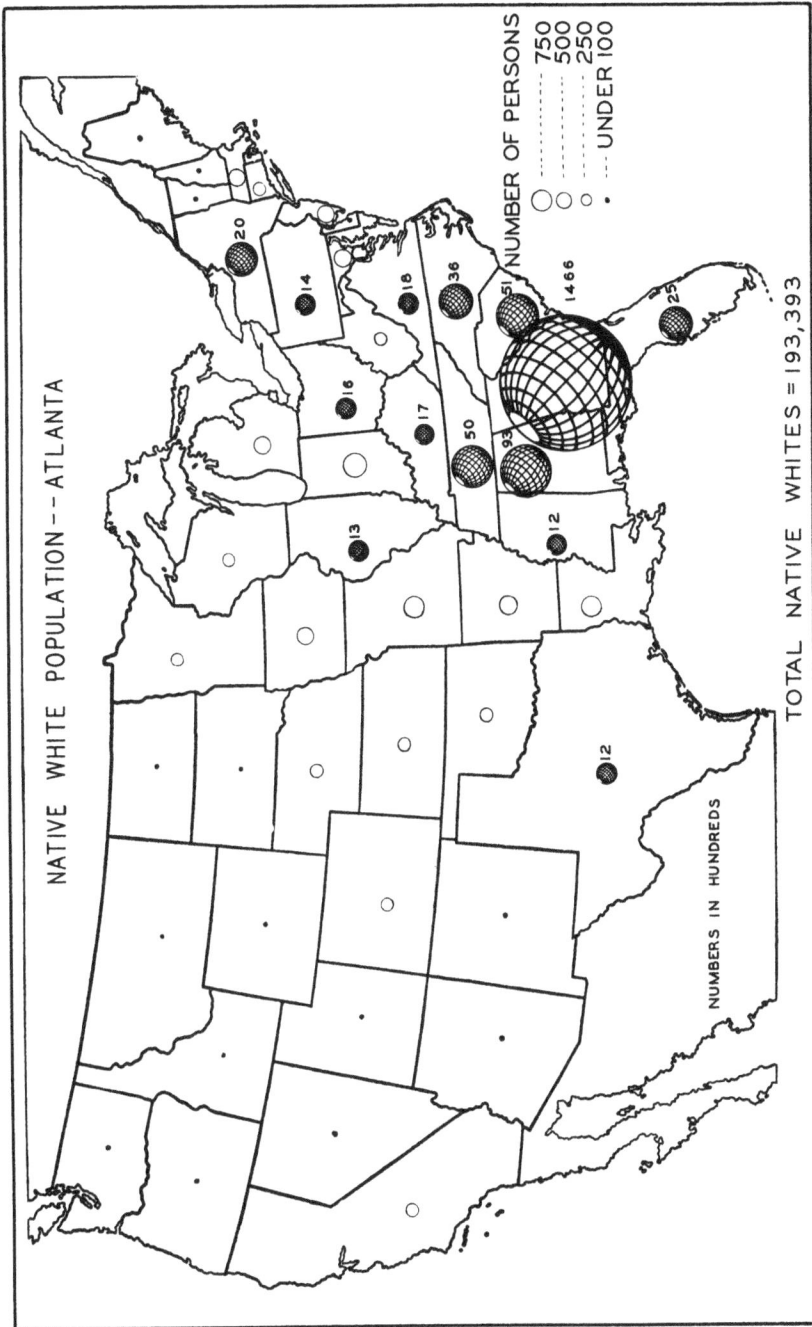

FIGURE 63. State of birth of the native white population of Atlanta, 1940.

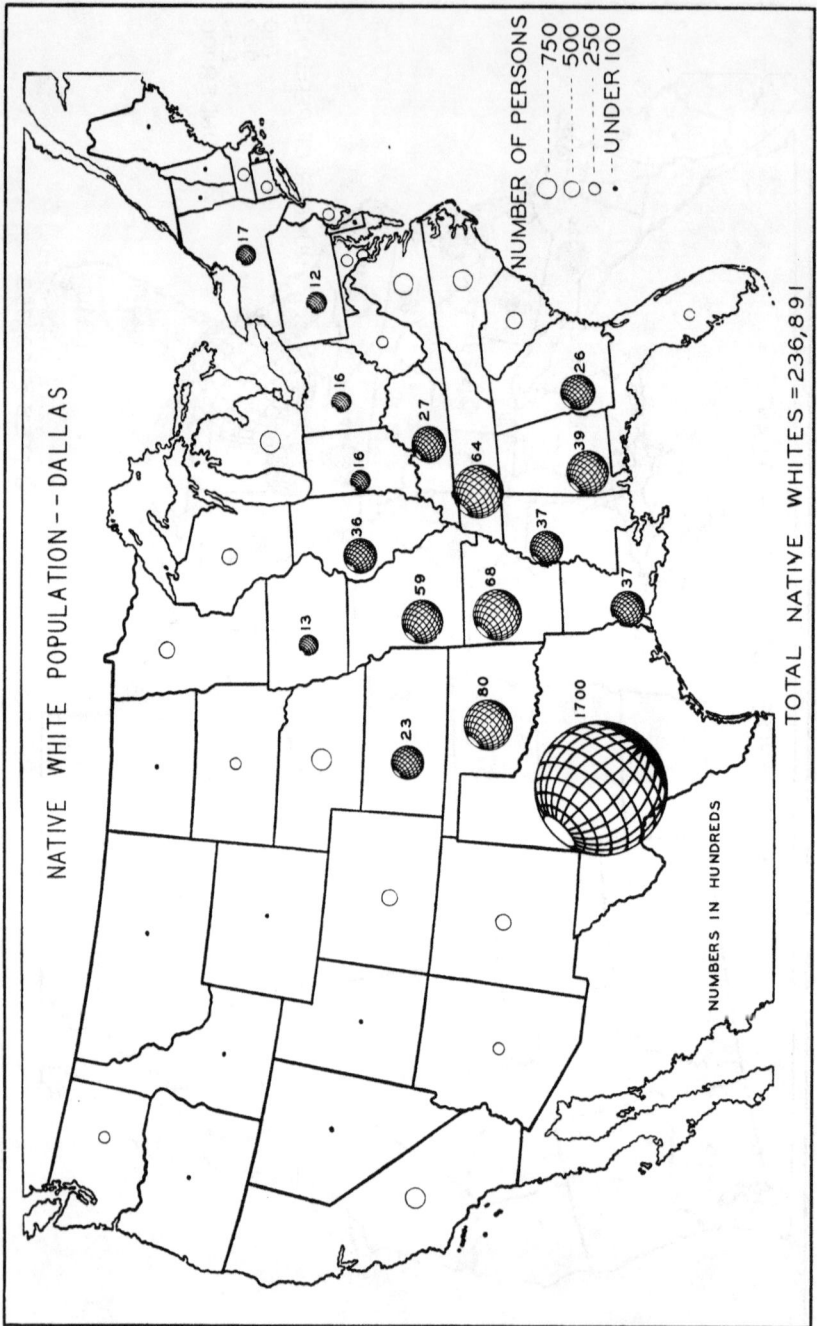

FIGURE 64.   State of birth of the native white population of Dallas, 1940.

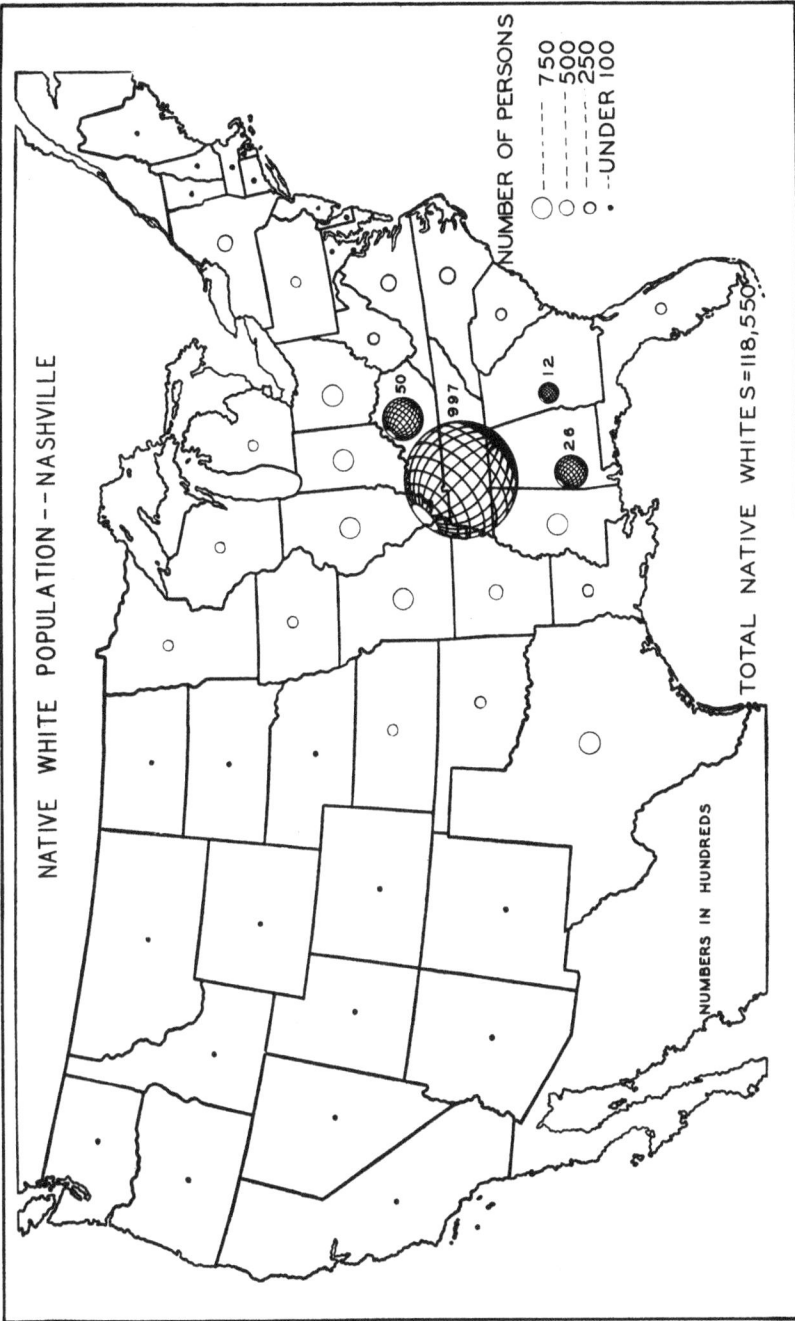

FIGURE 65. State of birth of the native white population of Nashville, 1940.

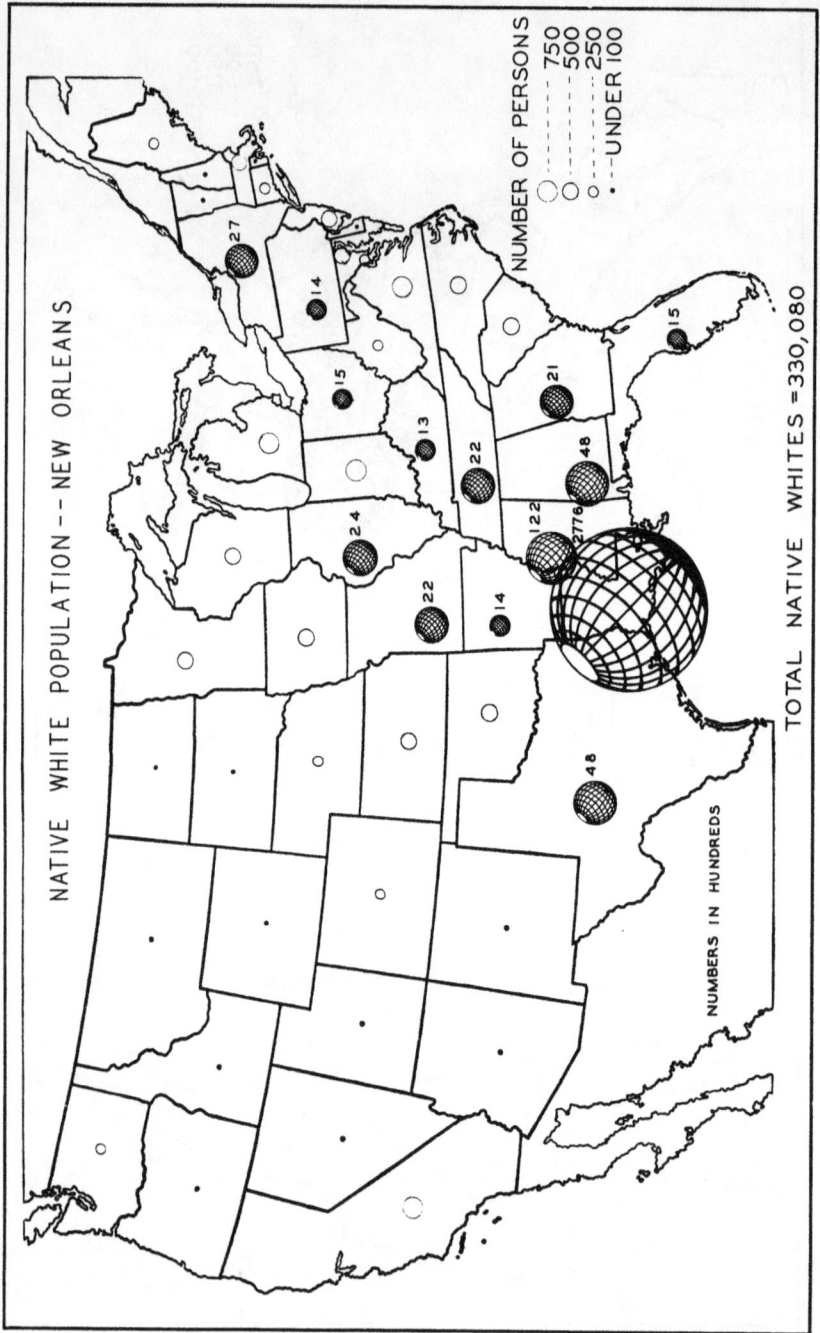

FIGURE 66. State of birth of the native white population of New Orleans, 1940.

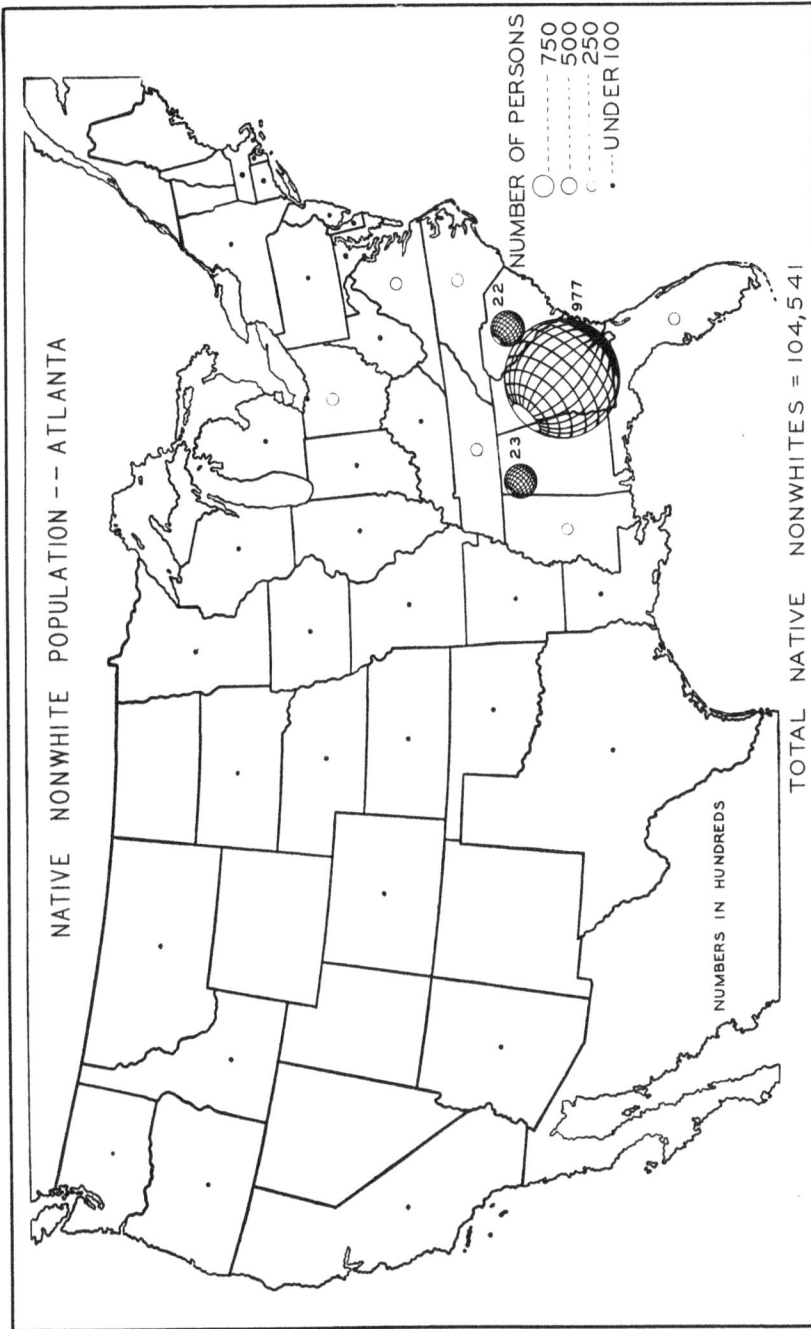

FIGURE 67. State of birth of the native nonwhite population of Atlanta, 1940.

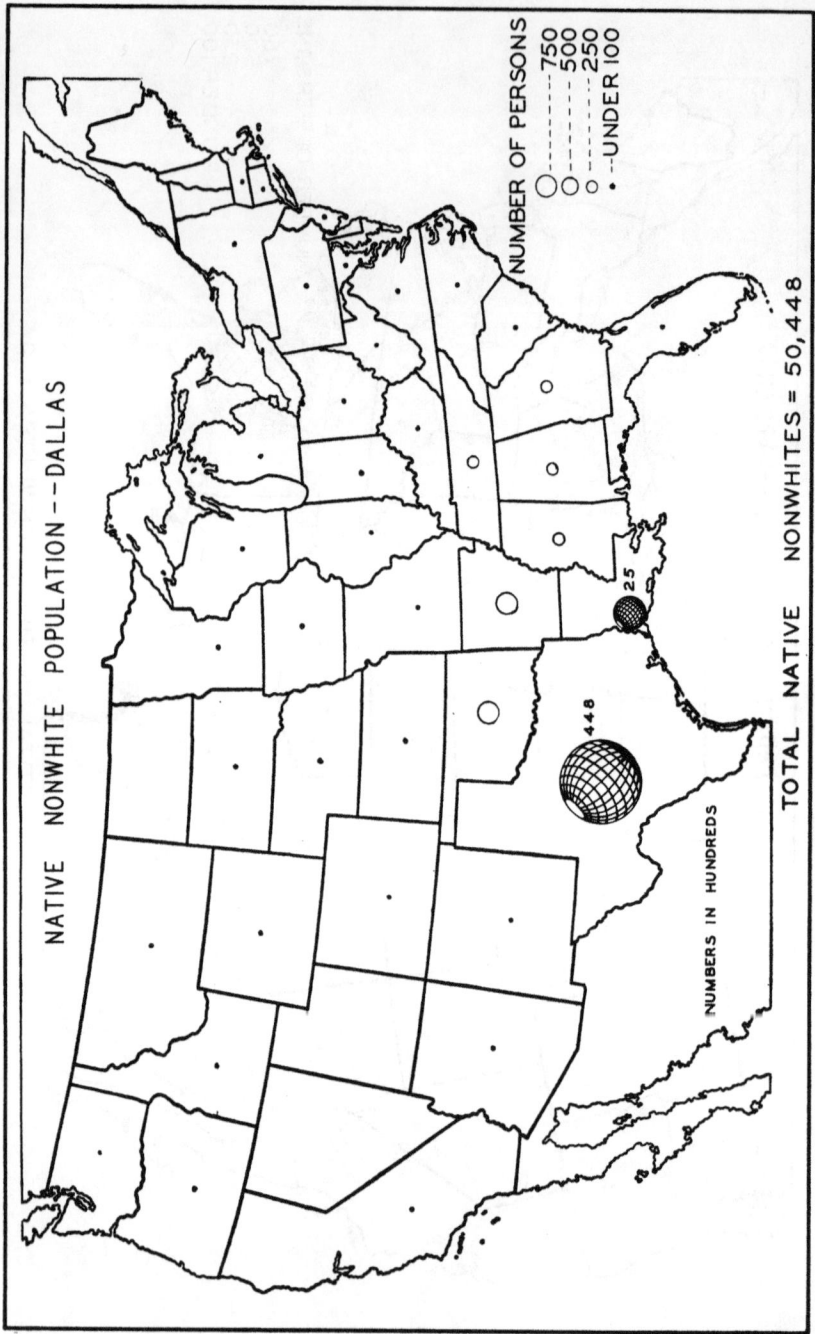

FIGURE 68. State of birth of the native nonwhite population of Dallas, 1940.

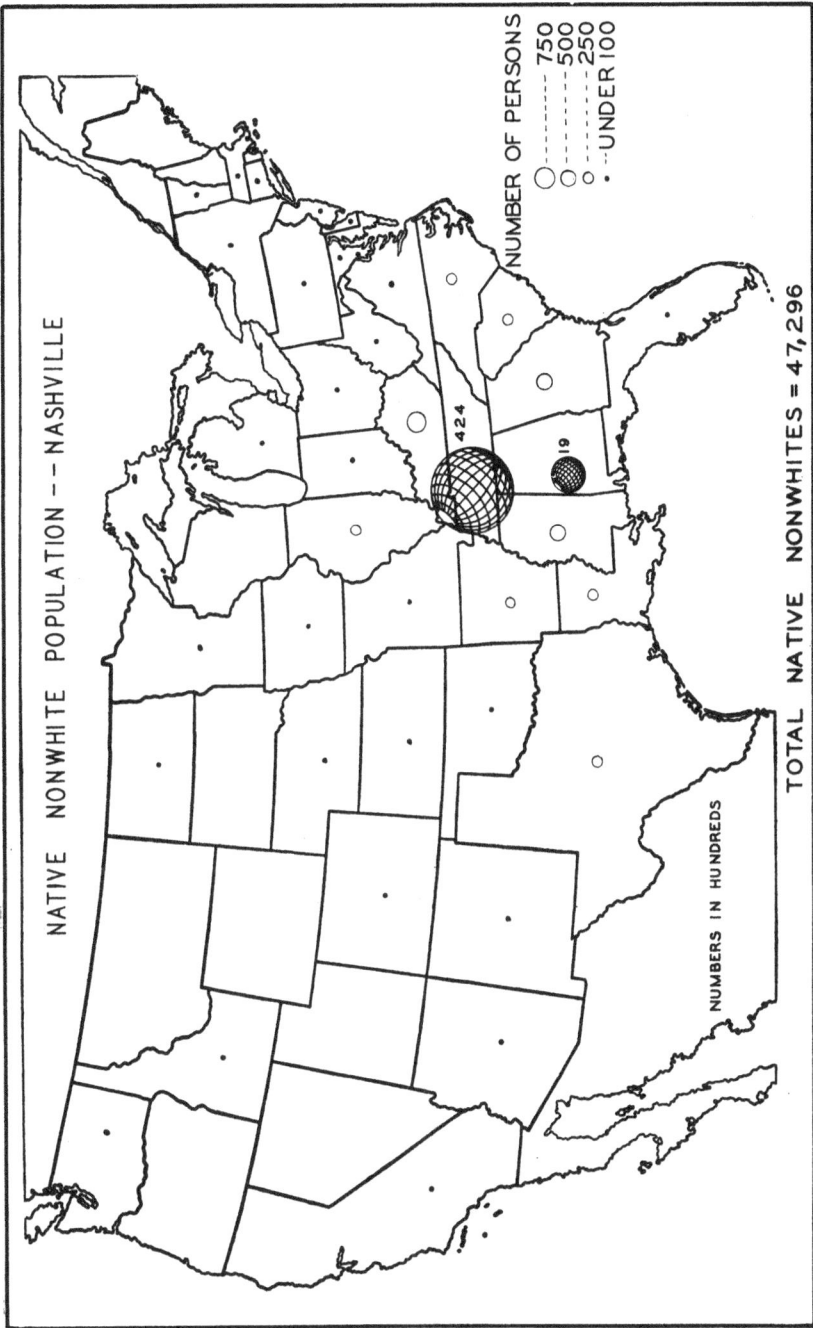

FIGURE 69. State of birth of the native nonwhite population of Nashville, 1940.

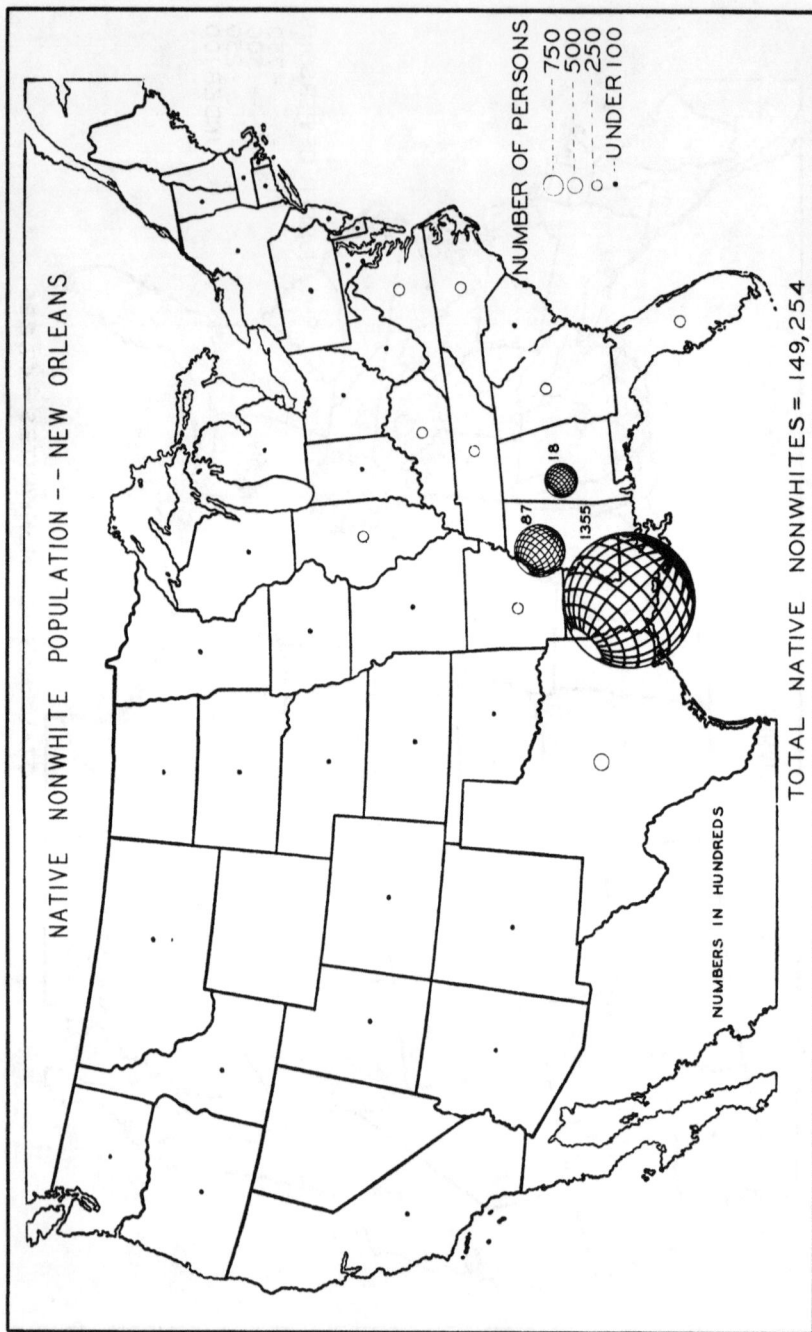

FIGURE 70.   State of birth of the native nonwhite population of New Orleans, 1940.

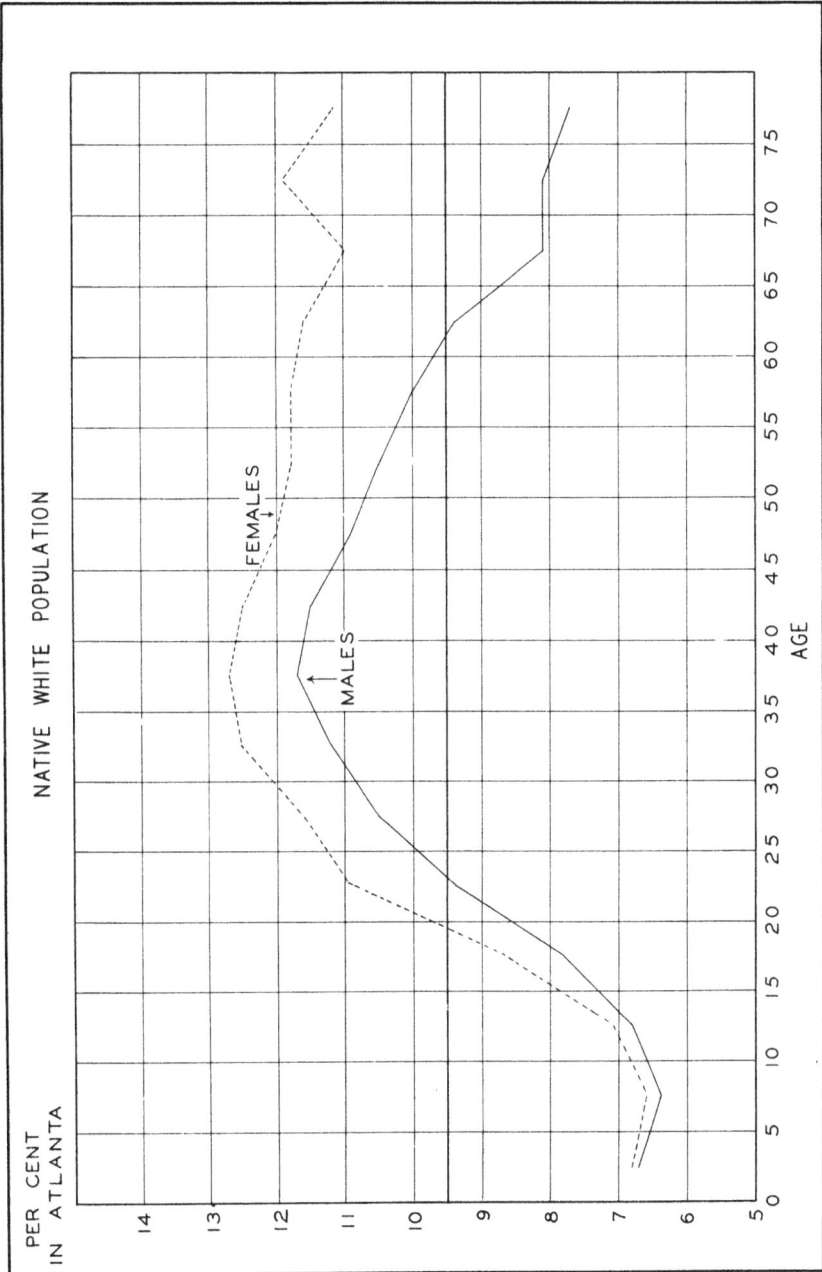

FIGURE 71. Percentages of the native white population of
Georgia residing in Atlanta, by age and sex, 1940.

189

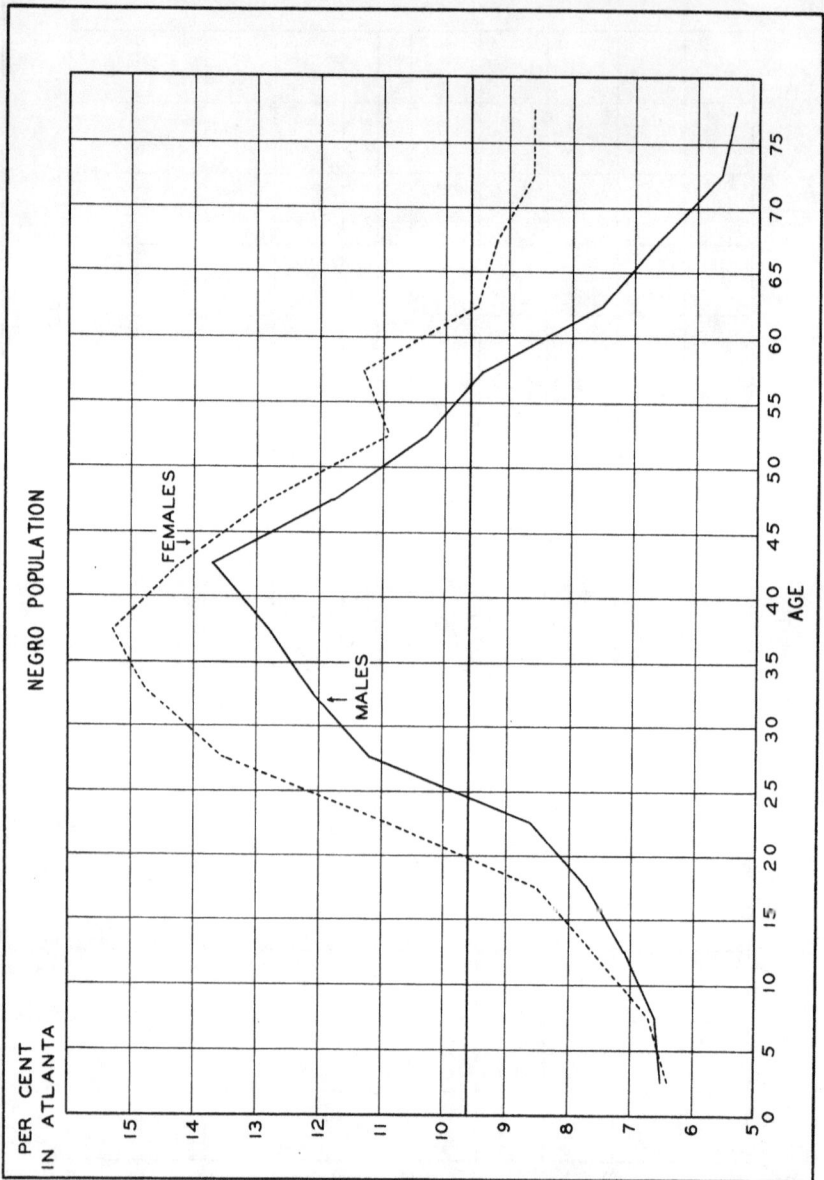

FIGURE 72. Percentages of the Negro population of Georgia residing in Atlanta, by age and sex, 1940.

than the Negro female. Much of this is probably due to longer expectation of life of the white race.

Again it should be pointed out that the only way such an age profile as shown here could possibly come about would be through migration, and these data agree generally with other data that the processes of migration cause a concentration of persons in the productive ages in the cities and a shortage of persons in the very young ages.[6]

It has not been possible because of limitations of the data to show migration trends within the city itself (that between census tracts). As pointed out previously, Atlanta has been a tract city only since 1940 (although there was some retabulation of the 1930 data). Significant migration trends within the city cannot therefore be determined. It is suggested that such information, if and when available will be valuable when Atlanta has been a census tract city for one additional census or possibly for two additional enumerations.

6. Noel P. Gist and L. A. Halbert, *Urban Society* (New York: Thomas Y. Crowell Company, 1947), pp. 263-299.

CHAPTER XIV

GROWTH OF POPULATION

THERE ARE TWO BASIC PARTS OF THE STUDY OF POPULATION growth: the study and analysis of what has already taken place and the speculation of what will occur in the future (forecasts). This study is limited almost entirely to the analysis of data relating to that which has already occurred. To trace the growth and to study the rate of growth of the total population of Atlanta from the time it first became a city (according to today's criteria) in 1850 to the present time; to study the growth and rate of growth of the white and the Negro population in order to determine how each has contributed to the over-all growth of the city; and to compare the rate of growth of Atlanta's populations (total, white, and Negro) with the rate of growth of the populations of other large southern cities are the aims of this chapter.

Many of the important problems facing the world today have arisen out of the differential rates of growth of various nations and "races." Much of the writing in regard to "population problems" has dealt with the growth of population although in many cases the authors were trying to make the data "fit" some mathematical law. The study of the growth of the population of Atlanta is an important part of this demographic analysis; however, one must keep in mind that there are only three basic factors which determine the number of persons at a given place at a given time; i.e., fertility, mortality, and migration. Any other factors (such as war; climate; level of living; the price of milk, eggs, or wheat; family) must influence the increase or decrease of a population by affecting the three basic factors mentioned above.

Atlanta reached the 2,500 mark for the first time in 1850 when her enumerated population was 2,572.[1] At the last census before the Civil War, taken in 1860, the population had grown nearly fourfold to 9,554. In the decade from 1860 to 1870, in spite of a war and a fire in 1864 which destroyed 700 of the 1,000 houses, Atlanta more than doubled its population; and when the census

---

1. *Seventh Census of the United States: 1850* (Washington: Robert Armstrong, Public Printer, 1853), p. 366.

was taken in 1870, 21,789 persons were enumerated.[2] The growth of the city was steady and by 1900 the total population was 89,872. Although the rate of growth in the twentieth century has not been quite so rapid as some decades of the nineteenth, by April 1, 1940, the Atlanta population had grown to 302,288 persons.[3] By July 1, 1948, it was estimated that the total population of Atlanta was 352,000.[4]

POPULATION GROWTH IN ATLANTA AND OTHER SOUTHERN CITIES

The growth of the population of Atlanta up to 1940 is presented in Figures 73 to 75 in a manner in which its rate of growth may be compared to other large southern cities.

All classes. The rate of growth of New Orleans has been the least rapid of the cities studied although it was the largest of the four cities in 1850 and still remained so in 1940. Dallas has grown most rapidly; this is especially true for the period of 1880 to 1890. For all classes the rate of growth appears to be in the following order: (1) Dallas, (2) Atlanta, (3) Nashville, and (4) New Orleans.

In the latter years of the ninteenth century the population of Atlanta increased more rapidly than that of Nashville, and around 1896 the Atlanta population equaled that of Nashville. Likewise, Dallas equaled and pulled ahead of Nashville about 1915. While Atlanta's growth has not been so spectacular as that of Dallas, it has been fairly steady with no significant spurts or plateaus. If the rate of growth for the years 1920-1940, for the four cities, is approximately maintained in the future, it appears likely that both Atlanta and Dallas may reach and even forge ahead of New Orleans, although no prediction is offered as

2. Atlanta City Council and the Atlanta Chamber of Commerce, *Handbook of the City of Atlanta* (Atlanta, Georgia: The Southern Industrial Publishing Co., n.d.), p. 5.
3. *Sixteenth Census of the United States: 1940*, "Population and Housing, Atlanta, Georgia," (Washington: Government Printing Office, 1942), p. 4.
4. W. E. Uzzell, *Estimated Population of Georgia, July 1, 1948* (Atlanta, Georgia: Georgia Department of Public Health, Division of Vital Statistics, 1949), p. 1.

to when these events might occur.[5]

Whites. For whites, Dallas is first in rate of growth; since 1910 Atlanta and Nashville have grown at about the same rate, and New Orleans whites have grown least rapidly.

Negroes. The Negroes of Dallas and Atlanta have grown at approximately equal rates; New Orleans ranks third and Nashville fourth in rate of growth of the Negro population. In 1890, the Negro population of Nashville was approximately the same as that of Atlanta; that is, just under 30,000. By 1940, Atlanta had more than 100,000 Negroes, whereas Nashville had about 45,000.

THE CAUSES OF ATLANTA'S GROWTH

It has been pointed out previously that the growth of Atlanta has been due largely to the migration of large numbers of persons into the city. Its growth has not been primarily the result of natural increase. It would be of interest to know the factors involved in producing the "attractive force" of cities and of that found in Atlanta particularly. It has been impossible to identify exactly the factors responsible for the growth of the city of Atlanta but what appear to be contributing developments can be mentioned.

By a process of gross over-simplification, the basic factors in the growth of the city of Atlanta might be listed as follows: (1) Atlanta is located at the intersection of the transportation systems of Georgia and much of the Southeast; (2) as a consequence of this strategic location, trade and commerce have flourished; (3) as a further consequence, owners, general managers, branch and regional offices have tended to locate in Atlanta in order to be near each other; (4) the movement of the capital of the state to Atlanta in 1868 (officially in 1877) added considerable impetus to its growth; (5) a great concentration of business, industry, institutions, and people has come about in order to provide goods and services for those persons congregated

5. This statement in no way implies that in 1950, or any other future date for that matter, Atlanta will be the largest city in the South. It is entirely within the range of possibilities that the 1950 census will show that Atlanta has fallen from the second largest southern city to the third, fourth, or even fifth city in the South. This latter eventuality depends to a great extent on the agressive annexation procedures of other southern cities in comparison to the attitudes toward annexation which have existed in the Atlanta area during recent years.

in Atlanta as a result of the aforementioned; and (6) as the city has overflowed its political boundaries, more and more territory has been annexed, and thus annexation has been a factor in the growth of the city.

Of the foregoing factors, the location of Atlanta seems of utmost importance. It lies near the foothills of the Blue Ridge mountains (elevation 1,050 feet above sea level) on a ridge which divides the watersheds of the Atlantic Ocean and the Gulf of Mexico. Furthermore, it is about midway on an airline route from Chicago to Miami; and in addition, although not unique in this position, is somewhat centrally located among the southern states south of Kentucky and east of the Mississippi River.

This strategic location of Atlanta was recognized early. In 1845 (Atlanta had only one railroad and a population of 100 persons), the eminent South Carolinian, John C. Calhoun, made the following remarks in the Southwestern Convention at Memphis:

> What, then, is needed to complete a cheap, speedy and safe intercourse between the valley of the Mississippi and the Southern Atlantic coast is a good system of railroads. For this purpose the nature of the intervening country affords extraordinary advantages. Such is its formation from the course of the Tennessee, Cumberland and Alabama riviers, and the termination of the various chains of mountains, that all the railroads which have been projected or commenced, although each has looked only to its local interest, must necessarily unite at a point in DeKalb county, in the State of Georgia, called Atlanta, not far from the village of Decatur, so as to constitute one entire system of roads, having a mutual interest each in the other, instead of isolated rival roads.[6]

Some of the fundamental factors in the growth of many cities must not be overlooked. The coming of the industrial revolution (including steam power and the factory system) has been basic in much city growth; closely associated has been the great improvement in production of agricultural products. Furthermore, the most rapid growth of Atlanta has taken place during a period characterized by rapid urbanization in Western Europe, the

6. Wallace P. Reed, editor, *History of Atlanta, Georgia* (Atlanta, Georgia: Byrd Printing Company, 1902), p. 19.

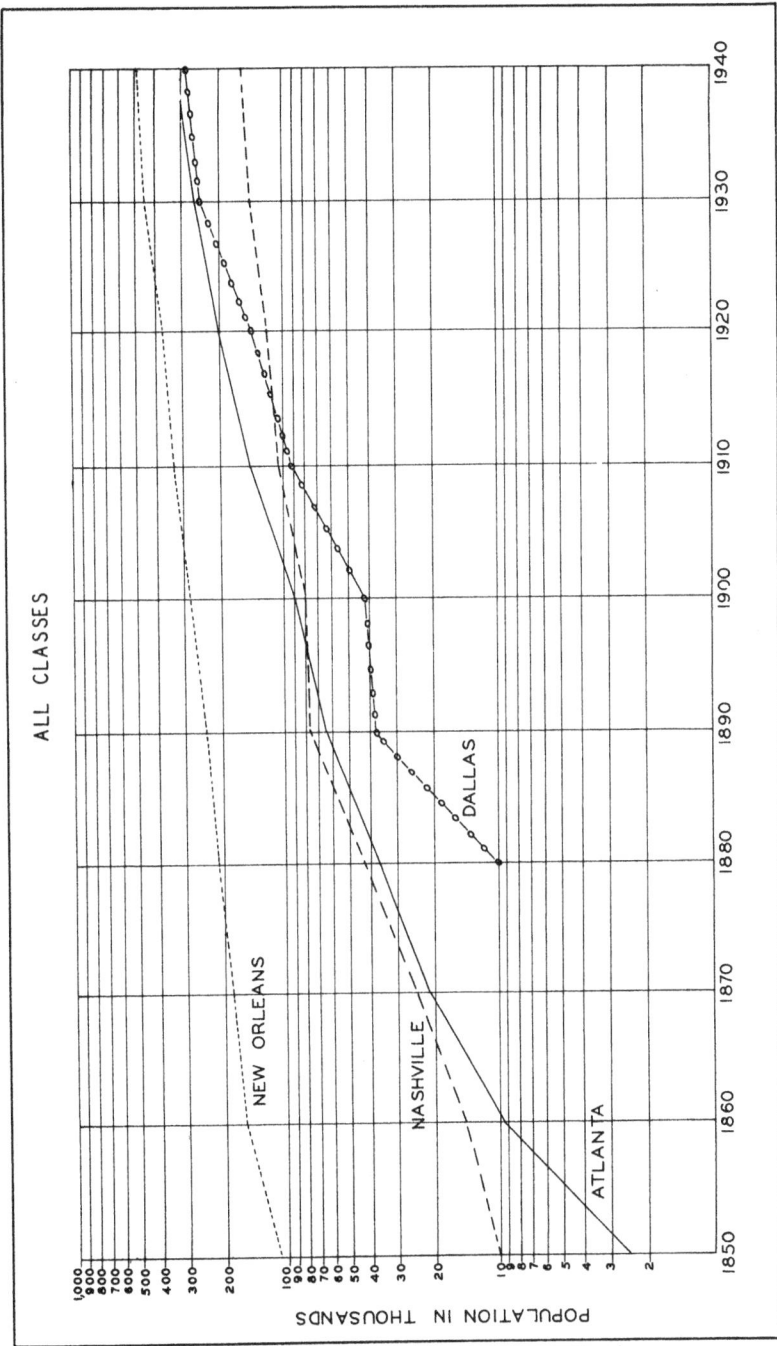

FIGURE 73. The growth of the total population in selected southern cities, 1850 to 1940.

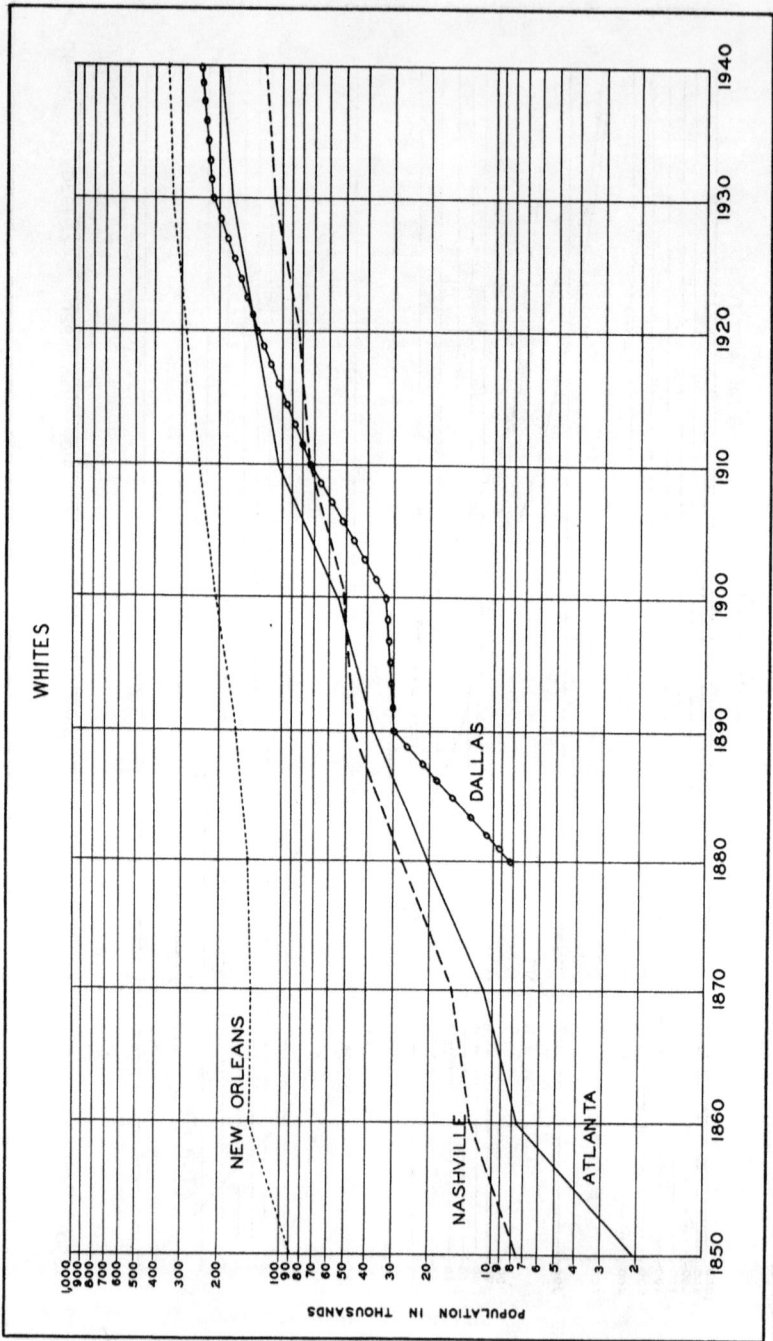

FIGURE 74. The growth of the white population in selected southern cities, 1850 to 1940.

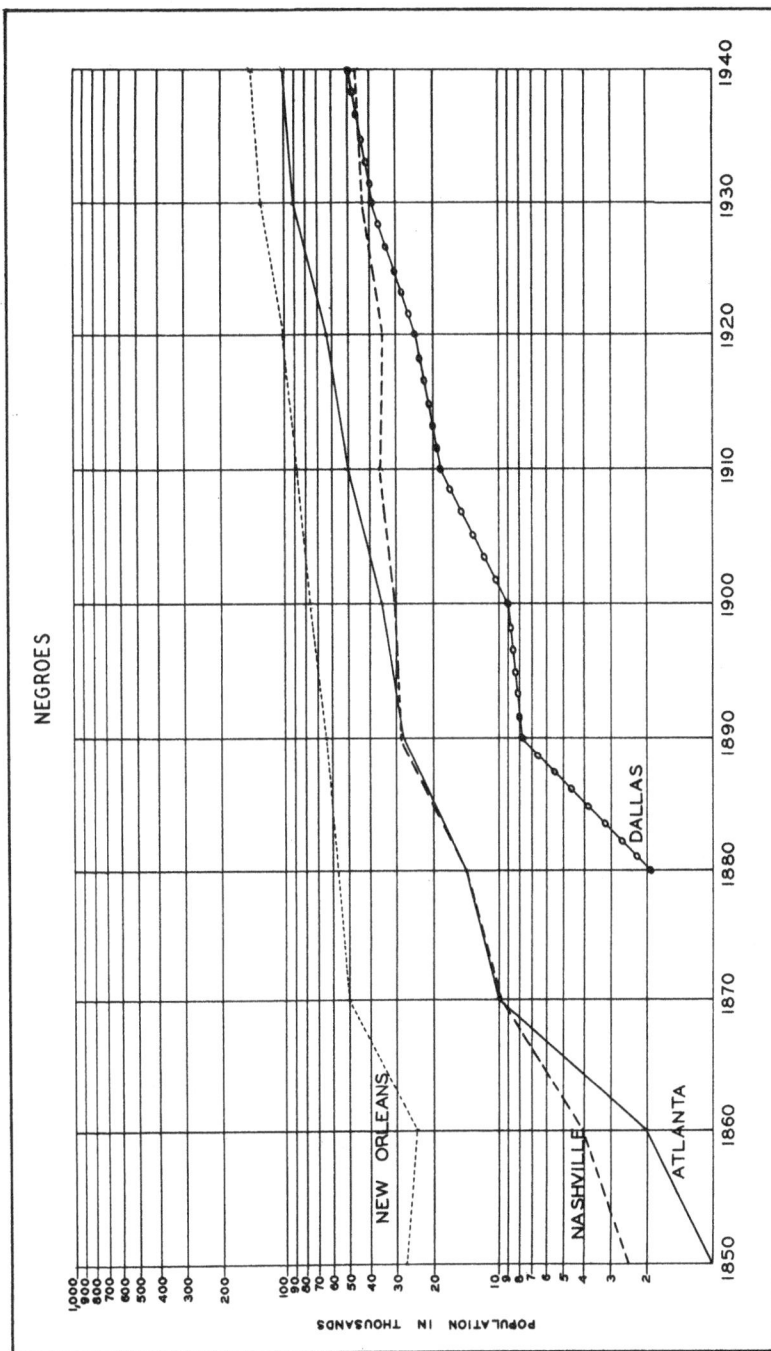

FIGURE 75. The growth of the Negro population in selected southern cities, 1850 to 1940.

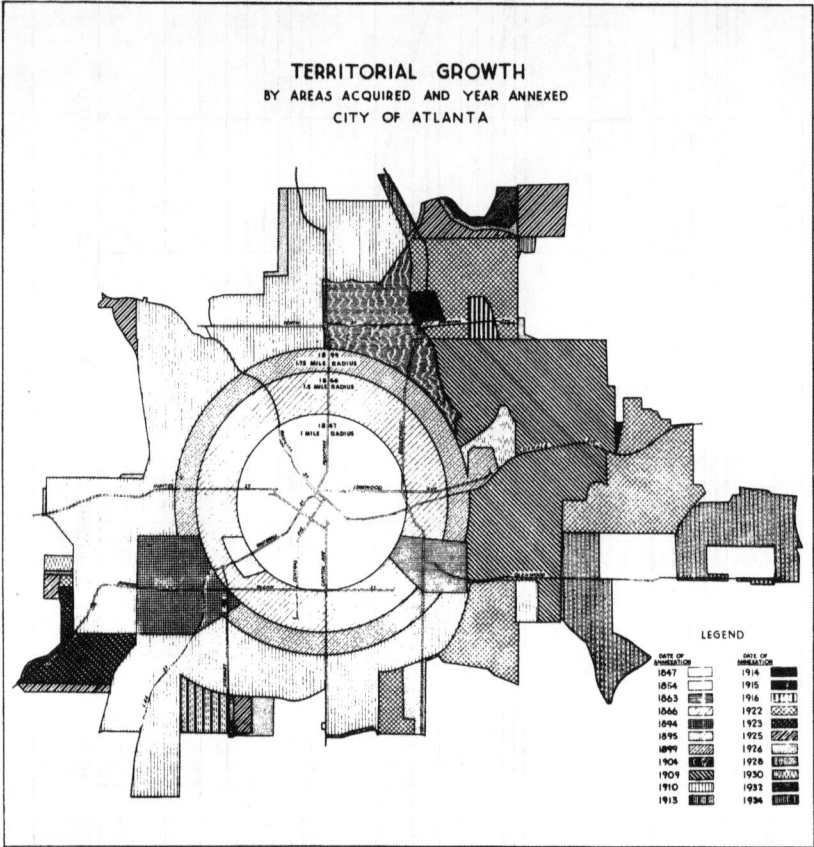

FIGURE 76. Territorial growth of the city of Atlanta, by areas acquired and year annexed. (Reproduced from WPA of Georgia official project 465-34-3-4.)

British Isles, and the United States. In the judgment of the writer, had these events not occurred, the growth of Atlanta would probably have not come about; however, those factors previously pointed out seem to be more directly related to Atlanta's growth.

Territorial Growth of Atlanta

Closely associated with the growth of population of the city of Atlanta is the territorial growth of the city. Figure 76 has been reproduced to afford a clear picture of this territorial growth and for use in studying the figures on the growth of population.

CHAPTER XV

SUMMARY AND CONCLUSION

Each of the findings of this study is best understood within the chapter and the context in which it is derived; therefore, the writer deems it advisable to leave most of these findings in their respective contexts and not repeat them in a concluding chapter. It is considered worthwhile, however, to list what seems to be the most pertinent findings, and to present these findings as briefly and with as little use of quantitative aids as possible. Thus this chapter is devoted to the non-technical discussion of the most relevant findings. Unless otherwise specified, the status in each item considered refers to the situation which existed in 1940.

In 1940 Atlanta was the twenty-eighth ranking city in point of size in the United States. It was more densely populated than the average urban community throughout the nation and even more so than the large cities of the South. There were two major races, the white and the Negro; the whites outnumbered the Negroes about two to one. Most of the population was native born but there was a very small percentage which was born in countries other than the United States; of this group, about one-fourth was from Russia.

The age distribution is typically urban; there is a shortage of children, a high concentration of persons in the working ages, and a shortage of old people. In regard to the shortage of old people, there is an outstanding shortage of old Negroes; this is probably due to migration and short life expectancy in comparison to the white race. The average age of the population has been rising; this is particularly true for the decade 1930-1940.

There are fewer men in proportion to the number of women in Atlanta than in any other large city in the nation. The high proportion of women to men comes about largely because of the high proportion of Negro women engaged in domestic service work in Atlanta, because of the longer expectation of life of females over males, and because of the low sex ratio at birth in the Negro population.

The chances are above average that the Atlanta man and the Atlanta woman will marry; and the chances are favorable that they will marry earlier in life than persons in the average of cities similar to Atlanta. Negroes do not support the marriage institution to quite the extent that white persons do. In contrast to what many people believe, Atlanta people do not marry later in life than their parents or grandparents; there are definite indications that they marry at a slightly earlier age.

In relation to other urban populations the educational status of the Atlanta population ranks fairly well. The white people in Atlanta, however, are considerably better educated than are the Negro people.

In the field of earning a living, a greater proportion of Atlanta men works for wages than in the average large city; that is, the likelihood of being an employer or working on one's own is less in Atlanta than in other southern cities. Negro women in Atlanta are self-employed or are employers to a much greater extent than white women. A high proportion of men in Atlanta is engaged in service work of all types, while a very high percentage of Negro women is engaged in domestic service work. A much smaller proportion of workers is employed in industrial work in Atlanta than in the urban United States.

A high proportion of Atlanta people is Protestant by religious faith and the highest ranking denomination in preference is the Baptist. The congregations are dominated by women; the proportion of women in the churches of Atlanta far exceeds the proportion of men.

Atlanta is like a colony; it has to be "repeopled" to some extent each year because its population fails to reproduce itself. Its rate of reproduction has been falling at least since 1890, and in 1940 the fertility rates in Atlanta were lower than the average large urban community in the nation. The Negroes fail to reproduce themselves to a greater extent than do the white people. In order to obtain people to replace those who die and to permit growth, the city must attract migrants largely from the other parts of the state of Georgia. Most of the persons who have come to Atlanta from outside of Georgia were former residents of adjacent states and more than likely came from one of the southern states; only occasionally do people outside the South come to Atlanta to live.

The death rate of Atlanta white people is comparatively low, but for Negroes it is exceptionally high. From the point of view of life expectancy, however, the Atlanta population ranks high.

In both races the female can expect to live much longer than the male; but people of the white race can expect to live longer than those of the colored race. The death rate among white children under one year of age is lower than the national average, and the rate for Negroes is approaching the average. These are indications that the quality of the Atlanta population is comparatively high because if people take care of their helpless offspring, they obviously will take care of themselves.

Atlanta has been growing rather steadily since it reached the 2,500 mark in 1850. If other southern cities continue at their present rates of growth, Atlanta will probably someday surpass New Orleans.

Conclusion. In many respects the Atlanta population is similar to other large urban populations of the South. The variations treated more fully in the main body of the study and summarized briefly in this chapter constitute to some extent at least the uniqueness of Atlanta, the things about the population of the city that make it distinctive and different from those of other cities.

APPENDIX A

TABLE A

Selected Urban Populations by Color, Nativity, and Parentage, 1890-1940

City, Color and Nativity	Population					
	1890	1900	1910	1920	1930	1940
Urban United States:	22,720,223	30,797,185	42,623,383	54,304,603	68,954,823	74,423,702
White	21,173,685	28,717,990	39,831,913	50,620,084	62,836,605	67,972,823
Native	15,538,263	21,895,860	30,196,544	40,263,101	52,109,746	58,838,505
Native parentage	9,022,289	12,380,669	17,849,644	24,556,729	33,497,232	———
Foreign or mixed parentage	6,515,974	9,515,191	12,346,900	15,706,372	18,612,514	———
Foreign parentage	———	———	8,791,920	11,304,886	12,959,015	———
Mixed parentage	———	———	3,554,980	4,401,486	5,653,499	———
Foreign born	5,635,422	6,822,130	9,635,369	10,356,983	10,726,859	9,134,318
Negro	1,481,142	2,005,972	2,689,229	3,559,473	5,193,913	6,253,588
Other Races	65,396	73,223	102,241	125,046	924,305	197,291
Atlanta:	65,533	89,872	154,839	200,616	270,366	302,288
White	37,416	54,090	102,861	137,785	180,247	197,686
Native	35,569	51,632	98,451	133,047	175,520	193,393
Native parentage	32,669	47,146	91,987	124,948	166,513	———
Foreign or mixed parentage	2,900	4,486	6,464	8,099	9,007	———
Foreign parentage	———	———	3,738	4,815	5,106	———
Mixed parentage	———	———	2,726	3,284	3,901	———
Foreign born	1,847	2,458	4,410	4,738	4,727	4,293
Negro	28,098	35,727	51,902	62,796	90,075	104,533

TABLE A (Continued)

SELECTED URBAN POPULATIONS BY COLOR, NATIVITY, AND PARENTAGE, 1890–1940

City, Color and Nativity	Population					
	1890	1900	1910	1920	1930	1940
Dallas:	38,067	42,638	92,104	158,976	260,475	294,734
White	30,006	33,575	74,043	134,888	215,720	244,246
Native	26,104	30,230	68,824	126,158	209,247	236,891
Native parentage	21,971	24,418	59,746	112,509	192,580	———
Foreign or mixed parentage	4,133	5,812	9,078	13,649	16,667	———
Foreign parentage	———	———	5,305	8,019	8,892	———
Mixed parentage	———	———	3,773	5,630	7,775	———
Foreign born	3,902	3,345	5,219	8,730	6,473	7,355
Negro .	7,993	9,035	18,024	24,023	38,742	50,407
Nashville:	76,168	80,865	110,364	118,342	153,866	167,402
White	46,773	50,796	73,831	82,703	111,025	120,072
Native	43,007	47,794	70,838	80,316	109,237	118,550
Native parentage	36,802	40,620	63,687	74,022	103,757	———
Foreign or mixed parentage	6,205	7,174	7,151	6,294	5,480	———
Foreign parentage	———	———	4,200	3,653	3,003	———
Mixed parentage	———	———	2,951	2,641	2,477	———
Foreign born	3,766	3,002	2,993	2,387	1,788	1,529
Negro.	29,382	30,044	36,523	35,633	42,836	47,318

TABLE A (Continued)

SELECTED URBAN POPULATIONS BY COLOR, NATIVITY, AND PARENTAGE, 1890–1940

City, Color and Nativity	Population					
	1890	1900	1910	1920	1930	1940
New Orleans:	242,039	287,104	339,075	387,219	458,762	494,537
White	177,376	208,946	249,403	285,916	327,729	344,775
Native	143,473	179,377	221,717	259,924	308,048	330,080
Native parentage	70,398	103,186	147,473	190,641	242,282	——
Foreign or mixed parentage	73,075	76,191	74,244	69,283	65,766	——
Foreign parentage	——	——	45,898	41,806	36,828	——
Mixed parentage	——	——	28,346	27,477	28,938	——
Foreign born	33,903	29,569	27,686	25,992	19,681	14,695
Negro	64,491	77,714	89,262	100,930	129,632	149,034

Sources: *Eleventh Census of the United States: 1890*, (Washington: Government Printing Office, 1892), pp. 672-673.
Twelfth Census of the United States: 1900, "Population, Vol. II," Part II (Washington: Government Printing Office, 1902), pp. 417-424.
Thirteenth Census of the United States: 1910, "Population, Vol. I," (Washington: Government Printing Office, 1913), pp. 184-224.
Fourteenth Census of the United States: 1920, "Population, Vol. II, General Report and Analytical Tables," (Washington: Government Printing Office: 1922), p. 79.
Fifteenth Census of the United States: 1930, "Population, Vol. II, General Report, Statistics by Subjects," (Washington: Government Printing Office, 1933), pp. 27, 34, 73-79.
Sixteenth Census of the United States: 1940, "Population, Vol. II, Characteristics of the Population," (Washington: Government Printing Office, 1934), pp. 20 and 114.

TABLE B

Number and Proportion of Negroes in Selected Urban Populations, 1850-1940

Year	United States Urban Population		Atlanta		Dallas		Nashville		New Orleans	
	Number of Negroes	Percentage of the total urban population	Number of Negroes	Percentage of the total population	Number of Negroes	Percentage of the total population	Number of Negroes	Percentage of the total population	Number of Negroes	Percentage of the total population
1850	----	----	512[1]	19.9	----	----	2,539[1]	25.0	26,916[1]	23.1
1860	----	----	1,393[1]	20.3	----	----	3,937[1]	23.2	24,074[1]	14.3
1870	----	----	9,929[2]	45.6	----	----	9,709[2]	37.8	50,456[2]	26.4
1880	----	----	16,330[2]	43.7	1,921[2]	18.5	16,337[2]	37.7	57,617[2]	26.7
1890	1,481,142	6.5	28,098	42.9	7,993	21.0	29,382	38.6	64,491	26.6
1900	2,005,972	6.5	35,727	39.8	9,035	21.2	30,044	37.2	77,714	27.1
1910	2,689,229	6.3	51,902	33.5	18,024	19.6	36,523	33.1	89,262	26.3
1920	3,559,473	6.6	62,796	31.3	24,023	15.1	35,633	30.1	100,930	26.1
1930	5,193,913	7.5	90,075	33.3	38,742	14.9	42,836	27.8	129,632	28.3
1940	6,253,588	8.4	104,533	34.6	50,407	17.1	47,318	28.3	149,035	30.1

1 Free Colored and Slaves.

2 Colored.

Sources: *Seventh Census of the United States: 1850* (Washington: Robert Armstrong, Public Printer, 1853), pp. 366, 474, 575. *Population of the United States in 1860* (Washington: Government Printing Office, 1864), pp. 74, 195, 467. *Ninth Census of the United States: 1870*, "Volume I, The Statistics of the Population of the United States," (Washington: Government Printing Office, 1872), pp. 102. *Statistics of the Population of the United States at the Tenth Census* (Washington: Government Printing Office, 1883), pp. 417-424. *Thirteenth Census of the United States: 1910*, "Population, Vol II," (Washington: Government Printing Office, 1913), pp. 173, 184, 400, and 790. *Fifteenth Census of the United States: 1930*, "Population, Vol. II, General Report, Statistics by Subjects," (Washington: Government Printing Office, 1933), pp. 73-76. *Sixteenth Census of the United States: 1940*, "Population, Vol. II, Characteristics of the Population," (Washington: Government Printing Office, 1943), pp. 20, 114, and 116.

TABLE C

SEX RATIOS AMONG WHITES AND NEGROES
IN ATLANTA FROM 1850 TO 1940

Year	Total Population	Whites	Negroes
1850	100	107	77
1860	103	108	84
1870	94	94	----
1880	----	----	----
1890	92	101	79
1900	85	96	71
1910	93	99	81
1920	93	96	86
1930	88	92	80
1940	86	89	79

Sources: *Seventh Census of the United States: 1850* (Washington: Robert Armstrong, Public Printer, 1853), p. 366.
Population of the United States in 1860 (Washington: Government Printing Office, 1864), p. 74.
Ninth Census of the United States: 1870, "Volume I, The Statistics of the Population of the United States," (Washington: Government Printing Office, 1872), p. 642.
Statistics of the Population of the United States at the Tenth Census (Washington: Government Printing Office, 1883).
Eleventh Census of the United States: 1890 (Washington: Government Printing Office, 1892), p. 672.
Twelfth Census of the United States: 1900, "Population, Vol. II," (Washington: United States Census Office, 1902), p. 122.
Thirteenth Census of the United States: 1910, "Population, Vol. I," (Washington: Government Printing Office, 1913), p. 263.
Fourteenth Census of the United States: 1920, "Population, Vol. III," (Washington: Government Printing Office, 1922), p. 222.
Fifteenth Census of the United States: 1930, "Population, Vol. III," Part 1 (Washington: Government Printing Office, 1932), p. 477.
Sixteenth Census of the United States: 1940, "Population, Vol. II, Characteristics of the Population," Part 2 (Washington: Government Printing Office, 1942), p. 198.

TABLE D

Per Cent Distribution by Major Occupation Group, for Male Employed Workers 14 Years Old and Over, for Selected Urban Populations of 100,000 or More, 1940

Urban Population	Total employed (except on public emergency work)	Professional workers	Semi-professional workers	Proprietors, managers, and officials except farm	Clerical, sales, and kindred workers	Craftsmen, foremen, and kindred workers	Operatives, and kindred workers	Domestic service workers	Service workers except domestic	Laborers except farm	Occupation not reported
Urban, United States (Male)	100.0	5.9	1.5	12.5	18.7	18.6	22.1	0.5	9.0	9.3	0.8
Atlanta	100.0	5.1	1.3	11.9	23.8	15.7	18.1	1.6	12.8	8.9	0.6
Dallas	100.0	5.0	1.5	15.2	26.0	16.7	16.6	1.6	10.5	6.1	0.5
Nashville	100.0	5.1	1.2	10.2	19.7	18.3	20.0	2.1	11.2	11.2	0.6
New Orleans	100.0	5.1	1.2	12.3	21.5	14.9	18.0	0.6	11.2	14.3	0.3

Source: *Sixteenth Census of the United States: 1940*, "Population, Vol. II, Characteristics of the Population," Part 1 (Washington: Government Printing Office, 1943), pp. 49 and 173.

Courtesy of The Atlanta Chamber of Commerce.

Aerial View of Atlanta Looking Northwest (Taken in 1948).

Atlanta Passenger Terminal at the Airport.

Courtesy Georgia Power Company.

Peachtree Street at Ellis Street Looking North

Courtesy Georgia Power Company.

Whitehall Street at Alabama Street Looking North.

Courtesy Georgia Power Company.
Intersection of Peachtree and West Peachtree Streets Looking
North, (1946).

"Five Points" Looking Northeast (December, 1946).

Courtesy Georgia Power Company

A Post-World War II Scene on Peachtree Street.

"Five Points" at Night Looking Southwest.

Courtesy Georgia Power Company.

TABLE E

PER CENT DISTRIBUTION BY MAJOR OCCUPATION GROUP, FOR FEMALE EMPLOYED WORKERS, 14 YEARS OLD AND OVER, FOR SELECTED URBAN POPULATIONS OF 100,000 OR MORE, 1940

Urban Population	Total employed (except on public emergency work)	Professional workers	Semi-professional workers	Proprietors, managers, and officials except farm	Clerical, sales, and kindred workers	Craftsmen, foremen, and kindred workers	Operatives, and kindred workers	Domestic service workers	Service workers except domestic	Laborers except farm	Occupation not reported
Urban, United States (Female)	100.0	11.6	1.0	3.7	32.5	1.1	19.6	16.4	12.1	0.8	1.0
Atlanta	100.0	8.0	0.7	2.6	30.0	0.8	13.8	31.2	11.9	0.5	0.6
Dallas	100.0	8.6	1.0	4.2	34.9	1.1	14.4	21.3	13.5	0.3	0.6
Nashville	100.0	10.1	0.7	2.4	26.7	0.9	18.7	26.8	12.1	0.7	0.9
New Orleans	100.0	10.2	1.0	3.3	28.7	0.8	15.2	27.3	12.1	0.8	0.4

Source: *Sixteenth Census of the United States: 1940*, "Population, Vol. II, Characteristics of the Population," Part 1 (Washington: Government Printing Office, 1943), pp. 59 and 174.

TABLE F

Per Cent Distribution of Employed Workers 14 Years Old and Over, by Industry Group and Sex, for Selected Urban Populations, 1940

Major Occupation Group	Urban United States			Atlanta		Dallas		Nashville		New Orleans	
	Total	Male	Female	Male	Female	Male	Female	Male	Female	Male	Female
Employed (except on public emergency work)	100.0	100.0	100.0	100.0	100.0	100.0	100.0	100.0	100.0	100.0	100.0
Agriculture, forestry, and fishery	1.1	1.5	0.3	0.5	0.1	0.8	0.1	0.5	0.1	1.2	0.2
Mining	1.0	1.4	0.1	---	---	0.6	0.2	0.2	---	0.2	---
Construction	4.8	6.8	0.3	9.2	0.4	9.9	0.4	9.5	0.3	8.9	0.3
Manufacturing	29.2	32.0	22.7	21.5	12.6	18.2	13.3	24.5	17.7	18.1	12.8
Transportation, communication, and other public utilities	8.7	11.0	3.4	13.2	4.4	11.5	4.4	12.7	3.0	18.9	3.5
Wholesale and retail trade	21.4	22.0	20.0	26.5	18.2	30.2	23.9	24.0	15.1	25.4	21.2
Finance, insurance and real estate	4.6	4.5	4.9	5.8	5.4	7.0	7.7	4.5	4.7	5.0	4.1
Business and repair services	2.2	2.9	0.8	2.9	0.8	3.7	1.1	3.1	0.5	2.9	0.6
Personal services	10.8	4.6	25.3	7.8	42.3	7.2	33.1	7.3	37.9	5.4	37.2

216

TABLE F (Continued)

PER CENT DISTRIBUTION OF EMPLOYED WORKERS 14 YEARS OLD AND OVER, BY INDUSTRY GROUP AND SEX, FOR SELECTED URBAN POPULATIONS, 1940

Major Occupation Group	Urban United States			Atlanta		Dallas		Nashville		New Orleans	
	Total	Male	Female	Male	Female	Male	Female	Male	Female	Male	Female
Amusement, recreation, and related services	1.2	1.3	0.8	1.3	0.7	1.8	1.0	1.1	0.5	1.9	1.2
Professional and re-lated services	8.6	5.4	16.1	4.8	11.3	4.4	12.1	5.7	15.3	5.3	15.4
Government	4.7	5.3	3.2	5.4	2.9	3.7	1.8	5.5	3.6	5.7	2.6
Industry not reported	1.6	1.5	2.1	1.1	1.0	1.0	0.9	1.3	1.4	1.3	1.0

Source: *Sixteenth Census of the United States: 1940*, "Population, Vol. II, Characteristics of the Population," Part 1 (Washington: Government Printing Office, 1943), pp. 49, 189-195.

TABLE G

NUMBER OF DIFFERENT DENOMINATIONS, IN SELECTED URBAN POPULATIONS, 1906-1936

Population	Year			
	1906	1916	1926	1936
Total United States	188	202	213	256
Atlanta	20	25	45	49
Dallas	19	21	46	45
Nashville	21	19	40	38
New Orleans	16	21	30	33

Sources: *Census of Religious Bodies: 1906*, Part 1 (Washington Printing Office, 1910), pp. 410-412, 430, 464-466, and 468.
Census of Religious Bodies: 1916, Part 1 (Washington: Government Printing Office, 1919), pp. 357-358, 387-388, 445, and 447.
Census of Religious Bodies: 1926, Vol. 1 (Washington: Government Printing Office, 1930), pp. 365-366, 401-402, 476-477, and 483-484.
Census of Religious Bodies: 1936, Vol. 1 (Washington: Government Printing Office, 1941), pp. 450-451, 494-496, 594, and 602.

TABLE H

PER CENT DISTRIBUTION OF DENOMINATIONS WITH 1000 MEMBERS OR MORE, IN SELECTED CITIES, 1936

Denomination	Atlanta		Dallas		Nashville		New Orleans	
	Total Membership	Per Cent of total Membership	Total Membership	Per Cent of total Membership	Total Membership	Per Cent of total Membership	Total Membership	Per Cent of total Membership
Total	152,083	100.0	119,446	100.0	78,446	100.0	264,370	100.0
Assemblies of God, General Council	———	———	2,221	1.9	———	———	———	———
Baptist Bodies: Southern Baptist Convention	28,358	18.7	16,458	13.8	12,290	15.7	3,029	1.1
Negro Baptists	32,044	21.0	21,170	17.7	5,597	7.1	18,822	7.1
Colored Primitive Baptists	———	———	———	———	1,331	1.7	———	———
Church of Christ, Scientist	———	———	1,043	0.9	———	———	———	———
Churches of Christ	1,804	1.2	2,279	1.9	7,413	9.5	———	———
Churches of God, Holiness	1,302	0.9	———	———	———	———	———	———
Church of the Nazarene	———	———	———	———	1,952	2.5	———	———
Disciples of Christ	3,158	2.1	8,315	7.0	2,317	3.0	———	———

TABLE H (Continued)

PER CENT DISTRIBUTION OF DENOMINATIONS WITH 1000 MEMBERS OR MORE, IN SELECTED CITIES, 1936

Denomination	Atlanta		Dallas		Nashville		New Orleans	
	Total Membership	Per Cent of total Membership	Total Membership	Per Cent of total Membership	Total Membership	Per Cent of total Membership	Total Membership	Per Cent of total Membership
Evangelical and Re-formed Church	----	----	----	----	----	----	4,573	1.7
Eastern Orthodox Churches: Greek Orthodox Church (Hellenic)	1,500	1.0	----	----	----	----	----	----
Jewish Congregations	12,000	7.9	10,400	8.7	4,200	5.4	8,700	3.3
Lutherans: Evangelical Lutheran Synod of Missouri, Ohio, and other States	----	----	1,107	0.9	----	----	7,489	2.8
Negro Mission of the Synodical Conference	----	----	----	----	----	----	1,554	0.6
Methodist Bodies: African Methodist Episcopal Church	10,281	6.7	----	----	2,398	3.1	3,286	1.2
Colored Methodist Episcopal Church	2,027	1.3	2,497	2.1	----	----	----	----

TABLE H (Continued)

PER CENT DISTRIBUTION OF DENOMINATIONS WITH 1000 MEMBERS OR MORE, IN SELECTED CITIES, 1936

Denomination	Atlanta		Dallas		Nashville		New Orleans	
	Total Membership	Per Cent of total Membership	Total Membership	Per Cent of total Membership	Total Membership	Per Cent of total Membership	Total Membership	Per Cent of total Membership
Methodist Episcopal Church	3,374	2.2	------	------	1,072	1.4	2,055	0.8
Methodist Episcopal Church, South	24,832	16.3	18,953	15.8	16,273	20.8	5,010	1.9
Old Catholic Churches in America: North American Old Roman Catholic Church	------	------	1,433	1.2			------	------
Presbyterian Bodies: Cumberland Presbyterian Church					1,458	1.8		
Presbyterian Church in the United States	9,957	6.6	5,850	4.9	5,014	6.4	3,966	1.5
Presbyterian Church in United States of America	------	------	3,307	2.8	1,270	1.6	------	------
Protestant Episcopal Church	4,420	2.9	2,245	1.9	3,462	4.4	8,377	3.2
Roman Catholic Church	8,430	5.5	14,498	12.1	7,644	9.8	191,933	72.7
All other denominations	8,596	5.7	7,670	6.4	4,759	6.1	5,576	2.1

Source: *Census of Religious Bodies: 1936*, Vol. I (Washington: Government Printing Office, 1941), pp. 450-451, 494-496, 594, and 602.

TABLE I

Denominational Membership of 1000 or More, by Age, In Selected Southern Cities, 1936

Denomination	Atlanta Total Membership	Atlanta Per Cent Under 13	Dallas Total Membership	Dallas Per Cent Under 13	Nashville Total Membership	Nashville Per Cent Under 13	New Orleans Total Membership	New Orleans Per Cent Under 13
Total	152,083	9.7	119,446	11.4	78,446	10.3	264,370	24.9
Assemblies of God, General Council	——	——	2,221	15.2	——	——	——	——
Baptist Bodies:								
Southern Baptist Convention	28,358	6.5	16,458	8.8	12,290	5.7	3,029	6.6
Negro Baptists	32,044	9.3	21,170	10.2	5,597	10.1	18,822	8.9
Colored Primitive Baptists	——	——	1,043	——	1,331	1.9	——	——
Church of Christ, Scientist	——	——	——	——	——	——	——	——
Churches of Christ	1,804	——	2,279	——	7,413	2.9	——	——
Churches of God, Holiness	1,302	24.8	——	——	——	——	——	——
Church of the Nazarine	——	——	——	——	1,952	8.8	——	——
Disciples of Christ	3,158	4.4	8,315	9.9	2,317	3.2	4,573	6.7
Evangelical and Reformed Church	——	——	——	——				
Eastern Orthodox Churches: Greek Orthodox Church (Hellenic)	1,500	——	——	——	——	——	——	——
Jewish Congregations	12,000	——	10,400	——	4,200	——	8,700	——
Lutherans: Evangelical Lutheran Synod of Missouri, Ohio, and Other States			1,107	21.0	——	——	7,489	22.6
Negro Mission of the Synodical Conference	——	——	——	——	——	——	1,554	31.4

222

TABLE I (Continued)

DENOMINATIONAL MEMBERSHIP OF 1000 OR MORE, BY AGE, IN SELECTED SOUTHERN CITIES, 1936

Denomination	Atlanta Total Membership	Atlanta Per Cent Under 13	Dallas Total Membership	Dallas Per Cent Under 13	Nashville Total Membership	Nashville Per Cent Under 13	New Orleans Total Membership	New Orleans Per Cent Under 13
Methodist Bodies:								
African Methodist Episcopal Church	10,281	17.9	—	—	2,398	13.2	3,286	16.2
Colored Methodist Episcopal Church	2,027	8.2	2,497	11.8	—	—	—	15.3
Methodist Episcopal Church	3,374	21.3	—	—	1,072	21.2	2,055	15.3
Methodist Episcopal Church, South	24,832	6.1	18,953	10.1	16,273	8.3	5,010	7.6
Old Catholic Churches in America: North American Old Roman Catholic Church	—	—	1,433	20.3	—	—	—	—
Presbyterian Bodies: Cumberland Presbyterian Church	—	—	—	—	1,454	16.3	—	—
Presbyterian Church in the United States	9,957	6.0	5,850	8.2	5,014	7.1	3,966	6.1
Presbyterian Church in the United States of America	—	—	3,307	6.0	1,270	4.2	—	—
Protestant Episcopal Church	4,420	9.2	2,245	10.0	3,462	15.9	8,377	18.1
Roman Catholic Church	8,430	27.0	14,498	21.1	7,644	20.3	191,933	29.4

Source: *Census of Religious Bodies: 1936*, Vol. I (Washington: Government Printing Office, 1941), pp. 450-451, 494-496, 594, and 602.

223

TABLE J

Denominational Membership by Age, in Atlanta, 1936

Denomination	Membership	Per Cent Under 13
Total	152,083	9.7
Adventist Bodies:		
Seventh-Day Adventist Denomination	624	2.9
American Rescue Workers	24	----
Assemblies of God, General Council	226	7.1
Baptist Bodies:		
Southern Baptist Convention	28,358	6.5
Negro Baptists	32,044	9.3
Colored Primitive Baptists	51	----
Primitive Baptists	328	0.4
Brethren, Plymouth:		
Plymouth Brethren II	24	----
The Christian and Missionary Alliance	192	2.1
Church of Christ (Holiness) U. S. A.	42	----
Church of Christ, Scientist	665	----
Churches of God:		
Church of God	188	4.8
Church of God (Headquarters, Anderson, Indiana)	149	43.6
(Tomlinson) Church of God	231	14.3
Church of God and Saints of Christ	200	24.0
Church of the Nazarine	252	12.3
Churches of Christ	1,804	----
Churches of God, Holiness	1,302	24.8
Congregational and Christian Churches	861	6.5
Congregational Holiness Church	144	0.7
Disciples of Christ	3,158	4.4
Eastern Orthodox Churches:		
Greek Orthodox Church (Hellenic)	1,500	----
Syrian Antiochian Orthodox Church	166	19.9
Evangelical and Reformed Church	163	----
Federated Churches	103	----
Jewish Congregations	12,000	----
Latter Day Saints:		
Church of Jesus Christ of Latter Day Saints	223	13.0

TABLE J (Continued)

DENOMINATIONAL MEMBERSHIP BY AGE, IN ATLANTA, 1936

Denomination	Membership	Per Cent Under 13
Lutherans:		
Evangelical Lutheran Synodical Conference of North America:		
Evangelical Lutheran Synod of Missouri, Ohio and Other States	101	33.7
Negro Mission of the Synodical Conference	34	----
United Lutheran Church in America	574	5.6
Liberal Catholic Church	30	----
Methodist Bodies:		
African Methodist Episcopal Church	10,281	17.9
African Methodist Episcopal Zion Church	759	11.7
Colored Methodist Episcopal Church	2,027	8.2
Free Methodist Church of North America	90	----
Methodist Episcopal Church	3,374	21.3
Methodist Episcopal Church, South	24,832	6.1
New Congregational Methodist Church	265	0.8
Wesleyan Methodist Connection (Or Church) of America	27	----
Pentecostal Assemblies:		
Pentecostal Fire-Baptized Holiness Church	41	----
International Pentecostal Assemblies	309	5.5
The Pentecostal Church, Inc.	17	----
Presbyterian Bodies:		
The General Synod of the Associate Reformed Presbyterian Church	288	5.9
Presbyterian Church in the United States	9,957	6.0
Presbyterian Church in the United States of America	695	15.0
Protestant Episcopal Church	4,420	9.2
Roman Catholic Church	8,430	27.0
Salvation Army	455	20.2
Triumph the Church and Kingdom of God in Christ	55	----

Source: *Census of Religious Bodies: 1936*, Vol. 1 (Washington: Governmı Printing Office, 1941), pp. 450-451.

TABLE K

Number of Births and Crude Birth Rate in Selected Urban Populations, 1940

	Cities of 100,000 or more		Atlanta		Dallas		Nashville		New Orleans	
	Births	Crude Birth Rate	Births	Crude Birth Rate	Births	Crude Birth Rate	Births	Crude Birth Rate	Births	Crude Birth Rate
All Classes	600,132	15.8	6,344	21.0	5,577	18.9	3,530	21.1	9,138	18.5
White	531,056	15.5	4,139	20.9	4,555	18.6	2,611	21.7	5,532	16.0
All other races	69,076	19.0	2,205	21.1	1,022	20.2	919	19.4	3,606	24.1

Sources: Forest E. Linder and Robert D. Grove, *Vital Statistic Rates in the United States: 1900-1940* (Washington: Government Printing Office, 1947), pp. 685, 800, 804, 818, 819 and 935; *Vital Statistics of the United States: 1940*, Part II (Washington: Government Printing Office, 1942), p. 69; *Sixteenth Census of the United States: 1940*, "Population Vol. II, Characteristics of the Population," Part 1 (Washington: Government Printing Office, 1943), p. 18.

TABLE L

NUMBER OF CHILDREN UNDER 5 PER 1,000 WOMEN AGED 15-44,
BY RACE, IN SELECTED URBAN POPULATIONS, 1890-1940

Urban Population	Year					
	1890	1900	1910	1920	1930	1940
Urban United States						
All Classes	------	------	374	381	315	257
Whites	------	------	382	392	316	258
Negroes	------	------	275	247	268	246
Atlanta						
All Classes	416	319	339	283	255	224
Whites	393	362	386	319	267	228
Negroes	343	269	264	215	233	218
Dallas						
All Classes	417	339	300	270	265	215
Whites	436	373	329	288	268	222
Negroes	348	238	204	183	205	189
Nashville						
All Classes	345	314	314	283	284	245
Whites	372	354	366	317	305	260
Negroes	307	257	226	242	235	210
New Orleans						
All Classes	403	388	340	305	302	239
Whites	413	422	371	331	310	225
Negroes	377	310	269	245	284	267

Source: *Eleventh Census of the United States: 1890*, "Population," Part II
(Washington: Government Printing Office, 1897), pp. 114, 118, 125, and 126.
Twelfth Census of the United States: 1900, "Population, Vol. II," Part II
(Washington: Government Printing Office, 1902), pp. 122, 127, 136, and 137.
Thirteenth Census of the United States: 1910, "Population, Vol. I, General
Report and Analysis," (Washington: Government Printing Office, 1913),
pp. 425-427, 450, 457, 458, 474, 476, and 486.
Fourteenth Census of the United States: 1920, "Population, Vol. II, General
Report and Analytical Tables," (Washington: Government Printing Office,
1922), pp. 312, 320, and 353.
Fourteenth Census of the United States: 1920, "Population, Vol, III, Composi-
tion and Characteristics of the Population by States," (Washington: Government Printing Office, 1922), pp. 206, 392, 960, and 988.
Fifteenth Census of the United States: 1930, "Population, Vol. II, General
Report, Statistics by Subject," (Washington: Government Printing Office,
1933), pp. 587, 757, 764, 789, and 790.
Sixteenth Census of the United States: 1940, "Population, Vol. II, Characteristics of the Population," (Washington: Government Printing Office, 1943),
pp. 23, 119-120, 125, 135, and 136.

TABLE M

COMPUTATIONS FOR GROSS AND NET REPRODUCTION RATES OF THE
WHITE POPULATION OF ATLANTA, 1939-1941

Age groups of mothers	Number of women in observed population July 1, 1940	3-year average number of female births, 1939-1941	Fertility rate for female births (2) ÷ (1) x 1,000	Number of years lived in age interval by cohort of 100,000 females	Number of female births to cohort, observed rates prevailing (3) x (4)
	(1)	(2)	(3)	(4)	(5)
15-19	9,177	297	32.364	465,576	15,133
20-24	10,747	689	64.111	464,571	29,784
25-29	1C,556	579	54.850	460,703	25,270
30-34	10,270	341	33.204	455,449	15,123
35-39	9,081	140	15.417	448,360	6,912
40-44	7,648	24	3.138	440,102	1,381
15-44	57,479	2,070	203.084	-----------	93,603

$$\text{Gross reproduction rate} = \frac{5(203.084)}{1,000} = 1.015$$

$$\text{Net reproduction rate} = \frac{93,603}{100,000} = .936$$

Sources: *Vital Statistics of the United States, Supplement: 1939-1940,* Part III (Washington: Government Printing Office, 1943), p. 176; *Vital Statistics of the United States: 1941,* Part II (Washington: Government Printing Office, 1943), p. 78; and life tables, this study.

TABLE N

COMPUTATIONS FOR GROSS AND NET REPRODUCTION RATES OF THE
NEGRO POPULATION OF ATLANTA, 1939-1941

Age groups of mothers	Number of women in observed population July 1, 1940	3-year average number of female births, 1939-1941	Fertility rate for female births (2) ÷ (1) x 1,000	Number of years lived in age interval by cohort of 100,000 females	Number of female births to cohort, observed rates prevailing (3) x (4)
	(1)	(2)	(3)	(4)	(5)
15-19	5,311	311	58.558	431,905	25,291
20-24	6,655	340	51.089	417,672	21,338
25-29	7,204	224	31.094	400,842	12,464
30-34	5,823	116	19.921	379,664	7,563
35-39	6,005	60	9.992	357,725	3,574
40-44	4,361	15	3.440	328,088	1,129
15-44	35,359	1,066	174.094	----------	71,359

$$\text{Gross reproduction rate} = \frac{5(174.094)}{1,000} = .870$$

$$\text{Net reproduction rate} = \frac{71,359}{100,000} = .714$$

Sources: *Vital Statistics of the United States, Supplement: 1939-1940*, Part III (Washington: Government Printing Office, 1943), p. 176; *Vital Statistics of the United States: 1941*, Part II (Washington: Government Printing Office, 1943), p. 78; and life tables, this study.

TABLE O

INDEXES OF NET REPRODUCTION OF THE WHITE AND NEGRO POPULATIONS
OF ATLANTA, 1939-1941

Population	Ratio of children under 5 to women 15-44	Ratio of children under 5 to women 20-44	Permanent replacement quota, 1939-1941*		Index of net reproduction per generation
White	228		357		.64
		272		430	.63
Negro	218		394		.55
		256		484	.53

* Based on stationary population derived from life table constructed by Reed-Merrell Method; see Chapter XII on mortality.

Sources: *Sixteenth Census of the United States: 1940,* "Population and Housing, Atlanta, Ga.," (Washington: Government Printing Office, 1942), p. 3; and life tables in this study.

TABLE P

ADJUSTED NET REPRODUCTION RATES FOR UNITED STATES URBAN
AND SOUTHERN URBAN WHITE AND NONWHITE WOMEN FOR
1935 TO 1940, 1930 TO 1935, AND 1905 TO 1910

Population	Period		
	1935 to 1940	1930 to 1935	1905 to 1910
United States Urban	726	747	937
White	731	756	977
Nonwhite	702	684	558
Southern Urban	712	742	764
White	726	766	874
Nonwhite	679	682	568

Source: *Sixteenth Census of the United States: 1940,* "Population, Differential Fertility, 1940 and 1910, Standardized Fertility Rates and Reproduction Rates," (Washington: Government Printing Office, 1944), pp. 20-21.

TABLE Q

NUMBER OF BIRTHS IN URBAN PLACES OF 100,000 OR MORE
AND THE CITY OF ATLANTA, BY RACE, 1937-1946

Year	Total all places of 100,00 or more in the United States			Atlanta		
	Total	White	Nonwhite	Total	White	Nonwhite
1937	565,130	----------	----------	5,605	--------	--------
1938	583,076	----------	----------	5,888	--------	--------
1939	574,502	510,298	62,088[1]	6,099	3,978	2,121
1940	600,132	531,056	66,745[1]	6,344	4,139	2,204
1941	660,005	584,700	72,775[1]	6,973	4,714	2,259
1942	792,625	711,780	80,845	7,443	5,150	2,293
1943	821,715	733,214	88,501	7,212	4,934	2,278
1944	762,954	672,889	90,065	7,218	5,033	2,185
1945	772,275	678,617	93,658	7,416	5,262	2,154
1946	937,505	825,283	112,222	9,599	6,951	2,648

[1] Negro.

Sources: *Vital Statistics of the United States: 1937*, Part II (Washington: Government Printing Office, 1939), pp. 13, 25.
Vital Statistics of the United States: 1938, Part II (Washington: Government Printing Office, 1940), pp. 14, 26.
Vital Statistics of the United States: 1939, Part II (Washington: Government Printing Office, 1941), pp. 36, 39.
Vital Statistics of the United States: 1940, Part II (Washington: Government Printing Office, 1943), pp. 69, 72.
Vital Statistics of the United States: 1941, Part II (Washington: Government Printing Office, 1943), pp. 26, 75.
Vital Statistics of the United States: 1942, Part II (Washington: Government Office, 1944), pp. 31, 20.
Vital Statistics of the United States: 1943, Part II (Washington: Government Printing Office, 1945), pp. 23, 24.
Vital Statistics of the United States: 1944, Part II (Washington: Government Printing Office, 1946), pp. 4, 16.
Vital Statistics of the United States: 1945, Part II (Washington: Government Printing Office, 1947), pp. 8, 20.
Vital Statistics of the United States: 1946, Part II (Washington: Government Printing Office, 1948), pp. 10, 36.

TABLE R

Specific Death Rates, by Age and Race, for Cities of 100,000 or Larger, for the United States and Selected Southern States, 1940

Area and Race	All Ages	Under 1 year	1-4 years	5-14 years	15-24 years	25-34 years	35-44 years	45-54 years	55-64 years	65-74 years	75-84 years	85 years and over
United States Cities of 100,000 or more	11.3	50.3	2.3	1.0	1.8	2.9	5.6	12.1	25.8	53.8	117.3	205.1
White	10.9	45.7	2.1	0.9	1.4	2.3	4.7	10.9	24.7	53.3	118.0	210.8
All other races	14.8	88.9	4.1	1.6	5.5	7.9	12.9	25.1	41.5	60.1	102.0	132.1
Georgia[1]	13.1	71.6	2.8	1.4	3.7	6.7	10.7	19.6	33.9	52.1	109.9	248.6
White	10.1	47.7	1.9	1.0	1.7	2.8	5.6	12.3	27.1	48.2	116.1	311.6
All other races	18.8	116.7	4.3	2.1	7.3	13.5	19.8	36.1	55.0	62.8	89.9	147.6
Louisiana[2]	13.5	78.6	3.5	1.3	2.5	4.1	7.6	18.8	34.6	61.5	127.9	190.4
White	12.4	52.2	3.2	1.0	1.4	2.8	4.8	14.1	31.2	62.5	134.9	229.4
All other races	16.0	127.1	4.0	1.8	5.0	6.9	13.6	30.7	46.1	58.1	94.8	103.3
Tennessee[3]	12.3	65.3	3.5	1.4	3.2	5.2	8.5	16.8	29.4	54.8	111.9	213.6
White	10.3	55.6	2.6	1.1	1.8	2.8	5.3	11.3	24.4	51.0	121.1	279.6
All other races	16.7	88.7	5.4	2.0	6.4	10.0	14.6	28.6	43.3	64.0	81.5	94.5
Texas[4]	11.5	91.3	6.0	1.5	3.0	4.0	7.0	13.5	28.2	52.1	110.1	216.6
White	10.8	84.5	6.0	1.4	2.4	3.2	5.5	11.1	25.5	52.0	113.7	235.5
All other races	15.1	134.2	6.2	2.0	5.8	7.8	13.4	26.3	48.9	53.0	74.9	117.6

1 Includes *Atlanta* only.
2 Includes *New Orleans* only.
3 Includes Chattanooga, Knoxville, Memphis, and *Nashville.*
4 Includes *Dallas*, Fort Worth, Huston, and San Antonio.

Source: Forrest E. Linder and Robert D. Grove, *Vital Statistics Rates in the United States: 1900-1940* (Washington: Government Printing Office, 1947), pp. 198, 200, 201, and 207.

COMPUTATIONS FOR CONSTRUCTING A STATIONARY POPULATION OF
1,000,000 FROM LIFE TABLES FOR WHITE MALES AND WHITE FEMALES,
ATLANTA, 1939-1941

Age Groups	Number of males in age interval in male life table population $_nL_{x_m}$	Number of males in age interval in stationary million $_nL_{x_m}$ $.081891 \, _nL_{x_m}$	Number of females in age interval in female life table population $_nL_{x_f}$	Number of females in age interval in stationary population $_nL'_{x_f}$ $.077113 \, L'_{x_f}$
(1)	(2)	(3)	(4)	(5)
0-4	471,044	38,574	475,955	36,702
5-9	464,959	38,076	471,381	36,350
10-14	461,496	37,792	469,609	36,213
15-19	456,850	37,412	467,576	36,056
20-24	452,125	37,025	464,571	35,824
25-29	446,612	36,574	460,703	35,526
30-34	439,891	36,023	455,449	35,121
35-39	431,085	35,302	448,360	34,574
40-44	416,584	34,114	440,102	33,938
45-49	395,343	32,375	428,756	33,063
50-54	367,820	30,121	412,098	31,778
55-59	329,296	26,966	389,231	30,015
60-64	277,228	22,702	356,934	27,524
65-69	217,203	17,787	314,327	24,239
70-74	155,883	12,765	257,162	19,831
75-79	94,008	7,698	184,592	14,234
80-84	42,916	3,514	107,369	8,280
85-89	14,057	1,151	44,443	3,427
90-94	2,635	216	10,999	848
95-99	474	39	2,922	225
All ages	5,937,509	486,229	6,662,539	513,768

Children under 5 = 75,276   Fertility ratio (women 20-44) = 430
Women 20-44   = 174,983   Fertility ratio (women 15-44) = 357
Women 15-44   = 211,039

Source: *Vital Statistics of the United States, Supplement: 1939-1940*, Part III (Washington: Government Printing Office, 1943), p. 20; *Vital Statistics of the United States: 1941*, Part II (Washington: Government Printing Office, 1943), p. 64; and life tables this study. (The average sex ratio at birth for the white population of Georgia during the period 1939-1941 was used in place of the sex ratio at birth of the Atlanta population.)

TABLE T

COMPUTATIONS FOR CONSTRUCTING A STATIONARY POPULATION OF 1,000,000 FROM LIFE TABLES FOR NEGRO MALES AND NEGRO FEMALES, ATLANTA, 1939-1941

Age Groups	Number of males in age interval in male life table population $_nL_{x_m}$	Number of males in age interval in stationary million $_nL_{x_m}$ $.110545\,_nL_{x_m}$	Number of females in age interval in female life table population $_nL_{x_f}$	Number of females in age interval in stationary population $_nL'_{x_f}$ $.107303\ L'_{x_f}$
(1)	(2)	(3)	(4)	(5)
0-4	445,797	49,281	453,069	48,616
5-9	436,118	48,211	443,594	47,599
10-14	432,761	47,840	440,397	47,256
15-19	424,967	46,978	431,905	46,345
20-24	407,929	45,095	417,672	44,817
25-29	382,612	42,296	400,842	43,012
30-34	351,348	38,840	379,664	40,739
35-39	317,323	35,078	357,725	38,385
40-44	279,035	30,846	328,088	35,205
45-49	232,902	25,746	292,350	31,370
50-54	185,053	20,457	250,661	26,897
55-59	141,462	15,638	203,168	21,801
60-64	100,689	11,131	158,181	16,973
65-69	70,496	7,793	122,637	13,159
70-74	49,835	5,509	93,749	10,060
75-79	28,306	3,129	63,326	6,795
80-84	11,779	1,302	34,507	3,703
85-89	3,369	372	12,753	1,368
90-94	472	52	2,616	281
95-99	75	8	196	21
All ages	4,302,328	475,600	4,887,100	524,400

Children under 5   = 97,897   Fertility ratio (women 20-44) = 484
Women 20-44   = 202,158   Fertility ratio (women 15-44) = 394
Women 15-44   = 248,503

Source: *Vital Statistics of the United States, Supplement: 1939-1940*, Part III (Washington: Government Printing Office, 1943), p. 20; *Vital Statistics of the United States: 1941*, Part II (Washington: Government Printing Office, 1943), p. 64; and life tables this study. (The average sex ratio at birth for the Negro population of Georgia during the period 1939-1941 was used in place of the sex ratio at birth of the Atlanta population.)

234

TABLE U

DEATHS FROM FIVE LEADING CAUSES (BY PERCENTAGES OF TOTAL DEATHS): UNITED STATES AND SELECTED SOUTHERN CITIES, 1946*

	Total deaths	Per cent of total	Diseases of the heart	Per cent of total	Cancer and other malignant tumors	Per cent of total	Intracranial lesions of vascular origin	Per cent of total	Nephritis	Per cent of total	Pneumonia (all forms) influenza	Per cent of total
United States	1,395,617	100.0	429,230	30.8	182,005	13.0	125,646	9.0	81,701	5.9	62,324	4.5
Atlanta1	3,679	100.0	922	25.1	448	12.2	378	10.3	324	8.8	171	4.6
Dallas	3,262	100.0	894	27.4	375	11.5	298	9.1	152	4.7	134	4.1
Nashville	2,149	100.0	522	24.3	236	11.0	204	9.5	132	6.1	124	5.8
New Orleans2	5,886	100.0	1,896	32.2	775	13.2	460	7.8	368	6.3	279	4.7

* Excluding "congenital malformations and diseases peculiar to the first year" and "other accidents."

1 Tuberculosis (all forms) ranked fifth with 173 deaths (4.7).
2 Tuberculosis (all forms) ranked fifth with 341 deaths (5.8).

Source: *Vital Statistics of the United States: 1946*, Part II (Washington: Government Printing Office, 1948), pp. 522-523, 536-537, 556-557, 604-605, and 608-609.

TABLE V

Infant Mortality Rates Per 1,000 Live Births, By Race, for Cities of 100,000 or Larger, for the United States And Selected Southern States, 1927-1940

Year	United States			Georgia[1]			Louisiana[2]			Tennessee[3]			Texas[4]		
	All Races	White	All Other Races	All Races	White	All Other Races	All Races	White	All Other Races	All Races	White	All Other Races	All Races	White	All Other Races
1940	39.3	36.1	64.0	48.1	32.1	78.0	58.5	41.6	84.6	50.9	43.5	68.7	64.7	60.5	89.2
1939	41.2	38.0	66.9	60.8	50.3	80.6	63.1	44.7	92.0	55.6	45.6	80.7	68.6	66.7	82.0
1938	44.3	41.1	73.6	68.5	59.9	86.2	80.9	68.0	102.6	77.9	72.5	93.0	63.0	59.9	86.0
1937	48.7	45.1	81.7	62.3	50.9	83.4	78.5	63.0	102.7	72.5	65.0	92.5	76.4	73.6	96.8
1936	52.2	48.1	89.8	77.1	61.2	108.0	93.1	74.3	123.6	85.6	79.0	103.5	77.3	74.7	97.2
1935	51.2	47.9	81.4	73.5	60.5	97.3	77.1	61.6	100.5	81.7	76.0	96.3	77.5	74.4	101.9
1934	55.5	——	——	82.9	71.0	104.4	81.6	63.9	108.5	98.1	85.9	130.1	83.4	72.9	113.6
1933	54.9	——	——	82.7	64.5	112.6	80.7	63.8	108.9	93.7	78.9	132.9	90.5	——	——
1932	54.6	——	——	69.3	56.3	92.1	74.8	60.8	99.3	86.3	76.1	113.2	——	——	——
1931	59.6	——	——	83.8	65.3	120.5	75.1	60.1	103.6	92.4	78.1	132.8	——	——	——
1930	61.1	——	——	93.6	65.3	148.2	87.9	71.4	120.4	98.5	84.3	139.3	——	——	——
1929	64.4	——	——	93.5	74.5	127.9	79.7	60.5	117.2	96.5	80.9	131.7	——	——	——
1928	68.3	——	——	99.7	70.7	156.1	78.2	61.7	111.3	94.3	77.2	132.7	——	——	——
1927	63.4	——	——	——	——	——	87.9	64.9	134.9	76.7	62.4	106.2	——	——	——

1 Includes *Atlanta* only.
2 Includes *New Orleans* only.
3 Includes *Chattanooga*, *Knoxville*, *Memphis*, and *Nashville*.
4 Includes *Dallas*, *Fort Worth*, *Houston*, and *San Antonio*.

Source: Forrest E. Linder and Robert D. Grove, *Vital Statistics Rates in the United States: 1900-1940* (Washington: Government Printing Office, 1947), pp. 578, 583, 587, 600 and 601.

TABLE W

INFANT MORTALITY RATES (PER 1,000 LIVE BIRTHS), BY COLOR,
FOR CITIES OF THE UNITED STATES OF 100,000 OR MORE
AND SELECTED SOUTHERN CITIES, 1941-1946

	United States Urban Cities of 100,000 or more	Atlanta	Dallas	Nashville	New Orleans
1946	31.4	31.0	39.8	34.4	33.9
White	29.1	22.3	32.7	28.1	28.5
Nonwhite	48.8	54.0	78.6	59.2	44.2
1945	34.8	41.5	44.5	54.6	37.2
White	31.9	32.3	37.8	49.5	29.6
Nonwhite	56.2	64.1	80.9	72.0	51.9
1944	36.0	45.9	35.9	48.3	43.0
White	33.1	32.8	30.7	42.0	35.2
Nonwhite	57.4	76.0	61.9	73.4	58.3
1943	36.3	46.2	39.8	48.6	45.9
White	33.2	33.6	33.6	39.9	35.9
Nonwhite	61.4	73.3	70.4	83.8	65.1
1942	34.5	40.8	37.2	41.9	44.3
White	31.8	29.9	31.9	37.9	35.7
Nonwhite	58.4	65.4	63.9	57.6	59.4
1941	37.0	------	------	------	------
White	33.7	------	------	------	------
Nonwhite	62.9	------	------	------	------

Sources: *Vital Statistics of the United States: 1946*, Part II (Washington: Government Printing Office, 1948), pp. 10, 36, 54, 93, and 97.
Vital Statistics of the United States: 1945, Part II (Washington: Government Printing Office, 1947), pp. 8, 20, 27, 45, and 47.
Vital Statistics of the United States: 1944, Part II (Washington: Government Printing Office, 1946), pp. 4, 16, 24, 43, and 45.
Vital Statistics of the United States: 1943, Part II (Washington: Government Printing Office, 1945), pp. 8, 34, 42, 60 and 62.
Vital Statistics of the United States: 1942, Part II (Washington: Government Printing Office, 1944), pp. 20, 31, 39, 57, and 59.
Vital Statistics of the United States: 1941, Part II (Washington: Government Printing Office, 1943), p. 10.

237

TABLE X

INFANT MORTALITY RATES FOR
THE CITY OF ATLANTA, BY RACE, 1930-1947

Year	Infant Deaths Per 1,000 Live Births		
	White	Negro	Total
1930	55.6	147.3	88.8
1931	57.8	114.1	77.6
1932	49.7	89.2	64.9
1933	57.2	111.2	79.4
1934	58.5	103.7	76.1
1935	54.5	95.6	70.6
1936	57.4	108.4	76.5
1937	42.8	83.8	58.5
1938	47.6	88.6	62.4
1939	44.1	87.3	58.4
1940	39.5	77.7	54.8
1941	34.2	68.4	47.0
1942	38.4	72.4	50.1
1943	37.9	75.6	51.9
1944	38.4	81.2	50.1
1945	34.5	66.7	45.9
1946	26.5	53.1	35.6
1947	23.7	52.1	34.3

Source: J. F. Hackney, *City of Atlanta Health Department, Annual Report: 1947* (Atlanta: City of Atlanta, Department of Health, 1948), p. 18.

APPENDIX B

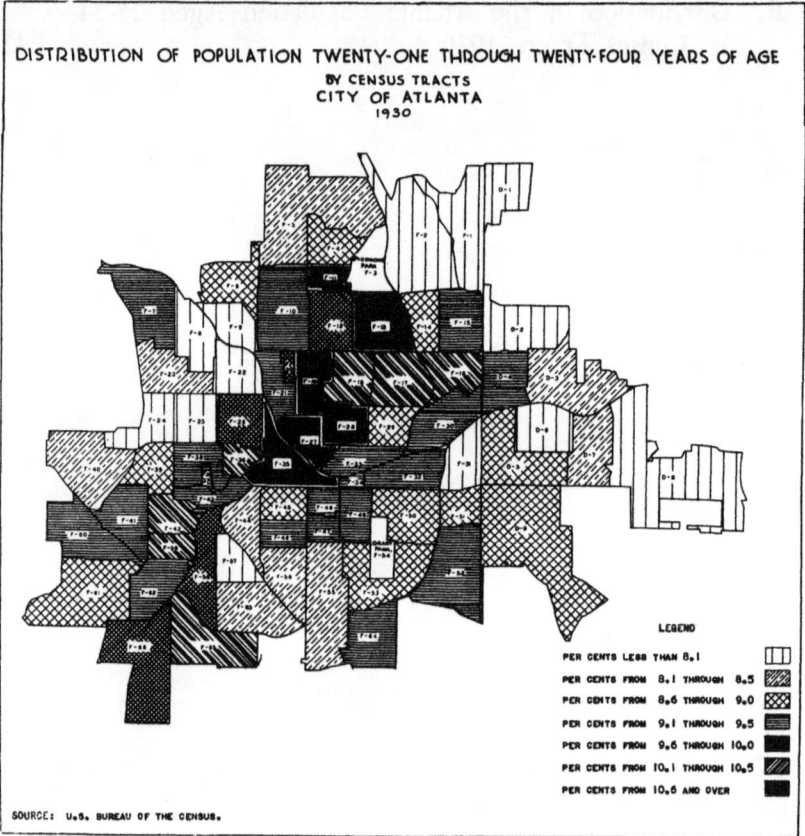

FIGURE A. Distribution of the Atlanta population aged 21-24, by census tracts, 1930. (Reproduced from WPA of Georgia official project 465-34-3-4.)

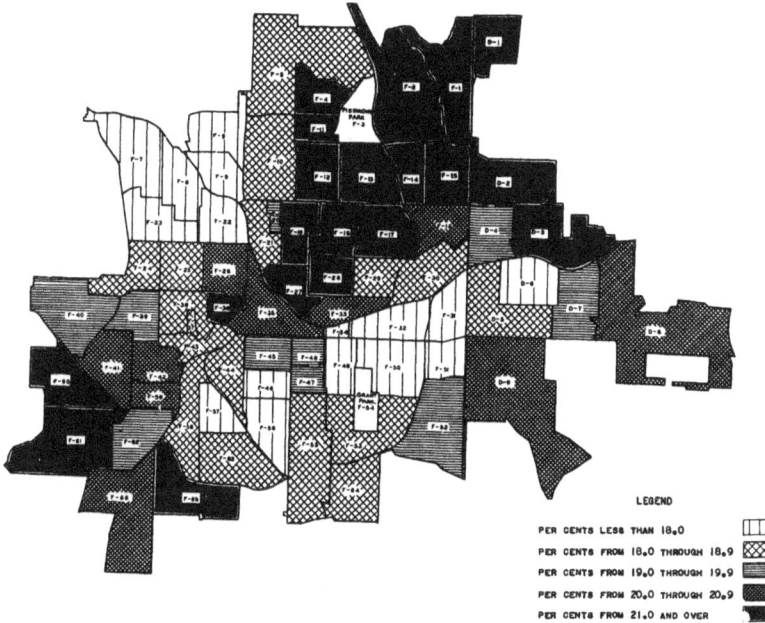

DISTRIBUTION OF POPULATION TWENTY-FIVE THROUGH THIRTY-FOUR YEARS OF AGE
BY CENSUS TRACTS
CITY OF ATLANTA
1930

SOURCE: U.S. BUREAU OF THE CENSUS.

FIGURE B. Distribution of the Atlanta population aged 25-34, by census tracts, 1930. (Reproduced from WPA of Georgia official project 465-34-3-4.)

BIBLIOGRAPHY

A. BOOKS

Atlanta City Council and the Atlanta Chamber of Commerce, *Hand Book of the City of Atlanta*. Atlanta, Georgia: The Southern Industrial Publishing Co., 1898. 111 pp.

Bateson, W., *Mendel's Principles of Heredity*. Cambridge: University Press, 1913. 413 pp.

Bonar, James, *Malthus and His Work*. New York: The Macmillian Company, 1924. 438 pp.

Carr-Saunders, A. M., *World Population: Past Growth and Present Trends*. Oxford: Clarendon Press, 1936. 336 pp.

City of Atlanta. Louisville, Kentucky: The Interstate Publishing Company, 1892-1893. 165 pp.

Darwin, Charles Robert, *The Descent of Man and Selections in Relation to Sex*. New York: D. Appleton and Co., 189?. 688 pp.

Dublin, Louis I., and Alfred J. Lotka, *Length of Life: A Study of the Life Table*. New York: The Ronald Press Company, 1936. 400 pp.

Durand, John D., *The Labor Force in the United States: 1890-1960*. New York: Social Science Research Council, 1948. 284 pp.

Fairchild, Henry P., editor, *Dictionary of Sociology*. New York: Philosophical Library, 1944. 342 pp.

Franquis, Juan Alvarado, *Comentarios Al VII Censo de Poplacion De Venezuela*. Caracas, Venezuela: Ministerio De Fomento, Direccion General De Estadistica, 1947. 90 pp.

Galton, Sir Francis, *Natural Inheritance*. London: The Macmillan Company, 1889. 259 pp.
———, *Hereditary Genius; An Inquiry into Its Law and Consequences*. New York: D. Appleton and Co., 1887. 390 pp.

Gist, Noel P., and L. A. Halbert, *Urban Society*. Second edition; New York: Thomas Y. Crowell Company, 1947. 629 pp.

Glass, D. V., *Population Policies and Movements in Europe*. Oxford: Oxford University Press, 1940. 490 pp.

243

Hagood, Margaret Jarman, *Statistics for Sociologists*. New York: Reynal and Hitchcock, Inc., 1941. 934 pp.

Hornady, John R., *Atlanta Yesterday, Today, and Tomorrow*. Atlanta, Georgia: American Cities Book Company, 1922. 442 pp.

Huber, H., H. Bunle, and F. Boverat, *La Population De La France—Son Evolution Et Ses Perspectives*. Paris: Librarie Hechette, 1939. 249 pp.

Kuczynski, Robert R., *The Balance of Births and Deaths*. 2 vols. New York: The Macmillan Company, 1928.
——, *The Measurement of Population Growth*. New York: Oxford University Press, 1936. 225 pp.

Landis, Paul H., *Population Problems*. New York: American Book Company, 1943. 500 pp.

Linder, Forrest E., and Robert D. Grove, *Vital Statistics Rates in the United States: 1900-1940*. Washington: Government Printing Office, 1947. 1051 pp.

Lynd, Robert S., and Helen M. Lynd, *Middletown*. New York: Harcourt, Brace and Company, 1929. 550 pp.

Marx, Karl, *Capital: A Critique of Political Economy*. Edited by Frederick Engels. New York: The Modern Library, 1936. 869 pp.

McKenzie, Roderick D., *The Metropolitan Community*. New York: McGraw-Hill Book Company, Inc., 1933. 352 pp.

Metropolitan Life Insurance Company, *State and Regional Life Tables: 1939-1941*. Washington: Government Printing Office, 1948. 265 pp.

National Resources Committee, *Our Cities*. Washington: Government Printing Office, 1937. 35 pp.
——, *Population Statistics, 1. National Data*. Washington: Government Printing Office, 1937. 107 pp.
——, *Population Statistics, 3. Urban Data*. Washington: Government Printing Office, 1937. 52 pp.

Newsholme, Sir Arthur, *The Elements of Vital Statistics in Their Bearing on Social and Public Health Problems*. London: George Allen and Unwin, Ltd., 1923. 623 pp.

Pearl, Raymond, *The Natural History of Population*. New York: Oxford University Press, 1939. 416 pp.

Pearson, Karl, *The Grammar of Science*. London: Adam and Charles Black, 1900. 548 pp.

The Pioneer Citizens' Society of Atlanta, *Pioneer Citizens' History of Atlanta*. Atlanta, Georgia: Byrd Printing Company, 1902. 400 pp.

Reed, Wallace P., editor, *History of Atlanta, Georgia*. Syracuse, New York: D. Mason & Company, Publishers, 1889. 491 pp.

Schmid, Calvin F., *Social Saga of Two Cities*. Minneapolis: Minneapolis Council of Social Agencies, 1937. 418 pp.

Smith, T. Lynn, *The Sociology of Rural Life*. Revised edition; New York: Harper & Brothers, 1947. 634 pp.
———, *Brazil: People and Institutions*. Baton Rouge, Louisiana: Louisiana State University Press, 1947. 843 pp.
———, *Population Analysis*. New York: McGraw-Hill Book Company, Inc., 1948. 421 pp.

Sorokin, Pitirim, and Carle C. Zimmerman, *Principles of Rural-Urban Sociology*. New York: Henry Holt and Company, 1929. 652 pp.
———, Carle C. Zimmerman, and Charles J. Galpin, *A Systematic Source Book in Rural Sociology*. Vol. I, 645 pp. Minneapolis: The University of Minnesota Press, 1930.
———, *A Systematic Source Book in Rural Sociology*. Vol. II, 677 pp. Minneapolis: The University of Minnesota Press, 1931.
———, *A Systematic Source Book in Rural Sociology*. Vol III, 752 pp. Minneapolis: The University of Minnesota Press, 1932.

Thomas, Dorothy Swaine, *Social and Economic Aspects of Swedish Population Movements, 1750-1933*. New York: The Macmillan Company, 1941. 487 pp.

Thompson, Warren S., *Population Problems*. Third edition; New York: McGraw-Hill Book Company, Inc., 1942. 471 pp.
———, and P. K. Whelpton, *Population Trends in the United States*. New York: McGraw-Hill Book Company, Inc., 1933. 415 pp.

Truesdall, Leon E., "Methods Involved in the Federal Census of Population," in Stuart E. Rice, editor, *Methods in Social Science*. Chicago: The University of Chicago Press, 1931. 822 pp.

Tylor, Sir Edward Burnett, *Anthropology: An Introduction to to the Study of Man and Civilization.* New York: D. Appleton and Company, 1898. 448 pp.

Vance, Rupert B., *All These People.* Chapel Hill, North Carolina: The University of North Carolina Press, 1945. 503 pp.

Whelpton, P. K., *Needed Population Research.* Lancaster, Pennsylvania: The Science Printing Company, 1938. 196 pp.

Whipple, George Chandler, *Vital Statistics.* Second edition; New York: John Wiley and Sons, Inc., 1923. 579 pp.

Willcox, Walter F., *Natural and Political Observations ʋade upon the Bills of Mortality by John Graunt.* Baltimore: The Johns Hopkins Press, 1939. 90 pp.

Works Progress Administration of Georgia Official Project 465-34-3-4, *A Statistical Study of Certain Aspects of the Social and Economic Pattern of the City of Atlanta, Georgia.* (n.p.): Works Progress Administration of Georgia, 1939. 187 pp.

Young, Kimball, *Personality and Problems of Adjustment.* New York: F. S. Crofts and Company, 1940. 868 pp.

B. PERIODICAL ARTICLES

Billings, J. S., "The Diminishing Birth Rate in the United States," *The Forum,* 15:467-477, June, 1893.

Dorn, Harold F., "The Natural Decrease of Population in Certain American Communities," *Journal of the American Statistical Association,* 34:106-109, March, 1939.

Dublin, Louis I., and Alfred J. Lotka, "On the True Rate of Natural Increase as Exemplified by the Population of the United States, 1920," *Journal of the American Statistical Association,* 20:305-339, September, 1925.

Edin, K. A., "The Birth Rate Changes," *Eugenics Review,* 20:258-266, January, 1929.

Green, Howard W., "Cultural Areas in the City of Cleveland," *American Journal of Sociology,* 38:356-367, November, 1932.

Hauser, Philip M., and Hope T. Eldridge, "Projection of Urban Growth and Migration to Cities in the United States," *The Milbank Memorial Fund Quarterly,* 25:293-307, July, 1947.

Hitt, Homer L., "The Use of Selected Cartographic Techniques in Health Research," *Social Forces*, 26:189-196, December, 1947.

Kemp, Louise, "A Note on the Use of the Fertility Ratio in the Study of Rural-Urban Differences in Fertility," *Rural Sociology*, 10:312-313, September, 1945.

Lamson, Herbert D., "Differential Reproduction in China," *Quarterly Review of Biology*, 10:308-321, September, 1935.

Metropolitan Life Insurance Company, *Statistical Bulletin*, 16:7, July 1935.

Notestein, Frank W., "The Differential Rate of Increase Among the Social Classes of the American Population," *Social Forces*, 12:17-33, October, 1933.

Pearl, Raymond, "Fertility and Economic Status," *Human Biology*, 4:525-553, December, 1932.

Princeton University, School of Public and International Affairs; Population Association of America, *Population Index*, 1935-1947.

Smith, T. Lynn, "A Demographic Study of the American Negro," *Social Forces*, 23:379-387, March, 1945.
———, and Homer L. Hitt, "The Misstatement of Women's Ages and the Vital Indexes," *Metron*, 13:95-108, 1939.

Weber, Adna Ferrin, "The Significance of Recent City Growth: The Era of Small Industrial Centres," *The Annals of the American Academy of Political and Social Sciences*, 23:223-236, March, 1904.

Williams, B. O., "Mobility and Farm Tenancy," *Journal of Land and Public Utility Economics*, 14:207-208, May, 1938.

Woodbury, Robert M., "Infant Mortality in the United States," *The Annals of the American Academy of Political and Social Sciences*, 188:97, November, 1936.

C. PARTS OF SERIES

Beegle, J. Allan and T. Lynn Smith, *Differential Fertility in Louisiana*, Louisiana Agricultural Experiment Station Bulletin 403, Baton Rouge, 1946.

Booth, Charles, *Life and Labour of the People of London.* 17 vols.; London: The Macmillan Company, 1892-1897.

Bureau of the Census, *Seventh Census of the United States: 1850.* Washington: Robert Armstrong, Printer, 1853. 1022 pp.

——, *Population of the United States in 1860.* Washington: Government Printing Office, 1864. 694 pp.

——, *Ninth Census of the United States: 1870,* "Vol. I, The Statistics of the Population of the United States." Washington: Government Printing Office, 1872. 804 pp.

——, *Eleventh Census of the United States: 1890,* Part I. Washington: Government Printing Office, 1892. 956 pp.

——, *Eleventh Census of the United States: 1890,* Part III. Washington: Government Printing Office, 1897. 1150 pp.

——, *Twelfth Census of the United States: 1900,* "Population, Vol. II," Part II. Washington: Government Printing Office, 1902. 754 pp.

——, *Twelfth Census of the United States: 1900,* "Special Reports, Occupations." Washington: Government Printing Office, 1904. 763 pp.

——, *Thirteenth Census of the United States: 1910,* "Population, Vol. I." Washington: Government Printing Office, 1913. 1369 pp.

——, *Thirteenth Census of the United States: 1910,* "Population, Vol. II." Washington: Government Printing Office, 1913. 1160 pp.

——, *Thirteenth Census of the United States: 1910,* "Population, Vol. III." Washington: Government Printing Office, 1913. 1225 pp.

——, *Thirteenth Census of the United States: 1910,* "Population, Vol. IV, Occupation Statistics." Washington: Government Printing Office, 1914. 615 pp.

——, *Fourteenth Census of the United States: 1920,* "Population Vol. II, General Report and Analytical Tables." Washington: Government Printing Office, 1922. 1410 pp.

——, *Fourteenth Census of the United States: 1920,* "Population Vol. IV, Occupations." Washington: Government Printing Office, 1923. 1309 pp.

——, *Fifteenth Census of the United States: 1930,* "Population, Vol. II, General Report, Statistics by Subjects." Washington: Government Printing Office, 1933. 1407 pp.

——, *Fifteenth Census of the United States: 1930,* "Population, Vol. V, General Report on Occupations." Washington: Government Printing Office, 1933. 591 pp.

———, *Sixteenth Census of the United States: 1940*, "Population, Vol. I, Number of Inhabitants." Washington: Government Printing Office, 1942. 1236 pp.

———, *Sixteenth Census of the United States: 1940*, "Population, Vol. II, Characteristics of the Population," Part 1. Washington: Government Printing Office, 1943. 977 pp.

———, *Sixteenth Census of the United States: 1940*, "Population, Vol. II, Characteristics of the Population," Part 2. Washington: Government Printing Office, 1943. 1002 pp.

———, *Sixteenth Census of the United States: 1940*, "Population, Vol. II, Characteristics of the Population," Part 3. Washington: Government Printing Office, 1943. 934 pp.

———, *Sixteenth Census of the United States: 1940*, "Population, Vol. II, Characteristics of the Population," Part 6. Washington: Government Printing Office, 1943. 1095 pp.

———, *Sixteenth Census of the United States: 1940*, "Population, Vol. III, The Labor Force," Part 1. Washington: Government Printing Office, 1943. 301 pp.

———, *Sixteenth Census of the United States: 1940*, "Population, Vol. III, The Labor Force," Part 2. Washington: Government Printing Office, 1943. 1052 pp.

———, *Sixteenth Census of the United States: 1940*, "Population, Vol. III, The Labor Force," Part 3. Washington: Government Printing Office, 1943. 1014 pp.

———, *Sixteenth Census of the United States: 1940*, "Population, Vol. III, The Labor Force," Part 5. Washington: Government Printing Office, 1943. 1082 pp.

———, *Sixteenth Census of the United States: 1940*, "Population, Vol. IV, Characteristics by Age," Part 1. Washington: Government Printing Office, 1943. 183 pp.

———, *Sixteenth Census of the United States: 1940*, "Population, Vol. IV, Characteristics by Age," Part 2. Washington: Government Printing Office, 1943. 945 pp.

———, *Sixteenth Census of the United States: 1940*, "Population, Vol. IV, Characteristics by Age," Part 4. Washington: Government Printing Office, 1943. 919 pp.

———, *Sixteenth Census of the United States: 1940*, "Population, and Housing, Atlanta, Georgia." Washington: Government Printing Office, 1942. 63 pp.

———, *Sixteenth Census of the United States: 1940*, "Population, State of Birth of the Native Population." Washington: Government Printing Office, 1944. 78 pp.

——, *Sixteenth Census of the United States: 1940,* "Population, Differential Fertility, 1940 and 1910, Standardized Fertility Rates and Reproduction Rates." Washington: Government Printing Office, 1944. 40 pp.

——, *Sixteenth Census of the United States: 1940,* "Population, Differential Fertility, 1940 and 1910, Fertility for States and Large Cities." Washington: Government Printing Office, 1943. 281 pp.

——, *Sixteenth Census of the United States: 1940,* "United States Life Tables and Actuarial Tables: 1939-1941." Washington: Government Printing Office, 1946. 151 pp.

——, *Sixteenth Census of the United States: 1940,* "Population, Internal Migration 1935 to 1940, Color and Sex of Migrants." Washington: Government Printing Office, 1943. 490 pp.

——, *Sixteenth Census of the United States: 1940,* "Population, Internal Migration 1935 to 1940, Age of Migrants." Washington: Government Printing Office, 1946. 382 pp.

——, *Sixteenth Census of the United States: 1940,* "Population, Internal Migration 1935 to 1940, Economic Characteristics of Migrants." Washington: Government Printing Office, 1946. 223 pp.

——, *Sixteenth Census of the United States: 1940,* "Population, Internal Migration 1935 to 1940, Social Characteristics of Migrants." Washington: Government Printing Office, 1946. 270 pp.

——, *Census Reports,* "Vol. III, Vital Statistics," Part I. Washington: Government Printing Office, 1902. 695 pp.

——, *Census Reports,* "Vol. III. Vital Statistics," Part II. Washington: Government Printing Office, 1902. 1055 pp.

——, "Deaths and Death Rates for Selected Causes, by Age, Race, and Sex United States, 1944," *Vital Statistics—Special Reports,* 25:263-299, November, 1946.

——, *Vital Statistics of the United States: 1937,* Part II. Washington: Government Printing Office, 1939. 186 pp.

——, *Vital Statistics of the United States: 1938,* Part II. Washington: Government Printing Office, 1940. 205 pp.

——, *Vital Statistics of the United States: 1939,* Part II. Washington: Government Printing Office, 1941. 283 pp.

——, *Vital Statistics of the United States: 1940,* Part II. Washington: Government Printing Office, 1943. 334 pp.

——, *Vital Statistics of the United States, Supplement: 1939-1940,* Part III. Washington: Government Printing Office, 1943. 581 pp.

——, *Vital Statistics of the United States: 1941*, Part II. Washington: Government Printing Office, 1943. 564 pp.

——, *Vital Statistics of the United States: 1942*, Part II. Washington: Government Printing Office, 1944. 533 pp.

——, *Vital Statistics of the United States: 1943*, Part II. Washington: Government Printing Office, 1945. 580 pp.

——, *Vital Statistics of the United States: 1944*, Part II. Washington: Government Printing Office, 1946. 595 pp.

——, *Vital Statistics of the United States: 1945*, Part II. Washington: Government Printing Office, 1947. 627 pp.

——, *Vital Statistics of the United States: 1946*, Part II. Washington: Government Printing Office, 1948. 647 pp.

——, *Religious Bodies: 1906*, Part 1. Washington: Government Printing Office, 1910. 670 pp.

——, *Religious Bodies: 1916*, Part 1. Washington: Government Printing Office, 1919. 594 pp.

——, *Religious Bodies: 1926*, Vol. 1. Washington: Government Printing Office, 1930. 769 pp.

——, *Religious Bodies: 1936*, Vol. 1. Washington: Government Printing Office, 1941. 943 pp.

Davies, Vernon, and John C. Belcher, *Mississippi Life Tables, By Sex, Race, and Residence: 1940.* Jackson, Mississippi: Mississippi Commission on Hospital Care, 1948. 11 pp.

Dublin, Louis I., "Causes of Death by Occupational Mortality Experiences of the Metropolitan Life Insurance Co., Industrial Department: 1911-1913." Washington: Government Printing Office, 1917. 88 pp.

Grove, Robert D., "Studies in Completeness of Birth Registration," *Vital Statistics—Special Reports*, 17:224-296, April, 1943.

Hackney, J. F., *City of Atlanta Health Department, Annual Report: 1947.* Atlanta, Georgia: City of Atlanta, Department of Health, 1948. 27 pp.

Hamilton, C. Horace, *Rural-Urban Migration in North Carolina 1920 to 1930*, North Carolina Agricultural Experiment Station Bulletin 295, Raleigh, 1934.

Hitt, Homer L., and Alvin L. Bertrand, *Social Aspects of Hospital Planning in Louisiana*, Louisiana Agricultural Experiment Station and the Office of the Governor, Louisiana Study Series No. 1, Baton Rouge, 1947.

251

Reed, Lowell J., and Margaret Merrell, "A Short Method for Constructing an Abridged Life Table," *Vital Statistics— Special Reports*, 9:681-712, June, 1940.

Smith, T. Lynn, *The Population of Louisiana: Its Composition and Changes*, Louisiana Agricultural Experiment Station Bulletin No. 293, Baton Rouge, 1937.

Thompson, Warren S., *Average Number of Children per Woman in Butler County, Ohio, 1930—A Study in Differential Fertility*. Washington: Government Printing Office, 1941. 81 pp.

University of Texas, *The Use of City Directories in the Study of Urban Population: A Methodological Note*. Austin, Texas: The University of Texas, 1942. 29 pp.

Uzzell, W. E., *Estimated Population of Georgia, July 1, 1948*. Atlanta, Georgia: Georgia Department of Public Health, Division of Vital Statistics, 1949. 2 pp.

Willcox, Walter F., *Introduction to the Vital Statistics of the United States*. Washington: Government Printing Office, 1933. 138 pp.

D. ENCYCLOPEDIA ARTICLES

Wolfe, A. B., "Population," Encyclopedia of the Social Sciences, First Edition, XII, 248-249.

E. UNPUBLISHED MATERIALS

McMahan, C. A., "A Study of the Population of Georgia by Sex, Age, Color, Residence, and Selected Socio-Economic Factors, 1940." Unpublished Master's thesis. The University of Georgia, Athens, 1946. 63 pp.

Turner, Charles C., "Births, Stillbirths, Infant Deaths, Total Deaths, Atlanta (Resident) Year 1947, by Census Tract and Race." Unpublished mimeographed report of the statistican of the City Health Department, Atlanta, Georgia, 1948. 1 p.

AUTHOR INDEX

A

Atlanta City Council, 43, 194, 243

B

Bateson, W., 36, 243
Batschelet, Clarence E., 7
Beegle, J. Allan, 25, 41, 247
Belcher, John C., 21, 145, 164, 167-170, 251
Bertrand, Alvin L., 43, 251
Billings, J. S., 39, 246
Bonar, James, 34, 243
Booth, Charles, 36, 248
Boverat, F., 62, 244
Bunle, H., 62, 244

C

Calhoun, John C., 196
Carr-Saunders, A. M., 243

D

Darwin, Charles Robert, 36, 243
Davies, Vernon, 21, 145, 164, 167-170, 251
Dublin, Louis I., 37, 243, 246, 251
Durand, John D., 243
Dorn, Harold F., 39, 246

E

Edin, K. A., 42, 246
Eldridge, Hope T., 246

F

Fairchild, Henry P., 4, 243
Franquis, Juan Alvarado, 62, 243

G

Galpin, Charles J., 33-34, 36, 245
Galton, Sir Francis, 36, 243
Gist, Noel P., 39, 62, 65, 191, 243
Glass, D. V., 243
Graunt, John, 26, 30-32, 246
Green, Howard W., 41, 246
Grove, Robert D., 4, 15, 18-22, 160, 174, 244, 251

H

Hackney, J. F., 176-177, 251
Hagood, Margaret Jarman, 10-11, 16, 20-21, 24, 244
Halbert, L. A., 39, 62, 65, 191, 243
Halley, Edmund, 33

Hamilton, C. Horace, 25, 39, 251
Hauser, Philip M., 246
Hitt, Homer L., 5, 43, 247, 251
Hornady, John R., 43, 244
Huber, H., 62, 244

K

Kemp, Louise, 41, 144, 247
King, Gregory, 33
Kuczynski, Robert R., 37, 244

L

Laidlaw, Walter, 6
Lamson, Herbert D., 42, 247
Landis, Paul H., 244
Linder, Forrest E., 4, 15, 20-22, 160, 174, 244
Livi, R., 36
Lotka, Alfred J., 37, 243, 246
Lynd, Helen M., 244
Lynd, Robert S., 244

M

McKenzie, Roderick D., 244
McMahan, C. A., 75, 252
Malthus, Thomas R., 34-35
Marx, Karl, 36, 244
Merrell, Margaret, 20, 40, 252
Metropolitan Life Insurance Company, 21, 163-164, 244, 247

N

National Resources Committee, 25, 40, 156, 244
Newsholme, Sir Arthur, 15, 244
Notestein, Frank W., 41, 153, 247

P

Pearl, Raymond, 15, 41, 244, 247
Pearson, Karl, 36, 245
Petty, William, 33
The Pioneer Citizens' Society of Atlanta, 43, 245
Plato, 29
Price, Richard, 34
Princeton University, School of Public and International Affairs, 247

R

Ravenstein, E. G., 36
Reed, Lowell J., 20, 40, 252

253

SUBJECT INDEX

New York, 6, 46, 65, 84, 141
North Carolina, 27
Number and distribution of population, 5, 45, 50
See also density

O

Occupational status, 13, 127-134
by sex, 128-130
change in structure, 133, 134
comparison with other large urban populations, 128
domestic service, 130
employment status
employers, 129, 131
government workers, 129, 131
salary workers, 129, 131
unpaid family workers, 129, 131
wage workers, 129, 131
personal services, 132
structure of, 129
trends in, 132
Orientation to the city, 26

P

Paris, 26
Peachtree Street, 27
Piedmont Park, 28
Poland, 52, 180
Population analysis, 42
"Population problems," 35

R

Race and nativity, 51-60
color, 56-59
Negroes, 56
nonwhites in metropolitan district, 55
nonwhites in suburban areas, 54
parentage, 56-59
data for religious bodies, 14
denominations, 135-137
Religious composition, 135-142
Baptists, 135, 136, 137
Catholics, 136, 137, 138
Episcopalians, 136, 137
Jews, 135, 136, 137
Methodists, 135, 136, 137

Presbyterians, 135, 137
grouping of, 140
growth in membership, 141
Protestant, 138
sex ratio among church members, 136, 138, 139
status, 204
trends in, 139
Replacement ratios, 16
See also fertility
Reproduction, rate of, 17, 143-157
See also fertility
Republic, 29
Russia, 52, 180, 203

S

Segregation, 28
Sex composition, 18, 83-90
See also sex ratios
by age, 84, 85, 86, 88, 89
by census tracts, 84-87
trends in, 87-90
Sex ratios, 18, 83-90, 203
See also sex composition
South Carolina, 25
State of birth, 181-188
Sylvan Hills, 28

T

Techwood, 75, 147
Tennessee, 160, 176
Texas, 160, 176
Tuberculosis, 160

U

Universities, Negro, 28
Urbanity, 41
Utah, 159

V

Vital processes, 14, 33, 143-177

W

Wales, 52, 180
Washington, D. C., 83
West End, 28
World War I, 87, 157
World War II, 157

257